Eight Myths of Student Disengagement

Classroom Insights from Educational Psychology Series

Classroom Insights from Educational Psychology

Eight Myths of
Student Disengagement

Creating Classrooms of Deep Learning

Jennifer A. Fredricks

A Joint Publication

CORWIN
A SAGE Company

CORWIN
A SAGE Company

FOR INFORMATION:

Corwin

A SAGE Company

2455 Teller Road

Thousand Oaks, California 91320

(800) 233-9936

www.corwin.com

SAGE Publications Ltd.

1 Oliver's Yard

55 City Road

London EC1Y 1SP

United Kingdom

SAGE Publications India Pvt. Ltd.

B 1/I 1 Mohan Cooperative Industrial Area

Mathura Road, New Delhi 110 044

India

SAGE Publications Asia-Pacific Pte. Ltd.

3 Church Street

#10-04 Samsung Hub

Singapore 049483

Printed in the United States of America.

A catalog record of this book is available from the Library of Congress.

ISBN 9781452271880

This book is printed on acid-free paper.

Acquisitions Editor: Jessica Allan

Associate Editor: Kimberly Greenberg

Editorial Assistant: Cesar Reyes

Project Editor: Veronica Stapleton Hooper

Copy Editor: Shannon Kelly

Typesetter: C&M Digitals (P) Ltd.

Proofreader: Dennis W. Webb

Indexer: Sheila Bodell

Cover Designer: Scott Van Atta

Marketing Manager: Stephanie Trkay

MIX
Paper from
responsible sources
FSC® C014174
www.fsc.org

14 15 16 17 18 10 9 8 7 6 5 4 3 2 1

Contents

Preface

"There are so many things schools can do to help kids think learning is fun. I think kids are naturally inclined to want to learn, but it kind of gets killed off slowly through school."

While doing my research I have listened to students talk about their experiences in school. The above quote is from a study I conducted comparing youths' experiences in school and in out-of-school contexts such as arts and sports. For many youths, school is boring, sometimes alienating, and has little relevance to their lives outside of school. Often these students only do what is required to do well on assessments and rarely exert the effort necessary for deep learning and engagement. In contrast, many of these same students report positive affective and behavioral experiences in out-of-school contexts. They talk about being excited, wanting to engage in their extracurricular activity all of the time, and being willing to exert the time and effort necessary to develop their skills in these domains.

I also have sat in classrooms and observed many students. I have seen classrooms in which students were off-task, bored, and using only superficial strategies to regurgitate the material for an upcoming test, seemingly with little hope for deep learning over time. It is painful to sit in these classrooms and know that students are not deeply engaged. On the other hand, I have had the pleasure to be in classrooms where students were actively participating, excited about learning, and using strategies to make deep connections between ideas.

My experiences talking to students and observing classrooms have raised several questions for me. Why is disengagement from school a shared experience for so many students? What can we learn about out-of-school settings that can be applied to classrooms? What differentiates engaging and disengaging classrooms? How do learning tasks, teacher interactions, and the peer dynamics in the classroom contribute to different levels of engagement? Is it possible to create classroom environments where all students are engaged? The purpose of this book is to tackle these questions.

I initially became an educational researcher because I wanted to create classrooms in which deep learning and engagement take place. Over time, however, I became increasingly frustrated by how disconnected research and practice are. Although the research community has made great advances in the understanding of motivation and engagement, much of this work has had a minimal effect on educational practice. This research is often too technical and complicated. Moreover, it often fails to account for the complex realities that teachers have to face on a day-to-day basis.

I was interested in writing this book because I saw it as a chance to present research in a way that would be accessible to teachers. To help bridge the gap between research and practice, I enlisted the help of three collaborators who teach in ethnically and economically diverse schools. They wrote vignettes describing how the research on engagement applied to their elementary, middle, and high school classrooms. I believe these sections are critical for showing other teachers that it is always possible to create more engaging classroom environments. The teachers also were instrumental in developing a list of resources that other professional educators can use to further their knowledge in each topic area. I believe we have succeeded in creating a book that is accessible to practitioners and that promotes positive change in classrooms. Our hope is that this book will help to create, classroom by classroom, schools in which deep learning and engagement become common shared experiences for students and their teachers.

Acknowledgments

There are several people I need to thank for making this book possible. First, I want to express my gratitude to the three collaborating teachers, Ellen, Melissa, and Michele, for their suggestions on how to make this book more accessible and relevant to educators. They wrote incredible *Engagement in Practice* sections, provided lists of books and Web sites that are relevant for educators, and gave me suggestions on ways to make the research more applicable to the day-to-day realities in schools. It was a pleasure to work with and learn from such gifted and reflective educators. I also want to thank Andrea Levinsky, my student at Connecticut College, who helped me with finding resources, writing *Text-to-Practice Exercises,* and editing the text. This book would have not been possible without the love, support, and encouragement of my husband, Harvey. Thank you for being my biggest fan and taking on extra responsibilities so I could write on the weekends. I also want to thank my two boys, Jacob and Dylan; my sister Rose; and my parents, Tom and Metty, for their ongoing love and support. I also want to acknowledge the countless teachers and students who have let me into their classrooms to observe, interview, and fill out surveys, so I could gain a better understanding of motivation and engagement. Finally, I want to thank all of the teachers who are working tirelessly each day to educate our youth. Being an effective teacher is the most difficult and underappreciated job in this world. I hope one day you will get the respect and admiration you deserve.

PUBLISHER'S ACKNOWLEDGMENTS

Corwin gratefully acknowledges the contributions of the following reviewers:

Patricia Baker, NBCT
Teacher, Gifted Education
Fauquier County Public Schools, Bealeton, VA

Ellen E. Coulson
7th Grade U.S. History Teacher
Sig Rogich Middle School, Las Vegas, NV

Patti Grammens
Teacher
Lakeside Middle School, Cumming, GA

About the Author

Photo courtesy of
Connecticut College.

Jennifer A. Fredricks is a professor of human development at Connecticut College, where she also directs the Holleran Center for Community Action and Public Policy. She has published over thirty-five peer-reviewed journal articles and book chapters on student engagement, family socialization, adolescent development, and extracurricular participation. She is currently working on a three-year grant on student engagement in math and science classrooms that is being funded by the National Science Foundation.

About the Contributors

 **Melissa Dearborn** is an educator, consultant, and instructional coach, with a special interest in how relationships impact student engagement. For the past sixteen years, she has been a teacher and instructional coach at the Integrated Day Charter School in Norwich, Connecticut. Over a twenty-year career, Melissa has worked with students from preschool through eighth grade and has taught a preservice literacy course for undergraduate students at Connecticut College. She received her undergraduate degree from Goddard College and her master's in teaching from Connecticut College. In addition to classroom teaching, Melissa has consulted on school climate, become a certified facilitator of the Expressive Arts through Salve Regina University, practiced Expressive Arts with Alzheimer's patients, and designed curriculum and teacher training for a girls' school in Kenya.

 **Ellen Cavanaugh** is in her third year as an English teacher at the Norwich Free Academy, an independent school in Norwich, Connecticut. She teaches five heterogeneously grouped students from urban and rural communities across a variety of socioeconomic and ethnic groups. Ellen enjoys experimenting with different teaching

methods, activities, and assessments to meet the needs of her students while at the same time challenging them to become active agents who use the resources provided for them to construct their own knowledge. She received her undergraduate degree in English and teaching certification from Connecticut College where she focused on critical pedagogy and teaching for social justice.

 **Michele Herro** has worked as a teacher in the Chicago public schools since 2006, teaching fifth grade her first year and then moving to fourth grade. Her pre-K-8 school has a diverse population, and her classrooms include many special education students and English language learners. Michele has led and participated in teacher study groups that focused on student engagement through inquiry in the areas of research, reading, and writing. Before teaching, she worked as an after-school program coordinator for middle and high school students. After graduating from college, Michele spent a year in the Philippines as a fellow with an educational NGO and school. She received her bachelor's in psychology from Duke University and her master's degree in education from the Harvard Graduate School of Education.

Introduction

DISENGAGEMENT IN EVERY CLASSROOM

Student disengagement is one of the biggest challenges teachers face each day in their classrooms. This disengagement can take many forms, including lack of participation and effort, acting out and disrupting class, disaffection and withdrawal, and failure to invest deeply in the academic content (e.g., not completing homework, not asking questions). Some educators have erroneously assumed that disengagement is just a problem of low-performing schools and does not apply to their classrooms. However, every school, regardless of its level, location, and demographic characteristics, has students who are disengaged. Recent evidence from national datasets in the United States indicates that as many as 40 percent to 60 percent of students are showing signs of disengagement (Steinberg, Brown, & Dornbush, 1996; Yazzie-Mintz, 2007). Nationwide, rates of disengagement are higher among males, youths from an ethnic group other than white or Asian, youths from lower socioeconomic status households, and youths in special education (Yazzie-Mintz, 2007). The reality is that students often view academics as boring and having little meaning in their lives. Many go through the motions and only do what is required. Although these students are on-task, or at least appear to be, they are not fully engaged and deeply invested in learning.

Student engagement is a complex but achievable goal for every teacher. This book presents a multidimensional construct of engagement that includes student behavior, emotion, and cognition. The book differs from other "quick guides to engagement" by arguing that it is necessary to consider all three of these dimensions to truly reach the deeper levels of learning needed for success in today's schools. Many states have adopted the Common Core and Next Generation Science Standards, which are designed to help students develop the knowledge and higher-order thinking skills necessary to be successful in college and high-skilled careers. This book will help K–12 teachers create the kind of environments of deep learning and engagement that are necessary to meet these new standards. Throughout this book, elementary, middle level, and high school teachers share their approaches for engaging students in a variety of ways that are supported by the research literature.

What's so important about engagement? There are several reasons why teachers at all levels should be concerned about the high levels of disengagement occurring in many classrooms. Increasing engagement is seen by both educators and policymakers as the key to addressing problems of low achievement, high levels of student boredom and alienation, and high dropout rates. For many students, dropping out of high school is the last step in a long process during which they become disengaged from school (Rumberger, 2011). Recent U.S. national reports estimate that every school day about 7,000 students decide to drop out of high school, resulting in a total of 1.2 million students dropping out each year (NEAP, 2009). These observations are troubling because youths need to be actively involved in school to acquire the knowledge and skills they will need to succeed in society and to be ready for college and careers. The consequences of disengagement are especially severe for low-income and African American, Hispanic, and Native American students. They are less likely to graduate from high school and face more limited employment prospects, which increases their risk for poverty, poor health, and involvement in the criminal justice system (National Research Council & Institute of Medicine, 2004).

Prior research has shown that engagement is a strong predictor of achievement-related outcomes. When students have higher engagement, they have higher grades, score better on standardized tests, and are more likely to finish high school and go on to college (Fredricks, Blumenfeld, & Paris, 2004). For students to succeed in today's increasingly global and complex economy and become career and college ready, they need to be able to think critically and solve cognitively complex problems. Students who just go through the motions but are not emotionally and cognitively engaged will not develop the higher-order thinking and problem-solving skills that will be necessary to compete for the jobs of the future.

Unfortunately, there is evidence that students' engagement steadily declines over the course of school. Moreover, prior research shows that many school practices are actually contributing to this decline over time (Fredricks et al., 2004).The decline begins as early as kindergarten and increases significantly over the transitions to middle and high school. It is most severe for boys, African American and Hispanic youths, and children from lower socioeconomic status households. Watching any young child play, it is clear that they are naturally curious and want to learn and explore. However, something happens when children enter school to dampen this natural interest in learning. This book will explore some of the factors that are responsible for this decline in engagement and outline practical, research-based strategies that teachers can use to create more engaging classroom environments where deep learning occurs.

How can student engagement be increased? A growing body of research shows that it is possible to increase engagement in schools by making changes to the social and instructional environment (Fredricks et al., 2004). Engagement is presumed to be malleable and responsive to changes in the environment. In fact, increasing engagement has been the central goal of many school improvement efforts, especially at the secondary level (National Research Council, 2004). Focusing on engagement as an explanatory variable for achievement and school completion offers more insight into intervention and prevention strategies than does focusing on unalterable demographic variables such as gender, ethnicity, and socioeconomic status. Although teachers cannot change the innate characteristics of their students, they can change the classroom environment. A student's engagement depends on the opportunities a teacher provides for that student to be engaged. It is clear from the intervention literature that teachers do have control and do play a powerful role in creating environments in which deep learning and engagement can take place.

How This Book Is Different
Than Other Books on Engagement

Many books have been written on how to increase engagement. Why should you read this book, and how is it different from these other texts? First, the author is one of the leading researchers in the field of engagement and motivation. She was one of the first to write about how engagement needs to be conceptualized as a multidimensional idea that includes behavior, emotion, and cognition. Many other texts simply equate engagement with on-task behavior, which neglects the emotional and cognitive dimensions that are so critical for deeper learning and achievement. Second, other books tend to emphasize classroom management techniques as the primary means for increasing engagement. This book also considers how instructional tasks, teacher-student relations, and peer dynamics help to create a culture of engagement in the classroom. Third, many of these other books present a simplistic list of strategies for increasing engagement in the short term, such as adding a fun activity or a hands-on task. This book acknowledges that there are no quick fixes or silver bullets to achieve full engagement. Rather, continuous efforts in creating a culture of engagement using research-based findings will result in powerful long-term changes to student engagement in every classroom. Finally, this book emphasizes that educators need to understand how student engagement fits within the broader context of a child's day and acknowledge the role that out-of-school time and families play in shaping engagement. Most other books neglect the reality that these factors affect what happens in the classroom.

Organization of the Book

The goal of this book is to expose both prospective and practicing K-12 educators to current advances in research on student engagement and to discuss implications for classroom practice. Readers will learn how to apply strategies that are supported by current research to help them reflect on and create more engaging classroom contexts where deep learning can take place. Examples will be provided for different age groups and content areas, as will ideas that are relevant to all ages and subject domains. In sections entitled *Engagement in*

Practice, three educators who teach in ethnically and economically diverse schools describe the strategies that they or their colleagues have used to increase engagement in elementary, middle, and high school classrooms.

Each chapter will describe an educational misconception and use research-based evidence to burst this myth. Hypothetical student cases are threaded throughout the text to illustrate the causes and consequences of disengagement and ways to improve engagement in the classroom. These cases will remind teachers of students they have either taught or observe daily in their classroom. Extensive opportunities for teachers to self-reflect through *Stop and Reflect* questions and *Text-to-Practice Exercises* are also provided in each chapter. These questions and exercises are designed to help readers connect the concepts to real-life examples and try some new approaches. *Key Terms and Concepts* are provided at the end of each chapter to enhance comprehension. Finally, each chapter includes a list of additional books and Web sites that educators can use to further their knowledge and understanding of student engagement.

Overview of Chapters

Chapter 1

MYTH 1: It's Easy to Tell Who Is Engaged: What Is Engagement and How Can I Assess It in My Classroom?

The first chapter introduces a multidimensional view of engagement that includes behavior, emotion, and cognition. Research evidence is provided to counter the myth that it is easy to tell which students are engaged by just observing their on-task behavior and compliance. Although these behaviors are important components of engagement, the greatest achievement and learning outcomes occur when students rank high on all three dimensions: behavioral, emotional, and cognitive. Educators can make more valid decisions about student engagement by collecting and evaluating data. Therefore, the chapter discusses why it is important and beneficial to assess engagement in the classroom. A variety of methods to assess engagement, including student self-reports, teacher ratings, observational measures, walkthroughs, and collecting data on early warning signs, are presented.

Chapter 2

MYTH 2: Some Students Just Don't Care: How Disengagement Is More Than Just a Lack of Student Motivation

One common misconception is that disengagement merely reflects a lack of student motivation. Research on how classroom practices, including the types of tasks assigned, quality of teacher-student relations, and peer dynamics, contribute to disengagement in the classroom is presented to counter this myth. The first section of this chapter outlines how the tasks that students typically do in school often bear little resemblance to how learning happens outside of the classroom, and, as a result, fail to result in deep engagement and learning. Next, the reasons why some teachers develop poor relations with their students and the consequences of these negative interactions for student engagement are outlined. Finally, the roles that peer rejection and negative peer dynamics play in disengagement are discussed.

Chapter 3

MYTH 3: What Happens Outside of School Competes With Academics: How Out-of-School Time and Families Affect Engagement in School

Youths spend over 50 percent of their waking hours outside of school. How students and their parents choose to spend this time has important implications for students' engagement in the classroom. In the first section, research on the benefits of participation in organized out-of-school activities such as sports or the arts for academic adjustment are outlined. Next, research on variations in engagement between school and out-of-school organized settings is presented. Possible reasons for the higher rates of engagement in out-of-school settings and the implications of these differences in engagement for classroom practice are discussed. Self-determination theory is presented as one theoretical approach for understanding why out-of-school contexts tend to be more engaging settings than school. In the final section, research on how parents can influence student engagement through the values they endorse and the experiences they provide in the home is presented. Practical strategies for working with families to increase engagement are provided.

Chapter 4

MYTH 4: Hands-On Is Minds-On: How to Create More Engaging Classroom Tasks That Result in Deep Learning

The tasks students complete in the classroom have important implications for motivation and learning. Chapter 4 provides a brief introduction to motivational theory, research on how children learn, and research on authentic instruction as the basis for creating more engaging classroom environments. This chapter addresses the common practice of emphasizing the motivational aspects of instructional tasks over the cognitive dimensions. Although developing fun and interesting tasks is part of the puzzle, deep learning and engagement will not occur unless educators also address the cognitive aspects of tasks that encourage higher-level thinking and reasoning. Authentic instructional models are presented as one pedagogical approach that incorporates the motivational and cognitive dimensions of engaging classrooms. Challenges in implementing this type of instruction in the classroom are presented. Finally, research-based recommendations for addressing both the motivational and cognitive demands of learning tasks are presented.

Chapter 5

MYTH 5: Focus on Content: Don't Make It Personal: How Relationships Matter for Student Engagement

Chapter 5 discusses why developing positive relations in the classroom is important for engagement. One misconception, especially among secondary school teachers, is that teaching content is more important for student success than developing relations with students. Prior research on how teachers' interpersonal and academic support influences students' engagement and learning is presented to counter this myth. Research on the effects of teacher involvement, autonomy support, and classroom structure on student engagement is presented. Challenges inherent in building relationships with difficult students are also discussed. Finally, research-based recommendations for fostering positive relationships with all students are provided.

Chapter 6

MYTH 6: Socializing With Peers Detracts From Student Engagement: How to Create a Peer Context That Supports Engagement

Chapter 6 focuses on the role peers play in student engagement. One common misconception is that a quiet classroom means that students are engaged and involved in productive learning. Another myth is that students learn best when working individually on tasks without the distraction of their peers. Research on the behavioral, emotional, and cognitive benefits of friendship in school and on how students collaborate and learn from their peers is presented to counter these myths. In addition, examples of cooperative and collaborative learning models are discussed. Some of the challenges inherent in cooperative group work are presented, along with research-based strategies to address each of these challenges. Finally, strategies for building stronger classroom communities are discussed.

Chapter 7

MYTH 7: There's Only So Much a Teacher Can Do: How to Help Those Students Still Struggling to Succeed

Chapter 7 addresses the view held by many teachers that even with changes to the social and instructional environment it is not possible to engage all students. A common assumption is that some students' success or failure is beyond the control of the teacher, especially that of students living in low-income and high-risk settings. Although many students do come to school facing significant challenges that can impact their learning and engagement, evidence from the intervention research shows that individual teachers, whole schools, and communities can make changes to help these disengaged students succeed in the classroom. In this chapter, the individual factors associated with higher levels of disengagement are outlined. Next, we outline strategies for engaging groups that have tended to have higher rates of disengagement, including boys, low achievers, students with a history of behavioral problems, and African American, Hispanic, and low-income youths. Practical, research-based recommendations for teachers to help reengage these students are presented. Finally, successful prevention and intervention programs for disengaged youths are discussed.

Chapter 8

MYTH 8: Student Engagement Is a Student Choice: Choosing to Make the Effort and Not Waiting for Engagement to Happen

The concluding chapter highlights the reasons why it so critical for teachers to address the level of disengagement in their classrooms. As educators, we can make the decision to invest our efforts towards increasing student engagement, or we can invest our efforts at students who are already disengaged. Being proactive rather than reactive has far more positive outcomes. Creating engaging classrooms that involve all students cognitively, emotionally, and behaviorally means transforming student learning for the long term. When students experience deep engagement, they become lifelong learners and seek out more engaging learning experiences over time.

A Challenge to Readers

Prior to the overview of the chapters, the argument was made that student engagement can be improved in every classroom for every student—a proposition most teachers would be wary of. However, this book challenges readers to examine any beliefs they hold and/or practices they engage in that may underlie one or all of the myths presented in this book. Changing the ways we think and talk about our students and the reasons we attribute to their engagement or disengagement are the first steps in improving student behavior, supporting positive emotions, and enhancing higher-level thinking.

CHAPTER ONE

MYTH 1: It's Easy to Tell Who Is Engaged

What Is Engagement and How Can I Assess It in My Classroom?

One of the most challenging tasks a teacher faces is to identify student engagement in the classroom. Can a teacher or classroom observer really tell who is engaged by just glancing around the room? Is a student looking out the window disengaged? Are the students who complete all of their assignments but do not participate in class truly engaged? This chapter reviews the reasons why it is important and beneficial to assess student engagement and outlines some of the different methods to assess this engagement in the classroom.

The chapter begins with six hypothetical cases of engagement. Although no one student will be exactly like those in the six cases described here, the portraits of engagement will likely remind the readers of students they have either observed or taught in their classrooms. These cases will be woven throughout the remainder of the book to illustrate the causes and consequences of different profiles of engagement. The major purposes of each chapter are to begin a journey of deconstructing the myths about engagement discussed in the introduction to this book and to take a stance to actively understand and evaluate the types of engagement in the classroom.

PORTRAITS OF ENGAGEMENT

Fully Engaged: Fiona and Franco

Fiona looks forward to going to school. She finds most academic subjects interesting and excels in math. She pays attention, enjoys challenging tasks, and tries hard to do her best work. She contributes her thoughts in discussions and asks good questions. She studies at home to make sure she understands the material even when she does not have a test. Her family is very involved in her education. They talk with her about how she is doing in school, monitor her homework, and attend school events. At home, she reads math and science books that her family has bought to supplement what she is doing in school. If she has trouble solving a problem, she goes over it until she understands it.

Franco likes school, likes being with his friends, and has a good relationship with his teacher. Most of the time, he is happy at school. He enjoys opportunities to be intellectually challenged and especially loves history. He works hard, listens attentively, and actively participates in class discussions. When he is studying for a test, he makes chapter outlines and tries to associate the material he is studying with what he already knows about the topic. His parents have high expectations for him and expose him to intellectually stimulating activities and experiences at home. He enjoys reading about history outside of school, going to museums, and discussing history with his family and peers.

Behaviorally Engaged Only: Beatrice and Benjamin

Beatrice is attentive, compliant, and participates in class activities. She follows the rules, does her work, and does not get in trouble. As a result, she does well in her classes and often goes unnoticed by the teacher. She has many friends and is socially active, but she finds her classes boring and is happier when she is with her friends outside of school. She believes school is important for her future, but few subjects retain her interest. She rarely reads anything that is not required and takes the safe route in all of her assignments. She is anxious and avoids challenging tasks for fear of making a mistake. When problems are hard, she gives up easily.

Benjamin pays attention, exerts effort, and comes to class prepared. He does his work, but he does not like going to school and is not interested in or excited by learning. He is motivated primarily by grades. He perceives a B as a failure and something to be avoided at all costs. As a result, he avoids challenging courses. He will do whatever he has to do to get a good grade, but he never does more than is required. He uses surface-level techniques such as memorization and rote recall to learn the material. He often gets right answers and gives the impression that he understands a subject or problem more deeply than he does. His parents have high expectations for him, but they do little to monitor his homework and time use. They work long hours and rarely attend school events.

At Risk: Rachel and Ryan

Rachel finds many of her subjects difficult and boring. Her mind often wanders in class and she rarely participates in class discussions. She has a poor relationship with her teacher. Her attendance and participation in class have been inconsistent. As a result, she is one of the lowest-performing students in her class. Although she acknowledges that she does need to do better in school, she lacks a successful strategy for overcoming her confusion. She has begun to assume that poor performance is inevitable. She wishes she did not have to go to school and does not see how it will help her in the future. She lives with her mother, who did not complete high school. Her mother believes strongly in the value of education, but she lacks the skills or confidence to help her daughter with school. Rachel has fun in school when she has extra recess or gets to talk with her friends. She also loves to sing and dance.

Ryan can sometimes be aggressive and often gets in trouble at school. He gives the impression that he does not care about school or getting in trouble. Sometimes he gets in trouble for not paying attention; other times, it is for fighting. He finds school an alienating and unsupportive context. He has a poor and often conflictual relationship with his teacher, and many of his peers don't like him. He often feels that the other students and his teacher wrongly accuse him of misbehaving. He often gets labeled as a disruptive and aggressive student, and he feels like he is given few opportunities to explain his behavior. He finds few subjects interesting and tries to get by doing as little as possible. He is having the most difficulty with math, which he finds boring and confusing. His parents have become increasingly frustrated with his poor behavior and academic performance, and they have tried a variety of forms of punishment. His favorite parts of the day are gym and recess. He likes playing sports, building things, and playing on the computer outside of school.

WHAT IS ENGAGEMENT?

At a school-wide level, increasing student engagement is seen as a key to addressing problems of low achievement, student boredom and alienation, and high dropout rates. In the classroom, disengagement can be identified through lower student effort in areas such as work completion and quality, as well as in student disruptions, participation, or absences. However, teachers cannot know if they have successfully increased engagement unless they know what it is and how to assess it.

The assessment of engagement has been made challenging by the large variation in how this construct has been defined and measured by researchers. Some researchers have focused on the behavioral dimension and have equated engagement with on-task behavior (Greenwood, Horton, & Utley 2002). Others argue that engagement needs to include both an emotional and a behavioral dimension (Finn, 1989; Skinner & Belmont, 1993). In a more recent review of the literature, my colleagues and I present a multidimensional view of engagement that includes **behavioral, emotional**, and **cognitive** engagement (Fredricks et al., 2004). We argue that including all three dimensions gives a richer picture of how students think, feel, and act in the classroom. However, even when researchers agree on the number and types of engagement dimensions, variation exists in how each specific dimension is defined. Table 1.1 outlines these different aspects of behavioral, emotional, and cognitive engagement (Fredricks et al., 2004).

It is important to note that there has been some overlap in the indicators included in definitions of behavioral, emotional, and cognitive engagement. One example of this overlap is student

Table 1.1   Definitions of Behavioral, Emotional, and Cognitive Engagement

Behavioral Engagement	
Positive conduct	1. Follows classroom and school rules
	2. Completes homework
	3. Comes to class with books and materials
Absence of disruptive behaviors	1. Does not skip school
	2. Does not get into trouble
	3. Does not get into fights
Involvement in classroom learning	1. Effort directed at completing tasks
	2. Participates
	3. Concentrates
	4. Pays attention
Participation in school-based extracurricular activities	1. Involvement in sports
	2. Involvement in school clubs
	3. Involvement in student government
Emotional Engagement	
Emotional reactions to classroom, school, or teacher	1. Enjoyment
	2. Interest
	3. Boredom
	4. Anxiety
	5. Happiness
	6. Sadness
Belonging	1. Liked by others
	2. Feels included
	3. Feels respected in school
Value	1. Perceives that task/school is important
	2. Perceives that task/school is useful for future
	3. Perceives that task is interesting
Cognitive Engagement	
Psychological investment in learning	1. Goes beyond requirements
	2. Prefers challenge
	3. Effort directed at understanding and mastering content
Cognitive strategy use	1. Metacognitive self-regulation (i.e., planning, monitoring, and evaluating thinking)
	2. Deep strategy use (elaborates, relates material to previous knowledge, integrates ideas, makes use of evidence)

effort. There is an important distinction between effort that is directed at doing the work versus effort that is directed at learning and understanding (Fredricks et al., 2004). In behavioral engagement definitions, student effort has been used to reflect compliance with the work required in school. In contrast, in cognitive engagement definitions, student effort has been used to describe the degree of psychological investment in learning.

STOP AND REFLECT

1. How do you currently define student engagement in your classroom?

2. What do you think of when you think of engaged and disengaged students? (What do they look like? Sound like?)

3. Which component of engagement do you think is most important: behavioral, emotional, or cognitive? Why?

4. How does your answer for question #3 impact your definition of engagement in question #1?

Why Engagement Is More Than On-Task Behavior

The reality is that in most classrooms, different configurations of behavioral, emotional, and cognitive engagement occur, and engagement in one dimension does not necessarily translate to others. Having a quiet and orderly classroom is an important goal for many teachers. As a result, many teachers equate compliance and on-task behavior with engagement. However, just because a student participates and follows the rules, it does not necessarily mean he or she is deeply invested in learning. Benjamin, one of the six students profiled at the beginning of this chapter, is an example of this type of student. Although he does his work and is on-task, he is bored and only using **shallow-learning strategies** that may help him regurgitate material for a test but will not lead to deep learning. Prior research has shown that the use of **deep-learning strategies**, such as relating new information to existing information and actively monitoring comprehension, leads to higher achievement than the use of shallow and surface strategies such as memorization and rote processing (Greene, Miller, Crowson, Duke, & Aley, 2004). Students who use rote strategies do not make as many mental connections, which in turn makes it more difficult for them to retrieve the information and apply it to new situations.

Beatrice is like many students who are only behaviorally engaged. These students are on-task and follow the rules. To an outside observer they look engaged. In many ways they are ideal students, well-behaved and dependable. However, although students like Beatrice are working on a task, they are not necessarily engaged in the effort necessary for deeper understanding. They are not deeply invested in the content and use only shallow- and surface-level strategies to study the material. In contrast, Fiona seeks out challenge, does extra work, and uses deep-learning strategies that will help her to learn and master the content. Prior research shows that students like Fiona have higher achievement because they are connecting and integrating content with their existing knowledge, which helps them to form richer mental representations (Greene et al., 2004).

Ideally, students are high on behavioral, emotional, and cognitive engagement. Fiona and Franco are examples of these fully engaged students. These types of students are easy to teach; they actively participate, are interested in school, and use learning strategies to help them master and learn the content. In turn, these students tend to elicit more positive interaction and support from both their teachers and peers, which can serve to further increase their engagement over time. It is clear that students who can form strong relationships in the classroom are at an advantage that grows exponentially as the academic year progresses. In contrast, at-risk students like Rachel and Ryan, who are showing signs of disengagement, are more difficult to teach. These students often receive less support from their teachers and peers, which serves to further dampen their engagement over time. Unfortunately, this results in a self-amplifying cycle in which individual differences in engagement are magnified over time (Skinner & Pitzer, 2012).

STOP AND REFLECT

1. What types of engagement and disengagement profiles do you see in your classroom?

2. Do you have students who are examples of fully engaged, behaviorally engaged only, or at risk? Who are your Fionas, Francos, Beatrices, Benjamins, Rachels, or Ryans? How do you interact with each type of student?

3. Do you have students who you don't know if or how they are engaged? How do you interact with these students?

WHY ASSESS ENGAGEMENT?

There are several reasons why teachers may want to assess engagement in their classroom. The first is to identify students who are at risk for disengagement and academic failure in order to provide better support to these students. Dropping out of school is not an instantaneous event; for many students it is the last step in a long process of disengagement from school (Finn, 1989). Teachers can play a critical role in identifying those students who show signs of disengagement and intervene to potentially prevent them from dropping out of school. Rachel and Ryan are examples of two students who are showing some early warning signs and could benefit from positive support and intervention. Chapter 7 outlines practical strategies for working with disengaged youth like Rachel and Ryan.

The second reason to assess engagement is to monitor how students are responding to the academic and social experiences in the classroom in order to see what is working and what might need to be changed. It is important for teachers to monitor both the variation in engagement within the same individual and across different individuals. The reality is not all students are engaged all of the time. Any given student may show different patterns of behavior, emotion, and cognition depending on the type of task, and he or she may even show different patterns with the same task if tired or distracted by something inside or outside of the classroom. At both the individual and class level, teachers can see how students respond to different classroom contexts (e.g., whole-class discussions, small-group work, and seatwork) and different subject areas.

Finally, a teacher or administrator may want to collect data on engagement as part of school improvement efforts. This might be accomplished through a teacher's classroom inquiry or as part of a professional learning community. Many school interventions focus on increasing engagement as a means to improving achievement and school completion rates. Collecting data on engagement can be used to evaluate the effectiveness of these school-wide reforms and can more effectively guide professional development efforts.

CONSISTENCY, DURATION, AND VARIATION IN ENGAGEMENT

There are a variety of questions that teachers might ask about the level of engagement in their classrooms, as the following three sections illustrate.

How consistent is student engagement in my classroom? An important question concerns the consistency of engagement across individual students. There are certain times of the day when students are more or less engaged in learning. For example, transitions between activities are a time when one often sees a drop in engagement. Furthermore, engagement varies across subject areas. Engagement tends to be higher in subject areas in which students think that they have high ability, find the content interesting, and/or see value in learning the content for their futures. Conversely, engagement tends to be lower in contexts where students are having academic difficulties, find the subject boring and unrelated to their lives, and/or do not see how learning more about the topic can help them in the future.

When and where are my students engaged? It is also important to consider the breadth, or variation, in engagement across different instructional settings. Prior research suggests that engagement varies across contextual factors (e.g., small-group work, large-group discussions, lecture, and seatwork) and characteristics of the task (e.g., complexity, challenge, time). For example, engagement has been found to be lower in classrooms where students spend the majority of their time in teacher-directed and passive activities. In contrast, engagement has been found to be higher in classrooms where students perceive instruction as challenging and when they are in cooperative grouping activities as opposed to large-group discussions (Shernoff & Csikzentmihalyi, 2009). Teachers can use information on variations in engagement to make adjustments to instruction.

How extensively are my students engaged? Finally, the duration or length of engagement is important to assess. Some students show high engagement throughout a whole lesson, while other students' engagement varies over time as a result of situational factors. For example, some students like Rachel and Ryan who are showing signs of disengagement may show an increase in engagement when they are working with their friends or working on a more creative project. For these students, teachers should try to identify the triggers that can either help to increase or decrease their engagement.

STOP AND REFLECT

1. What is your engagement goal for your classroom? Do you want to increase the percentage of students engaged, the time students are engaged, or the contexts in which students are engaged?

2. In what activities are students typically most engaged in your classroom? Why do you think these activities are engaging? When does students' attention waver? What do you believe triggers the disengagement?

3. At what times of the day are students most engaged? Least engaged? How do you explain the differences in engagement throughout the school day?

4. Do you have students like Ryan and Rachel who are behaviorally disengaged in your classroom?

   a. When, where, and with whom does their problem behavior occur?

   b. How do you react to the problem behavior? How do others react?

METHODS FOR ASSESSING ENGAGEMENT

Self-report measures. There are a variety of ways to assess engagement in the classroom. The most common way is to ask students to fill out self-report surveys that contain a series of questions about their behavior, emotion, and cognition. Some of these questions assess general engagement at the school level, while others measure engagement in a specific class. In these surveys, students circle their responses to **Likert-response items.** This is a fixed-response format to measure the level of agreement/disagreement with a particular statement. These items are usually measured on a 1-to-4, 1-to-5, or a 1-to-7 response scale, with responses that range from "strongly agree" to "strongly disagree" or "very true of me" to "not true of me." For younger students, scales can be a series of facial icons, such as ☺. If your students have easy access to technology, there are a variety of free resources for quickly and effectively surveying their perceptions (see Table 1.2). Scores can be either summed or averaged across items to form a scale or total score to describe the student on each dimension. **Scale scores** will more accurately represent behavioral, emotional, and cognitive engagement than any individual item.

Self-report methods are widely used because they are the most practical and easy to administer in classrooms. They can be given to large and diverse groups of students at a low cost, making it

Table 1.2   Common Survey Tools for Teachers

Product	Web Address	Company
Blackboard	www.blackboard.com	1997–2011 Blackboard, Inc.
Google Docs	www.google.com	Google
ProfilerPro	www.profilerpro.com	2003–2006 ALTEC
Quia	www.quia.com	2011 IXL Learning
Moodle	www.moodle.org	Moodle Trust
Survey Gizmo	www.surveygizmo.com	2005–2011 Widgix
Survey Monkey	www.surveymonkey.com	2009–2011 Survey Monkey
Zoomerang	www.zoomerang.com	2011 MarketTools, Inc.

possible to compare results across settings. Self-report methods are particularly useful for assessing students' perceptions of their emotional and cognitive engagement. These two dimensions of engagement are not directly observable (i.e., they are indirect measures of engagement) and need to be inferred from behavior or need to be reported by the student. One concern with self-report measures is that students may not answer honestly under some conditions, and, as a result, the self-report may not reflect actual behaviors, emotions, and cognitions. Another concern is that these measures often contain items that are worded too broadly (e.g., "I work hard in school") rather than worded to reflect engagement in particular tasks and situations.

Behavioral engagement can be measured with questions that ask students about their attention, effort, persistence, attendance, time spent on homework, preparation for class, participation in school-based activities, and risky behaviors (e.g., skipping school). **Emotional engagement** is measured with questions about emotions experienced in school, such as being happy or anxious. In addition, questions about students' level of interest, enjoyment, boredom, and perception of value of school, or how important school is, are also indicative of emotional engagement. Finally, **cognitive engagement** is measured with items that ask students about the use of deep-learning strategies, whether they like doing hard or challenging work, and whether they do more than is required either at school or at home (Fredricks et al., 2012). Table 1.3 includes some sample self-report items for behavioral, emotional, and cognitive engagement. These items may be on a 1-to-4, 1-to-5, or 1-to-7 Likert scale (1 = "never"; 4, 5, or 7 = "all of the time"; 1 = "not at all true"; 4, 5, or 7 = "very true").

Teacher ratings scales. Another method for assessing engagement is to have teachers rate individual students on a series of items about their behavior, emotion, and cognition. This technique can be particularly useful with younger children who have limited literacy skills and more difficulty completing self-report measures. It is also very useful when data needs to be collected on specific students. Teachers tend to be especially good reporters of student behaviors. However, accurately assessing emotional and cognitive engagement can be more difficult, especially if students mask their negative emotions and demonstrate compliant behavior, as in the cases of Beatrice and Benjamin.

Table 1.3 Sample Engagement Self-Report Items

Behavioral Engagement
1. I pay attention in class.
2. I work hard to do my best in class.
3. When I am in class, I listen very carefully.
4. When I am in class, I just act like I am working. (reverse coded)
5. I complete my homework on time.
6. I get in trouble at school. (reverse coded)
7. If I can't understand my schoolwork, I just keep doing it until I do.
Emotional Engagement
1. I feel happy to be part of school.
2. I enjoy learning new things.
3. When we work on something in class, I feel discouraged. (reverse coded)
4. I am bored at school. (reverse coded)
5. Most of things we learn in school are useless. (reverse coded)
6. School is one of my favorite places to be.
7. Sometimes I get so interested in school, I don't want to stop.
Cognitive Engagement
1. When I read a book, I ask myself questions to make sure I understand.
2. I classify problems into categories before I begin to work on them.
3. I check my schoolwork for mistakes.
4. Before I begin studying, I think about what I need to learn.
5. I work several examples of the same problem so I can understand problems better.
6. When I finish working a problem, I check my answers to see if they are reasonable.

Table 1.4 presents the Engagement versus Disaffection with Learning teacher ratings scale that was designed to measure behavioral and emotional engagement in the classroom (Skinner, Kindermann, & Furrer 2009). This survey has separate scales for engagement and disaffection (i.e., disengagement) in the classroom. This measure was initially developed for upper elementary

Table 1.4   Engagement Versus Disaffection Learning Survey—Teacher Report

Behavioral Engagement
1. In my class, this student works as hard as he/she can.
2. When working on classwork in my class, this student appears involved.
3. When I explain new material, this student listens carefully.
4. In my class, this student does more than is required.
5. When my student doesn't do well, he/she works harder.
Emotional Engagement.
1. In my class, this student is enthusiastic.
2. In my class, this student appears happy.
3. When we start something new in class, this student is interested.
4. When working on classwork, this student seems to enjoy it.
5. For this student, learning seems to be fun.
Behavioral Disaffection (i.e., Behavioral Disengagement)
1. When we start something new in class, this student thinks about other things.
2. In my class, this student comes unprepared.
3. When faced with a difficult assignment, this student doesn't even try.
4. In my class, this student does just enough to get by.
5. When we start something new in class, this student doesn't pay attention.
Emotional Disaffection (i.e., Emotional Disengagement)
1. When we work on something in class, this student appears to be bored.
2. When working on classwork, this student seems worried.
3. In my class, this student seems unhappy.
4. In my class, this student is anxious.
5. In my class, this student appears to be depressed.
6. In my class, this student is angry.
7. When working on classwork, this student appears frustrated.
8. When I explain new material, this student doesn't seem to care.
9. When working on classwork in my class, this student seems uninterested.

Source: Skinner, Kindermann, & Furrer (2009). Used with permission.

school classrooms but has since been used with older students. These questions can be applied to any subject area. All items are a 1-to-4 scale (1 = "not at all true"; 4 = "very true").

Few measures have been designed to measure engagement in specific subject areas. One exception is the Reading Engagement Index (REI; see Table 1.5), developed by Allan Wigfield and his colleagues at the University of Maryland (Wigfield et al., 2008). This teacher self-report measure was developed to assess behavioral, emotional, and cognitive engagement in reading in the elementary school years. All items are on a 4-point response scale from 1 ("not true") to 4 ("very true").

Observation measures. Another way to assess engagement is to directly observe individuals, targeted students, or the whole classroom. The majority of these observations measure aspects of behavioral engagement in terms of on-task behavior and participation. Table 1.6 presents some of these sample observational indicators. It is much more difficult to assess cognitive engagement with observational procedures because students may appear to be deeply thinking when in reality they are not. Peterson, Swing, Stark, and Swass (1984) found that some students that were judged to be on-task by observers reported in subsequent interviews that they were not thinking about the material while being observed. In contrast, many of the students who appeared to be off-task reported being very highly cognitively engaged. For example, a student who is looking out of the

Table 1.5   Reading Engagement Index

1. This student often reads independently.
2. This student reads favorite topics and authors.
3. This student is easily distracted in self-selected readings. (reverse scored)
4. This student works hard in reading.
5. This student is a confident reader.
6. This student uses comprehensive strategies well.
7. This student enjoys thinking deeply about the content of texts.
8. This student enjoys discussing books with peers.

Source: Wigfield et al. (2008).

Table 1.6   Sample Observational Indicators of Engagement

Engagement
• On-task
• Listens attentively
• Asks and answers questions
• Focuses on learning with minimum distractions
• Persists with a task, even when difficult or long
• Expresses interest and enthusiasm
Disengagement
• Inattention
• Aggressive behavior
• Inappropriate movement
• Inappropriate vocalization

window and tapping his or her pencil while deeply thinking about the content would be incorrectly rated as lower in engagement using these observational techniques than would a student who is diligently taking notes but not deeply engaged in understanding the ideas.

Although it is more difficult to directly assess emotional and cognitive engagement through observational methods, some indicators of these dimensions can be inferred from behavioral indicators. For example, a teacher could measure student preferences for challenge by their choice of task and their level of persistence. Emotional engagement can be observed when a student expresses enthusiasm and excitement or makes positive comments about an activity to either the teacher or a peer.

There are several ways to record observational data. The most common is to use a **time-sampling procedure** in which the observer records whether a certain behavior occurs for an individual during a specific time interval, which usually ranges from fifteen to thirty seconds. Table 1.7 presents a sample recording form for a time-sampling observation that measures on-task/off-task behavior for an individual student. For each time interval, the observer records whether the target student is on- or off-task. It is also important to record the time, subject, and setting to see if there are certain contexts or times of the day when the student tends to be more or less engaged.

Time-sampling procedures can also be used to assess the level of engagement at the classroom level. During each interval, the observer scans the classroom to count the number of students who are engaged and disengaged. This information can be used to create a percentage of students engaged during each interval and an average percentage of students who look disengaged. Another way to record observational data is to do an **event count** in which the observer records the number of times a predetermined behavior, such as inappropriate behavior, happens in a particular context. This data can be collected at either the individual or class level.

Teachers can also use a checklist or an inventory of behaviors to collect data on behavioral engagement. For each indicator, the observer checks whether the behavior occurred. Finally, observers can use a predetermined rating scale to record the level of engagement. The observer assesses the quality of a student's engagement either on individual indicators or on an overall measure of student engagement (1 = "not at all engaged";

Table 1.7 Sample Observational Form

Child Observed _____   Time of Observation _____

Date _____   Academic Subject _____

Observer _____   Setting _____

Moment	1	2	3	4	5	6	7	8	9	10
On-Task										
Off-Task										

Moment	11	12	13	14	15	16	17	18	19	20
On-Task										
Off-Task										

Total Intervals Observed _____   % On-Task _____

% Off-Task _____

Notes: _____

5 = "deeply engaged"). The observer assigns a value to each indicator along the continuum based on either direct observations or past documented observations.

Observations can either be conducted by a teacher or an outside observer such as an administrator, school psychologist, or a well-trained aide. However, observing your own students may be the most effective. Because teachers see students on a daily basis, they are better able to assess whether a behavior is typical or atypical for that particular individual. In addition, students may change their behavior if they know they are being observed by an outsider. It is also more efficient for a teacher to collect observational data for behaviors that occur at low rates or for behaviors that are unpredictable. On the other hand, conducting observations at the individual level can be difficult to do while teaching a lesson to a larger group of students.

Arrangements to support teachers who are asked to administer observational measures should be considered. Learning to reliably record data requires investments in training time, especially with more detailed observational measures. These trade-offs have to be weighed when deciding on the most appropriate observer. It is also important for the observer to collect enough data and to collect data across various academic settings (e.g., small groups, larger groups, individual seatwork) in order to get an accurate picture of engagement. For indicators of low behavioral frequency, the observer should try to identify the antecedents and consequences that can either prompt or reinforce behavior. This information can be used to determine both patterns and triggers of engagement and disengagement.

In the following **Engagement in Practice** section, Melissa discusses teachers' use of peer observations at her school.

ENGAGEMENT IN PRACTICE: PEER OBSERVATIONS

Melissa: For several years, teachers at our school have conducted peer visitations. Twice a year each teacher is visited and observed and also visits and observes a colleague. The two colleagues discuss specific goals they have and how they would like the observation to be followed. The focus may be on student behavior or teacher responsiveness. The educators conduct a follow-up discussion to share what they observed. These visits are nonevaluative. This is an informal way for colleagues to learn from one another and another means of data collection. Intentionally planning for visitation time and the follow-up discourse allows teachers to tap the resources of their peers. In turn, this may build the strength and capacity of the overall faculty.

Walkthroughs

Another method to collect data on student engagement is to do a **walkthrough**, which is defined as a brief, unscheduled, structured nonevaluative classroom observation. A walkthrough is often called a **learning walk**. These walkthroughs are usually done by an administrator or an outside evaluator and are sometimes collected as part of school improvement efforts. During a walkthrough, the observer writes a short narrative or fills out a short checklist that contains a variety of indicators of instruction and student engagement. A walkthrough is usually coupled with a process in which the observed teacher is given feedback about what was observed and how he or she can improve instruction.

A few observational systems have been developed to assist observers in collecting, managing, and recording data from walkthroughs. These include iObservation (www.iobservation.com), iWalkthrough (www.iwalkthrough.org), and Power Walkthrough (www.mcrel.org/products-and-services/featured-products-and-services/power-walkthrough). Table 1.8 provides some sample indicators of engagement that have been included in walkthroughs. These indicators include aspects of student behavior, emotion, and cognition; the quality of instruction; and the rigor of curriculum.

Early Warning Indicators

Finally, it is possible to use data already collected in school records to identify students who are showing signs of disengagement and are at risk of dropping out of school. A case study can be compiled using this data. Previous research has identified early

Table 1.8   Sample Indicators of Walkthroughs of Student Engagement

• Student is consistently on-task.
• Student is paying attention to the teacher and other students.
• Transitions between lessons are quick and efficient with minimum "downtime."
• Students exhibit interest and excitement.
• Teacher uses a variety of strategies to keep students engaged in lesson.
• Students are engaged in higher-order learning.
• Students are engaged in active conversations that construct learning.

warning indicators that signal higher odds that the student will get in trouble, struggle academically, and ultimately drop out of school (Balfanz, Herzog, & MacIver 2007). The predictive power of these early warning indicators is being used by many schools, districts, and organizations to guide prevention efforts. Examples of early warning indicators include:

- Tardiness
- Skipping school
- Absenteeism
- Behavioral referrals
- Detention
- Suspensions
- Failing classes
- Being behind in credits

In the following Engagement in Practice section, Ellen describes how early warning signs are being used to identify students at risk for disengagement at her school.

ENGAGEMENT IN PRACTICE: DATA WALL

Ellen: In the ninth grade at Norwich Free Academy, students are assigned a multidisciplinary team, consisting of four teachers, a guidance counselor, a special education teacher, and a school counselor, that is responsible for ensuring students have a successful ninth-grade experience. Members of the multidisciplinary team create a "data wall" or Google Doc spreadsheet to improve communication and to track data on students' behavioral engagement and achievement. This document is used to identify early warning indicators, to document interventions, and to track student improvement. Examples of early warning indicators on the "data wall" include achievement test scores, absenteeism, disciplinary referrals, and lost credits. This information is used to design intervention plans and to advocate for additional services in planning and placement team meetings.

Once information is collected on student behavior, it is important to have a mechanism to discuss this information and develop an intervention plan. In the next section, Melissa describes the importance of having a common meeting time to discuss students' academics and behavior.

ENGAGEMENT IN PRACTICE: COMMON TEAM MEETING TIME

Melissa: One way we support collaboration and discuss student engagement and performance at my school is to have common team meeting times. When schedules are created each year, we assure that grade-level teams and cross-grade levels have time to meet each week. While some of this is for planning, it is also used to discuss students' academics and behavior. Sometimes the student's previous teacher can offer insight, or my colleagues may offer ideas that have worked with students in their classrooms. Specialists such as the school social worker, instructional coaches, or special education teachers are invited to offer input. The routine frequency of these meetings is invaluable. Interventions can be collaboratively planned, implemented, and discussed as soon as seven days later. Common meeting times may seem like a simple strategy, yet intentionally scheduling time for colleagues to draw upon one another's expertise is empowering for teachers and beneficial for other students.

CHAPTER SUMMARY

This chapter began with the argument that engagement needs to be conceptualized as a multidimensional construct that includes behavior, emotion, and cognition. In addition to knowing how students act, it is critical to know how students feel about school and how they think. Six hypothetical cases were presented to illustrate how students vary on these different dimensions. The goal of this chapter was to counter the assumption that engagement is the same as compliance or on-task behavior. Students who are behaviorally engaged may look to the outside observer like they are fully engaged. However, these students may not be emotionally invested or using the cognitive strategies that are necessary for deep learning.

Next, the chapter outlined different reasons to assess engagement in the classroom, which include identifying students at risk for academic failure, monitoring how students are responding to the classroom environment, and evaluating school improvement efforts. Finally, different methods for assessing engagement in the classroom were reviewed, including student self-reports, teacher ratings, observational measures, walkthroughs, and collecting data on early warning signs. For each of these techniques, sample items that have been used in prior research were shared. The chapter concludes with *Text-to-Practice Exercises* to help educators apply these ideas to real classroom situations, a review of key terms and concepts, and a list of books and Web sites educators can consult for additional information.

TEXT-TO-PRACTICE EXERCISES

TPE 1.1: **Observe engagement:** Choose two students to observe across different contexts and subject areas. Note commonalities and differences in engagement. Document any patterns both within and across the students. Be sure to consider how individual and contextual factors impact engagement.

TPE 1.2: **Ask students about their engagement:** Ask a student about their engagement by using items from the self-report surveys listed in Table 1.2. Ask the child to explain his or her responses. Note that student feedback can be gathered over the course of several weeks.

TPE 1.3: **Identify disengagement in the classroom:** Identify students who are showing signs of disengagement in the classroom either by using observational techniques or by collecting data on early warning signs. How are these students' behaviors, emotions, and cognitions similar and different? What classroom practices and social experiences may be contributing to their disengagement?

KEY TERMS AND CONCEPTS

Behavioral engagement: Level of participation, task involvement, and prosocial conduct in school activities.

Cognitive engagement: Refers to the investment, thoughtfulness, and the willingness to exert the mental effort necessary in an activity.

Deep-learning strategies: Strategies that help students to deeply understand material. These strategies include finding connections, linking information to prior knowledge, and actively monitoring comprehension.

Emotional engagement: Includes positive and negative reactions to teachers, classmates, academics, and school. It reflects an individual's sense of belonging and sense of identification with school.

Early warning indicators: Behavioral and academic indicators that have been identified that put individuals at higher risk for academic failure and dropping out of school.

Event count: An observer records the number of times a predetermined behavior occurs.

Likert-response items: Specified response formats (such as "strongly agree" to "strongly disagree" or "very true of me" to "not very true of me").

Observations: A method of collecting data in which the behavior of individuals, targeted students, or classrooms is directly observed.

Scale scores: A set of items or questions intended to measure the same construct. A scale score is created by averaging or summing the individual items.

Shallow-learning strategies: Strategies that help students to memorize or reproduce knowledge with little attempt at deeper analysis or understanding.

Student self-report: Method for collecting data in which students respond to a series of Likert-response items.

Teacher ratings: Scores assigned to students based on teacher responses to a set of items using a specified response format (e.g., "very true of student" to "not very true of student").

Time-sampling procedures: Predetermined units of time (time sample) are used to guide an observer's attention throughout the observation period.

Walkthroughs/learning walks: Frequent, short, and unscheduled observations of student behavior and instruction. An important dimension of walkthroughs is providing teachers feedback and opportunities for reflection.

RESEARCH-BASED RESOURCES

Books and Reports to Read

Fredricks, J., & McColskey, W., with Meli, J., Mordica, J., Montrosse, B., & Mooney, K. (2010). *Measuring student engagement in upper elementary through high school: A description of 21 instruments.* Issues & Answers Report, REL 2010–No. 098. Washington, DC: U.S. Department of Education, Institute of Education Sciences, National Center for Education Evaluation and Regional Assistance, Regional Educational Laboratory Southeast. Retrieved from http://ies.ed.gov/ncee/edlabs/projects/project.asp?projectID=268.

Shapiro, E. S. (2004). *Academic skills problems: Direct assessment and intervention* (3rd ed.). New York, NY: Guilford Press.

Web Sites to Visit

1. **Direct Behavioral Ratings** (www.directbehaviorratings .org). This site provides resources for doing observations of behaviors in the classroom. Sample observations forms and information on how to plot data graphically and evaluate student behavior are presented.

2. **High School Survey of Student Engagement** (www.Indiana .edu/~ceep/hssse). This site provides information on the High School Survey of Student Engagement, a comprehensive national survey of student engagement and school climate taken by more than 400,000 secondary students. Information for schools interested in participating in the survey is available.

3. **Classroom Assessment Scoring System (CLASS)** (www .teachstone.org). This site provides information on the Classroom Assessment Scoring System (CLASS), a classroom observation tool developed by Robert Pianta at the University of Virginia.

4. **iObservation** (www.iobservation.com). iObservation is a data collection and management system for collecting data from classroom walkthroughs, teacher observations, and self-assessments. Sample observational forms are available on the site.

5. **iWalkthrough.org** (www.iwalkthrough.org). This site provides a set of resources developed by the Great School Partnership for conducting classroom observations and walkthroughs.

6. **Power Walkthrough** (www.mcrel.org/products-and-services/ featured-products-and-services/power-walkthrough). This site provides information on the Power Walkthrough software, a tool for collecting data on instructional practices and the level of school engagement.

CHAPTER TWO

MYTH 2: Some Students Just Don't Care

How Disengagement Is More Than Just a Lack of Student Motivation

T eachers who observe disengagement in their classroom often assume that something about the individual student is responsible for this disengagement and/or that a disengaged student just doesn't care and is not motivated to participate. Some teachers believe and often say that they would have a more engaging classroom if they just had the opportunity to work with a more motivated group of students. Individual characteristics of students do make it easier or more difficult to create a highly engaged classroom, and teachers can influence how student characteristics and learning tasks interact. Table 2.1 lists some of the individual characteristics that have been shown to be predictors of engagement. Research has linked achievement; **self-efficacy**, or an individual's beliefs about his or her ability to succeed in a situation; **intrinsic motivation**, or a motivation driven by an interest or enjoyment in the task; **mastery goal orientation**, or a focus on learning and understanding; and **utility value**, or perception of the importance of course work, to higher behavioral,

Table 2.1   Student Characteristics Related to Higher Behavioral, Emotional, and Cognitive Engagement

Student Characteristic	Definition by Example	Case Studies From Chapter 1
High prior achievement	"I earn high grades and test scores."	High: Fiona, Franco, Benjamin Low: Ryan and Rachel
Self-efficacy	"I feel like I can do this task."	High: Fiona and Franco Low: Ryan and Rachel
Intrinsic motivation	"I am doing this task based on pleasure in an activity rather than working towards an external reward."	High: Fiona and Franco Low: Beatrice, Benjamin, Ryan, and Rachel
Mastery goal orientation	"I am doing this task because I want to learn and understand."	High: Fiona and Franco Low: Beatrice, Benjamin, Ryan, and Rachel
Utility value	"It is important for me to learn what is being taught in this class for the future."	High: Fiona, Franco, Beatrice, and Benjamin Low: Ryan and Rachel

emotional, and cognitive engagement (Fredricks et al., 2004; Greene et al. 2004).

Teachers know that it is easier to engage students like Fiona and Franco, two of the students whose profiles were introduced at the beginning of Chapter 1. Fiona and Franco are successful in school, have high perceptions of their ability (i.e., self-efficacy), are intrinsically interested in learning, and approach tasks with a mastery goal orientation. In contrast, students like Ryan and Rachel are more challenging to engage because they do not believe that they have the skills to be successful (i.e., low self-efficacy), find school boring, and question the usefulness of school (i.e., low utility value) in their lives. Although teaching would hypothetically be easier if all students in the classroom were like Fiona and Franco, the reality is that students enter classrooms with a range of prior interests, abilities, and attitudes about school. The challenge for educators is to find a way to engage all of these different types of students.

Engagement is more than just motivation. Sometimes the terms *engagement* and *motivation* are used interchangeably; however, they are different and their distinctions are important. Motivation emphasizes psychological or internal processes that are more difficult to change, while engagement reflects an individual's interaction with his or her context (Fredricks et al., 2004). In other words, when an individual is engaged in something, it is difficult to separate their engagement from the environment. Moreover, it is possible for a student to be motivated but not actively engaged in a task (Connell & Wellborn, 1991). Motivation is necessary, but not sufficient, for engagement.

Engagement reflects an interaction between individual characteristics and contextual factors. The goals of this chapter are to counter the myth that disengagement merely reflects low motivation and to help teachers both identify and reflect on the elements of the instructional and social dynamics that may also be contributing to disengagement in the classroom. One reason many researchers and policymakers have begun to focus on engagement is that it possible to increase it through changes to the instructional and social environment of classrooms. Unfortunately, there also is evidence that many common practices in schools are actually leading to lower engagement among students. In this chapter, we review how traditional school tasks, poor relationships with teachers, and peer rejection contribute to disengagement.

SCHOOL VERSUS OUT-OF-SCHOOL TASKS

One reason students may be disengaged is that learning in school often bears little resemblance to how learning happens outside of the school context. Students like Benjamin may do their work and be behaviorally engaged because they have **extrinsic motivation** to get good grades and believe that doing well in school will help them in the future. However, it is more difficult to get these types of students emotionally and cognitively engaged in traditional school tasks that have little relevance to their own lives and are not structured in a way to support deep learning. Table 2.2 lists some important differences between learning in school and in out-of-school contexts that researchers have identified over more than two decades.

In school, students spend a large portion of their time in **direct instruction**, a pedagogy that emphasizes explicit instruction of skills through lectures, demonstrations, and individual seatwork. A large-scale study of over 2,500 classrooms showed that fifth graders spent 90 percent of their class time listening to a teacher or working alone and only 7 percent of their time in small-group activities (Pianta, Belsky, Houts, & Morrison, 2007). Paper-and-pencil worksheets and other passive learning activities are common in many of these classrooms. In these environments, teachers are in control. They determine the structure, routines, and learning activities, and students have limited opportunities to make decisions related to their learning. School learning is primarily based on symbols and is decontextualized from objects and events outside of school. The content often has little relation to students' lived experiences. Although the benefits of direct instruction have been identified as contributing to higher scores on low-level tests of basic competencies, this instructional approach will likely have a less positive effect on student engagement and the conceptual outcomes outlined in the Common Core and Next Generation Science Standards.

A growing body of research on learning in organized out-of-school settings, including after-school and community-based programs and learning in practical and work situations, suggests that the mental activity outside of school is very different than that which occurs in traditional classrooms (Larson, 2000; Resnick, 1987). These outside environments tend to be more **child-centered**. Individuals have some choice over learning activities and often participate in designing rules, consequences, and rewards for good behavior. Outside of school, individuals use objects, events, and actions directly in their reasoning, rather than just using symbols to represent ideas. Much of learning outside of school also occurs in groups. Knowledge is socially distributed, as each individual depends on what others do and know. These groups work together to try and solve cognitively complex real-world problems. These activities often occur over an extended period of time and culminate in a public presentation of findings.

One of the key differences between learning in school and in out-of-school settings is how information is shared. In traditional classrooms, the goal of many activities is for students to reproduce knowledge in assignments that are only shared with their teacher.

Table 2.2   Differences Between Learning in School and in Out-of-School Contexts

Traditional School Contexts	Out-of-School Contexts
• Teacher-directed	• Child-centered
• Passive	• Active
• Individual knowledge	• Socially shared knowledge
• Limited time	• Extended time
• Decontextualize	• Real-world context
• Reproduction of knowledge	• Creation of knowledge

For the most part, a student's success is independent of what other students do in the classroom. In contrast, in out-of-school settings, individuals often work together, and the knowledge that is created is shared with a larger community.

In the following *Engagement in Practice* section, Michele describes one strategy she has used to change how knowledge is distributed and shared in her classroom. She uses a "reading buddies" program to work on literacy and arts activities that are shared with the larger school community.

ENGAGEMENT IN PRACTICE: READING BUDDIES

Michele: At my pre-kindergarten through eighth grade elementary school, each younger grade classroom pairs up with an older grade classroom to work together as reading buddies throughout the school year. This collaboration also involves the older students helping the younger ones with writing. The collaborative work is displayed in the main hallways of the school. The older students read a book or two to their younger buddies, and as the year progresses, they listen to the younger buddies read out loud to them. Each year, my fourth graders pair up with a kindergarten class and the buddies work on projects that relate to the kindergarten-themed units. A couple of times a year, our class also invites the younger

(Continued)

(Continued)

buddies for a reading buddies author's share, where the fourth graders take turns reading aloud a piece of writing they have written during our writer's workshop. The fourth graders choose an excerpt to read to their audience, just like real-world authors do when they are on a book tour. The author's share with our reading buddies helps students to practice reading aloud for a writing celebration that we have in our classroom when we invite parents to come in and listen to our finalized pieces. It is a great way for the class to share their writing with other students and families in the larger school community.

STOP, REFLECT, AND TRY

1. Using Table 2.2, how would you characterize the tasks in your classroom?

   a. Do your students spend most of their time listening to the teacher?

   b. How often do your students have opportunities to work in small groups?

   c. Do students spend most of their time reproducing knowledge or constructing knowledge?

   d. How much time do your students have to work on assignments in class?

   e. What type of feedback do you give students on assignments?

   f. Do your students have opportunities to share their knowledge with their classmates, the larger community, or with a virtual community?

   g. Are your students given any opportunities to choose assignment topics or how or when they complete an assignment?

2. What changes could you make to your instruction to incorporate the aspects of learning in out-of-school contexts listed in Table 2.2? Incorporate one of these changes into your instruction. Track how students respond.

Unfortunately, this emphasis on traditional school tasks has been exacerbated by accountability movements. In many classrooms, students spend much of their time on drill and practice and on tasks that require recall or repetition of procedures. Students like Fiona, Franco, Beatrice, and Benjamin will be behaviorally engaged in these classrooms. They will pay attention, stay on task, and use shallow-learning strategies such as rehearsal or underlining to complete assignments. However, this type of work does not lead to emotional engagement, cognitive engagement, or deeper learning. Students quickly become bored with the repetition of these activities, making it less likely that the information will be stored in long-term memory (Willingham, 2009). Moreover, these types of tasks are less likely to require intensive effort, self-regulation, or higher-level learning strategies that promote deep understanding and flexible use of knowledge. For some students, such as Rachel and Ryan, the focus on achievement test preparation can actually backfire and lead to lower achievement test scores because they find the classroom environment so disengaging. Ironically, the desire of educational policymakers to bring about immediate increases in student achievement is having the unintended consequence of inhibiting classroom practices that have been found to be most likely to increase student engagement and result in deeper learning. Whereas behavioral engagement may be important in low-level tasks, as schools move to new and more highly conceptual standards, emotional and cognitive engagement will be essential.

TEACHER–STUDENT RELATIONS AND DISENGAGEMENT

A sizeable research literature demonstrates the importance of high-quality teacher-student relationships for increasing behavioral, emotional, and cognitive engagement (Fredricks et al., 2004). Teachers who form positive relationships with their students are creating classroom environments where deep learning can take place, while at the same time supporting students' social and emotional development. Relationships with teachers are particularly important for students who display academic and behavioral problems (Hamre & Pianta, 2006). Positive relations with teachers can protect students at risk for school failure. Unfortunately, poor-quality relations between students and teachers can actually increase the level of academic risk (Ladd & Burgess, 2001). Strategies for developing stronger relationships with students are outlined in more detail in Chapter 5. In this section, the groundwork is laid for understanding why teacher-student relations are essential for engagement.

The importance of developing positive relations with teachers continues as students get older. Although students spend less time with teachers during the middle and high school years, having a positive personal connection with a teacher is predictive of higher classroom participation, higher interest and enjoyment, and lower dropout rates (Fredricks et al., 2004).

However, as students transition from elementary to middle school, the quality of their relationships with their teachers tends to decline. Eccles and her colleagues (1993) suggest that this decline is a result of a mismatch between youths' developmental needs and the context of middle schools. At a time when students would benefit developmentally from close relationships with teachers, the size and structure of middle schools often does not facilitate a sense of connectedness and may instead lead to greater feelings of alienation. In middle schools, students have multiple teachers and spend limited time each day with any one teacher. Furthermore, the emphasis in many middle schools is on management and control rather than on supporting students' social and emotional needs. This can make it even more difficult for teachers and students to develop these connections.

Although many teachers have positive relationships with the students in their classrooms, others do not. Some teacher-student relationships can be characterized as **conflicted teacher-student relationships**. In these relationships, teachers and students are angry, show little warmth, do not communicate, and appear disconnected from each other (Pianta, 1999). Prior research has found that teacher conflict with students predicts lower levels of classroom participation and achievement (Ladd, Birch, & Buhs, 1999). Although teachers are frequently troubled by their relationships with students, they often do not know how or feel unable to better meet these students' needs.

Why do some students and teachers develop poor relations? Which types of students are most at risk for developing poor relations? Table 2.3 lists some factors that place students at risk for

Table 2.3   Student Risk Factors for Problematic Student-Teacher Relationships

Risk Factor	Case Study
Aggression	Ryan
Disruptive behavior	Ryan
Inconsistent attendance	Rachel
Male	Ryan
Lack of participation	Ryan and Rachel
Problems with family relationships	Ryan
Behavioral problems at home	Ryan
Referred to special education	
Mental health problems	

problematic teacher-student relationships. Students like Ryan and Rachel who are behaviorally disengaged (disruptive, hostile, aggressive, or disconnected) tend to have poorer relations with their teachers. Teachers prefer students like Fiona, Franco, Beatrice, and Benjamin who are academically competent, responsible, and conform to school rules. In addition, boys typically have more conflict and less close relationships with their teachers than do girls (see Chapter 7 for more information on supporting boys' engagement). This finding may reflect the limited number of male teachers in elementary and middle schools and the fact that girls tend to be more compliant and less disruptive in the classroom. A student's experiences at home also matter. Students with poorer family relationships and more behavioral problems at home tend to have less close relationships with teachers (Murray & Murray, 2004). Finally, there is evidence that students with intellectual and emotional disabilities experience less positive teacher relationships than students who have more typical development (Baker, 2006).

These poor student-teacher relations are perpetuated over time. Chronic student-teacher conflict predicts increased behavioral problems and less positive attitudes toward school (Hamre & Pianta, 2006). Ryan is an example of this type of student. He can be disruptive and unmotivated and has failed to develop positive relations with teachers at his school. The disruptive behavior and lack of motivation will likely further evoke negative responses and less positive support from his teacher. In turn, these negative responses will further increase his disengagement over time.

STOP AND REFLECT

1. Do you have conflicted relations with any of your students?

   (Identify students like Ryan or Rachel in your classroom.)

2. What words come to mind when you think of students with whom you have a conflicted relationship?

3. What might you have done to contribute to these conflicted relationships?

4. How do you feel and react when these students show signs of disengagement?

5. Are there times when you have reconnected with students with whom you have had a conflicted relationship? What helped to foster this connection?

Although it can be difficult, teachers play a critical role in breaking a negative interaction cycle between themselves and students. The first step is for teachers to recognize the important role that positive teacher-student relationships play in academic adjustment, especially among students who are most academically at risk. Although it takes more effort to develop relationships with difficult students, the benefits of positive relationships for student engagement are the greatest for these youths. It is also important that teachers reflect on their own feelings about these students and how through their beliefs and actions they may be inadvertently contributing to and perpetuating these negative relations. For example, teachers often label students like Ryan as disruptive or aggressive and interpret all of their actions in light of these perceptions. This can result in students feeling that they are being treated unfairly and judged more critically than their classmates. Teachers should reflect on both the implicit and explicit messages they are providing to disengaged students about their behavior and abilities.

Second, teachers need to change the way they view disengagement. They should not view disengagement as a character flaw of the student or a shortcoming of the teacher. They should view it instead as a signal that this student needs more support and often a different type of support than they are currently receiving. For some students, teachers may need to seek advice or assistance from other staff at the school, such as social workers, school psychologists, and special educators, on how to interact more effectively with these students. Additional strategies for improving relationships with students are discussed in Chapter 5. In the following *Engagement in Practice* section, Ellen describes how she intervened to improve a poor relationship with a student.

ENGAGEMENT IN PRACTICE: IMPROVING TEACHER–CHILD RELATIONSHIPS

Ellen: Last year, I had a very challenging class. This class was difficult to manage largely because of one student who constantly disrupted lessons, talked to her friends while I was trying to address the class, and almost always disregarded my attempts to redirect her. After weeks of conflict, I asked her to see me after school. At first, I planned to use this meeting as a punishment and to talk with her about her behavior and how she could change it to benefit her classmates' learning experience. However, we never got a chance to discuss her behavior. She arrived early for her detention, and, rather than being upset with me for giving her a detention, she was happy to spend time with me. The first thing she said to me was, "What is your mom like?" I told her that my mom was supportive, caring, and motivating. Then I asked her what her mom was like. Sadly, she told me something very different. She proceeded to tell me her entire family history, which was one of the saddest stories to date. After our meeting, which lasted a couple of hours, my greatest opponent became my greatest ally. She was almost always on-task and even reprimanded her classmates for off-task and disrespectful behavior. I realized that she was looking for a strong, consistent, supportive, female role model.

PEER RELATIONS AND DISENGAGEMENT

The peer dynamics in the classroom can also either promote or undermine engagement. Students who are accepted by their peers tend to have more positive attitudes towards school, have higher interest, and behave in more socially acceptable ways (Fredricks et al., 2004). However, whereas positive peer relationships can enhance engagement, peer rejection and low peer acceptance negatively impacts engagement and achievement (see Chapter 6 for more discussion of the positive effects of peers on engagement). Low peer acceptance and **peer rejection**, or being actively disliked by peers, is predictive of indicators of school disengagement, including behavioral problems, negative school attitudes, and school avoidance (Fredricks et al., 2004). The relation between peers dynamics and disengagement is likely to be reciprocal over time. Students who do not conform to school rules and dislike school are less likely to perceive their peers as supportive (Ladd et al., 1999). Ryan's case provides an excellent example of this reciprocal process. His aggressive behaviors have resulted in many of his peers actively disliking him. In turn, this rejection from his peers has resulted in further behavioral problems and alienation from the school context.

There are several explanations for why poor peer relations can have a negative impact on student engagement. Students who are actively disliked by classmates are subjected to peer-imposed mal-treatments (e.g., ignoring, avoiding, and excluding) and actual peer abuse (e.g., ridicule, harassment, and physical harm) (Ladd, Herald-Brown, & Reiser, 2008). Furthermore, students with poor peer relations participate less in classroom activities because they are either ignored or actively excluded from activities. It is also likely that rejected students further disengage from activities and interacting with their classmates as a way of avoiding more nega-tive treatment from their peers. As a result of being excluded from social situations, rejected children also have fewer opportunities to develop and practice **prosocial behaviors**, which are volun-tary behaviors that are made with the intention of benefiting oth-ers (Eisenberg & Fabes, 1998). Examples of prosocial behaviors include: cooperation, sharing, helping a peer with schoolwork, and comforting a peer who is upset. The effect of peer rejection can be particularly problematic during adolescence. Crosnoe

(2011) theorized that feeling like one does not belong to the peer group at school has a negative impact on adolescents' academic adjustment because adolescents use counterproductive coping strategies to deal with their feelings (e.g., using drugs, disengaging from school).

Which students are most at risk for being rejected by their peers? Table 2.4 lists social characteristics that put students at risk for peer rejection and behaviors teachers might see in their classroom that

Table 2.4   Risk Factors for Peer Rejection

Risk Factor	Indicators in the Classroom
Low level of prosocial behavior	1. Difficulty cooperating 2. Difficulty sharing 3. Does not offer instrumental help to peers (e.g., helping with homework) 4. Does not offer emotional support to peers
Low emotional regulation	1. Easily upset 2. Difficulty controlling extreme emotions 3. Emotions inappropriate for situation
Reactive aggression	1. Difficulty interpreting social cues 2. Easily provoked and irritated by other students 3. Overestimates hostility from others and underestimates own level of hostility 4. Views aggression as acceptable way to solve problems
Socially immature	1. Difficulty reading social and physical cues 2. Difficulty understanding jokes and games 3. Responds inappropriately to peers 4. Difficulty making friends own age
Social anxiety	1. Avoids social situations 2. Afraid to speak up in class or social situations because of fear of embarrassing self 3. Fear of situations involving new people 4. Prefers to work alone

are indicative of each of these risk factors. These students exhibit few prosocial behaviors and have difficulty regulating their emotions and managing more extreme emotional states. They can get easily frustrated, irritated, and angry at their peers.

One of the biggest risk factors for peer rejection is **reactive aggression**. Reactive aggression occurs in response to a perceived threat and is often based in fear and is impulsive in nature. Students who display reactive aggression have more difficulty interpreting social situations and generating possible solutions to social problems (Crick & Dodge, 1996). They tend to overestimate hostility in others, are more likely to interpret ambiguous situations as aggressive, are more easily provoked, and are more likely to view aggression as an appropriate means for resolving conflict. Students who are socially immature and have difficulty controlling their behavior also are at a greater risk for peer rejection. These children often act before they think because they are less able to self-regulate their behavior. Finally, students who are fearful and socially anxious are often awkward in social situations, and, as a result, are more likely to be rejected by their peers (Bierman, 2004).

STOP AND REFLECT

1. Have any of your students been actively rejected by their peers?
   a. How did you react to their rejection?
   b. What words come to mind when you think of these students?
   c. Which risk factors for peer rejection outlined in Table 2.4 did they exhibit?
   d. What are some of the triggers that antagonized these students?

2. How are the triggers that antagonize students related to ways in which you organize your classroom, support student interactions, or deliver instruction?

In order to intervene early, it is important to identify students' social skills and areas in need of improvement. Observing peer interactions in the classroom, cafeteria, on the playground, during passing periods, or at school events can provide insight into how students interact with their classmates across a variety of settings. These observations can provide specific details on students' interactive styles and the treatment received from their peers. It is important to observe students in less structured times of the day because it is during these times that more casual conversations and important observations can occur. As students navigate free time, they often need to solve problems, compromise, or stand up for themselves and others. Lunch, transition periods, and recess are also working times for teachers. It is during these times that teachers can model prosocial behaviors. These informal settings are also times that teachers can engage their students in conversations that they may not have been able to have in class.

Teachers should intervene early before the relation between peer rejection and disengagement becomes perpetuated over time. Table 2.5 outlines some practical strategies for working with students who have been rejected by their peers. Positive teacher-student relationships can provide these students with skills that can help them in social interactions with their classmates. For aggressive youths, developing a positive relationship with their teacher has been associated with fewer behavioral problems and greater peer acceptance (Hamre & Pianta, 2006). Teachers also play a key role in modeling interactions towards these students. Students' social preferences have been found to be influenced by their observations of whether the teachers think a peer is desirable (Hughes & Kwok, 2006).

The **Responsive Classroom** is one instructional approach where teachers can model appropriate behavior and teach social skills. This approach emphasizes social, emotional, and academic growth in a safe community (www.responsiveclassroom.org). Developed by classroom teachers in the early 1980s, it is now being used in urban, rural, and suburban classrooms across the nation. The approach consists of practical strategies for helping students to build academic and social-emotional competencies. Responsive classrooms are based on the assumption that a classroom's social dimensions are as important as its academic dimensions. An important focus of these classrooms is teaching students social skills such as cooperation, self-control, empathy, and responsibility. Researchers at the University of Virginia (Rimm-Kaufman, 2012) have shown that schools using Responsive Classroom practices have experienced improved student-teacher interaction, higher

Table 2.5   Practical Strategies for Working With Rejecting Youths

1. *Model appropriate behavior.* Teachers should be a role model for how to regulate emotions and deal with conflict, advocating techniques such as calming down and seeking help when necessary. Children can also benefit from observing either their classmates or other children interact and solve conflicts.

2. *Teach and model problem-solving and conflict resolution skills.* Teachers should explicitly teach and model pro-active language for problem solving. Teaching children to acknowledge both sides of an issue, use "I" messages, and to attack the problem not the person gives them skills for peaceful resolution. These procedures and language must be modeled, taught, and practiced routinely. Peers can also be trained as mediators to help others resolve conflicts.

3. *Provide opportunities for social success.* Having successful social interactions provides positive reinforcement, especially for students who have experienced difficulty in this domain. Set up situations where the child has a good chance of being socially successful. Enlist the help of students with well-developed social skills to help the child interpret social situations. Teachers can use learning buddies, peer mediators, or one-on-one tutoring where a student with difficulty is paired with a younger student and given a leadership role.

4. *Provide positive feedback.* Provide positive, immediate, and informative feedback when the child behaves appropriately. Effective praise should be informative rather than evaluative and controlling (see Chapter 4 for strategies for effective praise). Do not single out a student for misbehavior. Never humiliate a child in front of his or her peers.

5. *Help students learn to manage and regulate emotions.* Instruct children on how to handle emotions and manage anger. Techniques include using self-talk, reframing the problem, identifying alternative solutions that do not involve aggressive responses, seeking help, and avoiding situations where aggressive behavior is more likely.

6. *Develop a personal relationship with the student.* Prior research shows that developing a close relationship with a teacher can be a protective factor for these youths. Get to know the student and show that you care about him or her as an individual. Ask the student about his or her interests and experiences outside of school. Attend a sporting event or other event outside of the school in which the student is participating. Celebrate his or her accomplishments.

7. *Seek out advice from school psychologists, school social workers, and school counselors.* A growing body of study shows that aggressive youths can benefit from social-skills training, social-cognitive interventions, and parent-focused interventions (Bierman, 2004). Most schools have some form of individual or group training for students with social-emotional and behavioral problems. These mental health professionals can also connect students to resources and potential interventions outside of the school.

academic achievement, improved social skills, more positive feelings towards school, and fewer disciplinary problems. (You can download their research brief at http://curry.virginia.edu/uploads/resourceLibrary/Research_brief_SALS.pdf.)

One important classroom practice in the Responsive Classroom model is the **Morning Meeting**. In these meetings, students come together to greet each other and do activities that either help to build community, promote caring among individual students, or resolve a conflict that is occurring among peers. In the following *Engagement in Practice* sections, Michele and Melissa describe how they use a Morning Meeting in their elementary and middle school classrooms to teach social skills and set a positive social tone so all students can feel welcome.

Another concern with peer relations is that the norms of some peer groups do not support engagement and academic achievement. Some ethnographic research has suggested that an

ENGAGEMENT IN PRACTICE:
MORNING MEETING

Michele: In my fourth-grade classroom, we start off every day with a Morning Meeting. We sit in a circle and shake our hands with the neighbors on either side of us, saying "good morning." One or two students spend a couple of minutes sharing news or a story about something that recently happened. Then we do either an ice-breaker or a community-building game and end the meeting by sharing any announcements for the day. A couple of days each week, instead of a group activity, we spend time getting to know one student who is featured for that week. This is a great way to get know our classmates better. With over thirty students in the class, it lasts nearly the entire year. At the first Morning Meeting of the week, the featured student gets to share a poster that they've created about themselves. On these posters, they share information about their families, favorite things, and anything else they would like us to know about them. Another day that week, the featured student brings a letter from home that their parent or a family member has written about them, which shares some interesting things we might not know

(Continued)

(Continued)

about the student (the instructions are sent home to the family the week before). During that day's Morning Meeting, I read the letter aloud to the class. This is one of my class's favorite Morning Meetings of the entire week. Families really enjoy being able to participate in our class through these letters.

Melissa: It is eight o'clock. Twenty-two students and their teacher gather in a circle for Morning Meeting. This group sets a positive tone for the day by welcoming each other with respectful greetings, sharing news and announcements, and playing a community-building game. In the older grades, students lead the meeting, choosing activities that allow students to practice social skills in a safe environment. On this morning, Amanda leads the group in a spider web greeting. A ball of yarn is tossed student to student. As it unrolls, each child is greeted and together the class constructs a web through cooperation and teamwork. Eye contact, listening, speaking, and being noticed are all parts of this daily activity as well as the reminder that we welcome, include, and support all our fellow classmates. After sharing the day's agenda, news, and announcements, Amanda gets the group ready for a cooperative game of marble roll. Holding recycled cardboard troughs, the class passes a marble around the circle. They cheer each other on and encourage each other if the marble falls. Feeling known, safe, and competent, the class is ready to begin the day.

anti-academic culture predominates among African American and low-income youth, who are more likely to be ridiculed by their peers for trying to excel in academic work (Fordham & Ogbu, 1986; National Research Council, 2004). As a result, the hypothesis is these students disengage from school because they fear peer rejection. An anti-academic peer culture has been observed in some ethnographic studies, though large-scale survey research suggests that it is not pervasive among African American or low-income students (National Research Council, 2004). In fact, in many high schools, students report that their peers actually encourage rather than discourage engagement and academic achievement (Brown & Larson, 2009). However, although an anti-academic orientation is not pervasive, it does exist among some students. It is important for teachers to investigate the reasons why these students hold these beliefs. Often these views reflect more about the individual student than the larger peer culture. Rachel is an example of this type of student. Her anti-academic orientation is likely more a result of her fear that she does not have the skills to be successful and a belief that the value of figuring out how to succeed is not worth the effort required.

CHAPTER SUMMARY

The goal of this chapter was to counter the myth that disengagement merely reflects a lack of motivation. Instead, we asked teachers to consider how aspects of both the academic and social environments also play a role in the high levels of disengagement we see in many classrooms. Chapter 2 began with an overview of how engagement encompasses more than just motivation. The remainder of the chapter reviewed the different characteristics of schooling that are contributing to disengagement among today's elementary, middle, and high school students, including an overview of differences between in-school and out-of-school learning, poor teacher-student relationships, and peer rejection. One reason why many students are disengaged is that the structure of school tasks bears little resemblance to how learning happens outside of the classroom. Another reason students are disengaged is that they develop conflictual relationships with their teachers and fail to develop positive relations with their peers. This lack of support contributes to disengagement over time. The chapter concludes with *Text-to-Practice Exercises* to help educators apply these ideas to real classroom situations, a review of key terms and concepts, and a list of additional books and Web resources that teachers can use to explore ways to show their students that they care and to help students care about each other.

TEXT-TO-PRACTICE EXERCISES

TPE 2.1: **Evaluate a lesson:** Evaluate a lesson for the opportunities for learning (see Table 2.2). Describe whether and how the lesson addresses each dimension. How could you improve this lesson to include more of the following dimensions?

    a. Opportunities for students to work in groups

    b. Opportunities for active learning

    c. Real-world topics

    d. Opportunities for public presentation

    e. Opportunities for decision making

TPE 2.2: **Evaluate quality of teacher-student relationships:** Think of students in your classroom that you have had both positive and less positive relationships with. For each student, describe your relationship and how you feel about having this student in your classroom. Using material in this chapter, attempt to explain the reasons for the differences in the quality of the relationships. What strategies could you use to improve the quality of the less positive relationships?

TPE 2.3: **Assess social behavior:** Compare the social behavior of two children with different social profiles (e.g., rejected versus accepted, aggressive versus nonaggressive). Compare these children on the different dimensions outlined in Table 2.4. Observe these children in different settings. Compare how they interpret social cues, regulate emotions, demonstrate prosocial behaviors, and resolve conflicts. Using the material in this chapter, attempt to explain the differences in their peer relations. What strategies could you use in your classroom to model and practice prosocial behaviors?

KEY TERMS AND CONCEPTS

Child-centered: A type of instruction that is focused on each student's needs, abilities, interests, and learning styles. Opportunities for students to make decisions about their learning experiences are central to this instructional method. Teachers play a more facilitative role in these classrooms.

Conflicted teacher-student relationships: Relationship in which teachers and students display anger, limited warmth, and poor communication.

Direct instruction: A type of instruction that is teacher directed and emphasizes carefully articulated lessons in which skills are broken down into small units, deliberately sequenced, and taught explicitly.

Extrinsic motivation: Refers to motivation that comes from external factors outside of the individual, such as grades or rewards.

Intrinsic motivation: Motivation that comes from an internal interest or enjoyment in the task, as opposed to from external factors.

Mastery goal orientation: A focus on learning and understanding as opposed to relative performance.

Morning Meeting: A component of the Responsive Classroom in which students come together to do activities that either help to build community, promote caring among students, or resolve a conflict that is occurring among students.

Peer rejection: Occurs when a student is actively disliked by his or her peers.

Prosocial behaviors: Voluntary behaviors that help others. Examples include sharing, instrumental help, and emotional support.

Reactive aggression: An aggressive response that is impulsive and driven by a perception of hostile responses in others.

Responsive Classroom: A practical approach to teaching that integrates academic and social learning. It incorporates ten classroom practices: 1) Morning Meetings, 2) rule creation, 3) interactive model, 4) positive teacher language, 5) logical consequences, 6) guided discovery, 7) academic choice, 8) classroom organization, 9) working with families, and 10) collaborative problem solving.

Self-efficacy: Individuals' beliefs about their ability to succeed in a situation.

Utility value: Perception of the importance of schoolwork.

RESEARCH-BASED RESOURCES

Books and Reports to Read

Bierman, K. L. (2004). *Peer rejection: Developmental processes and intervention strategies.* New York, NY: Guilford Press.

Brady, K., Forton, M. B., & Porter, D. (2010). *Rules in school: teaching discipline in the responsive classroom.* Turner Falls, MA: Northeast Foundation for Children.

Charney, R. (2002). *Teaching children to care.* Turner Falls, MA: Northeast Foundation for Children.

Crosnoe, R. (2011). *Fitting in, standing out: Navigating the social challenges of high school to get an education.* New York, NY: Cambridge University Press.

Crowe, C. (2012). *How to bullyproof your classroom.* Turner Falls, MA: Northeast Foundation for Children.

Denton, P., (2007). *The power of our words: The teacher language that helps children learn.* Turner Falls, MA: Northeast Foundation for Children.

Denton, P. & Kriete, R. (2000). *The first six weeks of school.* Turner Falls, MA: Northeast Foundation for Children.

Kriete, R. (2002). *The morning meeting book.* Turner Falls, MA: Northeast Foundation for Children.

Pianta, R. C. (1999). *Enhancing relationships between children and teachers.* Washington, DC: American Psychological Association.

Rimm-Kaufman, S. (2012). *Social and academic learning study.* University of Virginia, Curry School of Education. http://curry.virginia.edu/uploads/resourceLibrary/Research_brief_SALS.pdf.

Willingham, D. T. (2009). *Why don't students like school? A cognitive scientist answers questions about how the mind works and what it means for classrooms.* San Francisco, CA: John Wiley and Sons.

Web Sites to Visit

1. **Education.com** (www.education.com). This site includes articles on bullying and improving teacher-student relationships.

2. **Edutopia.com** (www.edutopia.com). This site includes research on social and emotional learning and features profiles of schools that are improving the way students learn using social and emotional learning.

3. **My Teaching Partner** (www.mtpsecondary.net). This site provides information on My Teaching Partner, an individual

professional development program designed to help teachers improve their relationships with their students.

4. **Responsive Classroom** (www.responsiveclassroom.org). This site provides information on the Responsive Classroom model, an instructional approach in the elementary school grades that is designed to help students develop social and emotional competencies.

5. **Origins** (www.originsonline.org). This site includes resources related to the Responsive Classroom model for elementary schools and Developmental Designs, an intervention to teach social, emotional, and academic skills during the middle school years.

6. **Collaboration for Academic, Social, and Emotional Learning (CASEL)** (www.casel.org). This site includes resources on social and emotional learning in schools, including activities, research, and professional development opportunities.

CHAPTER THREE

MYTH 3: What Happens Outside of School Competes With Academics

How Out-of-School Time and Families Affect Engagement in School

In the United States, students are only in school for seven hours each day, for an average of 180 out of 365 days a year. Therefore, it makes little sense to discuss how to engage students in classroom learning without considering the settings in which students live and spend their time. The reality is that youths spend a greater percentage of their waking hours in activities outside of the classroom than those inside in the classroom. Students can spend this out-of-class time in settings and with people that support learning, engagement, and positive development, or they can spend this time in contexts that negatively impact their engagement in the classroom. In this chapter, research related to two places where students spend their out-of-school time is presented. First, the chapter begins with a discussion of the research on the consequences of extracurricular activity participation. Second, research on parent involvement and engagement is presented.

EXTRACURRICULAR ACTIVITY PARTICIPATION AND ACADEMIC OUTCOMES

One way that many children and adolescents choose to spend their out-of-school time is by participating in school- and community-based extracurricular activities such as sports, the arts, and school clubs. In national surveys, over 80 percent of children and adolescents reported involvement in at least one school-based extracurricular context over the past year (Mahoney, Harris, & Eccles, 2006). Although extracurricular participation is a common developmental experience for many youths, some educators question the value of schools investing in these contexts. In an era of accountability and fiscal constraints, many schools have limited their resources to those aspects of the curriculum that were mandated as part of the No Child Left Behind Act. It is estimated that in the 2009–2010 school year, over $2 billion dollars were eliminated from after-school budgets (Fredricks, 2011).

Some educators assume that activities such as sports and the arts are just "extras" and are only useful for fun and recreation. Another common assumption is that participating in extra-curricular activities competes for students' time and attention and can take away from time that they can spend on schoolwork. This is a myth. Several studies have shown that youths who participate in extracurricular activities have higher grades, score higher on achievement tests, are more engaged in school, and are more likely to attend college (Feldman & Matjusko, 2005). Furthermore, participants in these activities are less likely to drop out of school. Some research suggests that the benefits of extracurricular activity involvement are greatest for academically at-risk students (Mahoney & Cairns, 1997). The reality is that for some students, the opportunity to participate in organized non-academic contexts such as sports and the arts is the only reason they come to school, stay in school, and do their school work. Cuts to extracurricular programming are devastating for these youths.

Why do students who participate in extracurricular contexts do better in school? Several explanations have been proposed. One is that involvement in these activities helps to organize out-of-school time. The after-school hours are a period of both risk and opportunity for positive development. The more time children and adolescents are involved in extracurricular activities, the less time they have to be involved in unstructured and unsupervised contexts. Spending time in unsupervised or unstructured contexts during the after-school hours has been shown to be related to poorer academic achievement, poorer psychological adjustment, and higher-risk behaviors (Feldman & Matjasko, 2005). Participation in extracurricular activities also can strengthen youths' relations with adults and peers. Youths who participate in school-based extracurricular contexts have been found to have stronger relations with their teachers and to have more academically oriented peers than those who are not involved in extracurricular activities (Broh, 2002; Fredricks & Eccles, 2005). High-quality organized activities are also structured in a way to support the development of **initiative**, or the capacity for devoting effort over time towards achieving a goal. Qualitative research suggests that when activities are youth-based and involve challenging tasks, adolescents develop skills such as organizing time, contingency thinking, and problem solving (Larson, 2000).

Through organized participation, youths can also develop a wide range of competencies and prosocial values, many of which are more difficult to develop in traditional academic settings. In a study comparing youths' developmental experiences in school and in out-of-school organized contexts, youths reported that organized activities offered more experiences related to managing emotions, interpersonal development, and developing social skills than did school (Larson, Hansen, & Moneta, 2006). Organized activities tend to have a smaller adult-student ratio and are less structured than school-based settings, thus giving youths more opportunities to interact with their peers and adult leaders and more opportunities to develop social skills. Furthermore, in organized-activity contexts, children's social relations are often directed towards solving a challenging problem. This is very different than most school contexts where youth have few opportunities to interact with their peers outside of lunch, transition periods, or recess.

Differential Access to Benefits of Extracurricular Participation

Some research suggests that the benefits of extracurricular participation are greatest for low-income youths (Marsh & Kleitman, 2002). Participation in such activities can provide these students with developmental supports in a safe and supervised context and can also reduce the likelihood that they will develop problems associated with poverty. Unfortunately, those youths who are in greatest need of these opportunities and who would benefit most from participating are less likely to be involved than their more advantaged peers. Children in low-income families are less likely to participate in sports, clubs, and lessons than children in higher-income families (Mahoney & Eccles, 2007). In poor urban neighborhoods and rural areas, fewer school- and community-based extracurricular activities are available for youths to participate in, and those that are available vary significantly in their level of quality (Halpern, 1999). These communities also have fewer parks, community centers, and playing fields for children to use. The cost of activity involvement, lack of access to transportation, and competing work responsibilities are additional barriers to participation in organized activities for low-income youths.

VARIATION IN ENGAGEMENT ACROSS CONTEXTS

Many students who show signs of disengagement in school show more positive emotion and stronger behavioral engagement in out-of-school contexts such as athletics and the arts. It is not uncommon to see students like Rachel and Ryan, who were profiled as disengaged in school at the beginning of Chapter 1, showing a very different profile of behavior, emotion, and cognition in settings outside of school time. The differences in engagement across these two contexts raise important questions. Why are schools such disengaging places for these students? Why do these same students show higher engagement in other settings?

One way researchers have examined variations in engagement across settings is to use **experience sampling methods** (ESM). This is a technique in which students carry beepers for one week. When they are randomly beeped, they report on what they are doing and how they are feeling. Using ESM techniques, researchers have documented that classrooms are not very engaging settings. In fact, high school students report the lowest levels of engagement in school and the highest levels of engagement in structured out-of-school contexts such as sports and the arts (Larson, 2000). This method of sampling student experiences has been also used to compare engagement across different classroom settings. Researchers have found that students are more likely to report low intrinsic motivation and high levels of boredom in classrooms where they spend more of their time in teacher-directed and passive activities. In contrast, student engagement is higher in classrooms where students perceive instruction as challenging and when they are in cooperative grouping activities as opposed to large-group discussions (Shernoff & Csikzentmihalyi, 2009).

In the following *Engagement in Practice* section, Melissa describes how teachers at her school reached a difficult student through sports.

ENGAGEMENT IN PRACTICE: REACHING STUDENTS THROUGH SPORTS

Melissa: A student in my school had little connection to peers or academics. He was often disruptive in class and mean to his peers or much younger students. He was a bright student, although he struggled with reading comprehension. Most teacher-student interactions were negative, which produced little change in this student's behavior, and perhaps even fueled more negative behavior. His teachers were frustrated. It was difficult to find something positive to build on and nurture in this student because he was destructive to the community-building going on in class. The only thing that seemed to excite him was sports. When he talked about soccer there was a different light in his eye. I decided to attend a game. I stayed for the game and afterwards talked with him about his play and teammates. When he came to school on Monday, I provided him with the sports page from several newspapers to engage him with silent reading. The sports page became a tradition each week, and he became more receptive to his teachers. He was less disruptive in class and much more receptive to redirection. Was this a magic bullet? Certainly not. The adjustment issues and family concerns surrounding this student did not magically disappear, nor did his uncooperative behaviors. But a door had been opened slightly. The next step was a series of parent, student, and teacher meetings during which they developed specific goal-setting and monitoring plans. In the meantime, this student read high-interest material each day from which I could build upon to develop his comprehension skills.

Increasing the availability of organized activities in the school will require resources and administrative support. Teachers can communicate to administrators the impact that extracurricular participation has on students' experiences in the classroom by sharing examples of students that have benefited from this involvement. Teachers can also play an important role in identifying students who they think will benefit from extracurricular participation and encouraging these students to participate.

SELF-DETERMINATION THEORY AND ENGAGEMENT

Why do out-of-school contexts tend to be more engaging settings than school? **Self-determination theory** is one theoretical perspective that can be used to explain the differences in engagement across these two contexts. According to self-determination theory (Ryan & Deci, 2000), engagement will be higher in contexts where an individual's needs for relatedness, autonomy, and competence are met. This theory is presented in Figure 3.1. Self-determination theory assumes that individuals have 1) a basic need to feel connected to others (i.e., relatedness), 2) a basic need to experience their behavior as self-initiated rather than controlled by external incentives (i.e., autonomy), and 3) a basic need to feel that they can effectively interact with their environment and know what they need to do to be successful (i.e., competence). In classrooms, the need for relatedness is supported when students develop caring and close relationships with their teachers and their peers. The need for autonomy is supported when students experience autonomy support, or freedom in determining their own behaviors, as opposed to being controlled by external factors. Finally, the need for competence is supported when classrooms are optimal in **classroom structure**, which refers to the amount of information in the context regarding what strategies will be effective in achieving school success. In a classroom that lacks structure, students are unclear about the expectations and the consequences of their behavior.

One reason organized out-of-school settings tend to be more engaging contexts is they have more elements of self-determination theory that support an individual's need for relatedness, autonomy, and competence (Fredricks, Hackett, & Bregman, 2010). In organized out-of-school settings, individuals often work together as a team to achieve a common goal. Developing social skills, encouraging teamwork, and giving youths greater decision-making opportunities are central to the mission of many of these activities. In contrast, in most traditional school-based settings, students are expected to work by themselves on activities and have limited opportunities to interact with their peers. As a result, it is easier to develop relationships in out-of-school settings. Additionally, youths in out-of-school settings have greater opportunities to make decisions and have input on how activities are structured. In contrast, in school settings, teachers make the majority of decisions. As a result, the need for autonomy is less supported in school settings. Another important difference between school and out-of-school settings is opportunities for youths to receive feedback on their abilities. In many out-of-school contexts, individuals work on challenging and interesting tasks and are given immediate feedback on their performance. In school, students often reproduce knowledge that is only shared with their teacher. Feedback is less frequent and generally less informative. This makes it more difficult for students to know what they need to do to be successful, which supports the need for competence.

STOP, REFLECT, AND TRY

1. How do the tasks in your classroom support students' needs for relatedness, autonomy, and competence?

2. What types of feedback do you provide to students? How frequently do you provide feedback? How informative is that feedback?

3. What changes can you make to your classroom to increase the support for the following?

   a. Relatedness

   b. Autonomy

   c. Competence

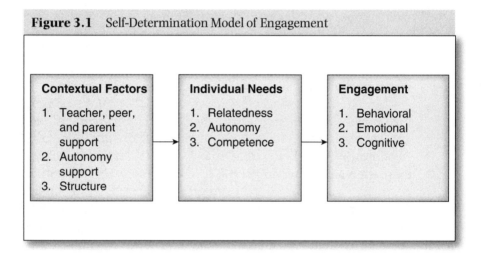

Figure 3.1   Self-Determination Model of Engagement

FAMILIES AND ENGAGEMENT

A substantial body of research over the last three decades has shown that family involvement is associated with a variety of positive academic outcomes (Gonzalez-DeHass, Willems, & Doan Holbein, 2005; Henderson & Mapp, 2002). Children with more involved families are more likely to:

- Earn higher grades
- Receive higher achievement test scores
- Have better attendance
- Have fewer behavioral problems
- Have lower dropout rates
- Report more positive attitudes towards school
- Report higher intrinsic motivation

The effects of parent involvement may vary by type of involvement. For example, Hill and Tyson (2009) examined the relations between three types of parental involvement and academic achievement in middle school. They found that academic socialization (e.g., communicating expectations, discussing the value of education) was the aspect of parent involvement that was most predictive of achievement, followed by school-based involvement (e.g., parent-teacher conferences, PTA). Involvement in activities at home was related to higher achievement if the focus was on enrichment, such as visiting museums and providing books in the home. In contrast, parent help with homework was the only aspect of parental involvement that was negatively associated with achievement. This finding may reflect the fact that some parents increase their involvement in homework only when their children are struggling academically.

Despite the growing evidence of the benefits of parent involvement for children's engagement and achievement, parents are not as involved as they or their teachers want them to be. In surveys with both elementary and secondary teachers, increasing parent involvement is listed as a top priority (Langdon & Vesper, 2000). In this next section, the different ways families can influence student engagement, barriers to this involvement, and practical strategies for increasing parent involvement in the classroom are outlined.

Parent involvement. One of the most visible aspects of parent involvement for teachers is having parents attend conferences and school events. However, this is only one dimension of parent involvement. Parents can also support children's engagement by creating an environment to support learning in the home and through their involvement in other aspects of the school. Joyce Epstein, Coates, Salinas, Sanders, and Simon (1997) have developed the most comprehensive framework for understanding the different types of parent involvement. Table 3.1 provides an overview of Epstein's typology of parent involvement, descriptions of the ways that teachers can support each type of involvement, and sample parental indicators.

In addition to direct forms of parent involvement, parents can also influence student engagement through their parenting style and through the transmission of educational values (Bempechat & Shernoff, 2012). One important dimension of

Table 3.1   Epstein's Typology of Parent Involvement

Type of Involvement	Descriptions of Supporting Strategies	Sample Parental Behaviors
Parenting	Help families establish home environments to support children as students	Parent supervises time use and behavior. Parent discusses with child interests, courses at school.
Communicating	Design effective forms of school-to-home and home-to-school communications	Parent initiates contact about academic performance.
Supporting school	Recruit and organize parent help and support	Parent volunteers at school and attends activities.
Learning at home	Provide ideas about how families can help children with homework and other school-related activities	Parent monitors schoolwork. Parent communicates expectations regarding schoolwork. Parent signs up child for academic lessons outside of school.
Decision making	Include parents in school decisions.	Parent is member of school committee.
Collaborating with community	Identify and integrate community resources and services to strengthen school programs, family practices, and children's learning and development.	Parent uses community resources. Parent takes part in community groups.

Source: Epstein et al. (1997). Used with permission.

STOP AND REFLECT

1. How would you characterize the level of parent involvement in your classroom?

   a. Which parents are most involved? Why?

   b. Which parents are least involved? Why?

(Continued)

(Continued)

2. Using Table 3.1, describe the types of parent involvement in your classroom.

   a. Which types are most prevalent?

   b. Which types are least prevalent?

   c. Which types are easiest to increase?

   d. Which types are most difficult to increase?

3. Using Table 3.1, outline strategies you could use to increase the level of parent involvement in your classroom.

parenting style is autonomy support versus control. **Autonomy-supportive parents** allow children to explore their own environment, to initiate their own behavior, to take an active role in solving their own problems, and to express their points of view. This is especially important in adolescence when youths have an increasing desire for autonomy and decision making. Autonomy support seems to be particularly important for low-achieving children (Ng, Kenney-Benson, & Pomerantz, 2004), and especially if mothers stress the importance of effort and using learning strategies as they help their children with homework (Pomerantz, Grolnick, & Price, 2005). Such practices may help low-achieving children feel both competent and socially supported.

In contrast, **controlling parents** exert pressure to regulate children's behaviors through commands, directives, or love withdrawal. These types of parents deny their children chances to solve problems and ignore their points of view (Pomeranz, Moorman, & Litwack, 2007). In Ryan's case, introduced in Chapter 1, Ryan's parents are an example of this controlling type of parenting. They use punishment and give him few opportunities to explain his behavior. Their attempts to control his behavior have resulted in Ryan feeling coerced and lacking agency. There is evidence that perceiving a lack of control leads to a higher level of problem behavior and disengagement (Raftery, Grolnick, & Flamm, 2012). In the following *Engagement* *in Practice* section, Ellen shares an example of a controlling parent in her classroom.

ENGAGEMENT IN PRACTICE: CONTROLLING PARENTING

Ellen: This past year, I had a student who appeared to be engaged. He completed his homework on time and did fairly well on assessments. Midway through the school year, his core teachers and I began to notice a change in his affect and a decline in his performance. His grades began to slip, so we decided to contact his parents to schedule an intervention meeting. Upon meeting his mother, it was obvious that his academic slip was more of an attempt to gain some sort of agency, as it was apparent that his mother controlled his life. His mother wanted him to pursue a top-notch college, while he wanted to learn a trade and play his guitar. Rather than listening to her son's wishes, the mother continued to pressure her son to improve his grades and motivation. She sent lengthy e-mails almost daily to his teachers about his physical health, his progress on specific projects, and even on the exact weight of his backpack. As her communication increased, her son's academic performance tanked to the point where he was failing multiple classes. He stopped doing his homework completely, disregarded classroom rules, wrote papers in orange crayon, and fell asleep every other class. Had his mother listened to and supported his interests, perhaps he would have had a much more successful second semester. However, due to the restrictive nature of his home life, he wasn't able to achieve the success that he was more than capable of achieving.

Several studies have shown a positive relation between parental autonomy support and behavioral engagement (e.g., higher time on homework, lower problem behavior), emotional engagement (e.g., intrinsic motivation, positive attitudes toward school), and cognitive engagement (e.g., persistence in the face of challenge) (Pomerantz et al., 2007). This positive relation also may be explained by self-determination theory;

autonomy-supportive practices help to support children's need for autonomy, which in turn leads them to be more engaged with their environments.

Parents' own attitudes about education and learning can also help to shape children's beliefs and values, which influences classroom engagement. Parents communicate these beliefs both implicitly and explicitly. Benjamin, profiled in Chapter 1 as a student who is behaviorally but not emotionally or cognitively engaged, illustrates the importance of parental support and communication. His parents have high expectations and verbally communicate that school is important. However, because they are not involved in his education, their actions may actually be communicating the message to him that school is not really that important. In contrast, the parents of Fiona and Franco, who hold high expectations, provide intellectual resources, and help with schoolwork, are communicating verbally and nonverbally to their children that their schoolwork is important.

BARRIERS TO PARENT INVOLVEMENT

Many teachers report being dissatisfied with the level of parent involvement in their classrooms. If parent involvement is so important for children's success in school, why are so many parents not engaged? Lack of parent involvement can stem from a variety of family, child, and school factors. Table 3.2 outlines some barriers to parent involvement that have been identified in prior research. Low-income and less educated parents have been found to be less involved in their children's schooling than parents with higher income and education (Laureau, 2000). Lower socioeconomic families are less likely to have flexible work hours, transportation options, access to child care, and other resources that are more readily available to middle-class families and that make it easier to be involved in a child's education. Another reason these families may be less involved is that these parents have lower **parental efficacy**, or confidence in their intellectual abilities and ability to help their child with homework. Parents must feel competent to provide assistance with homework and believe that their assistance can help to increase children's perceptions of their competencies. Rachel's mother is an example of a parent who feels she lacks the skills to help her daughter with schoolwork.

Families in racially or ethnically diverse groups are also often less involved in school activities than are white families. Language barriers and cultural variations in views of parent involvement may help to explain these ethnic differences in the level of parent involvement. In many Asian and Hispanic families, respect for teachers is considered paramount (Valdés, 1998). However, these displays of respect can be perceived by some educators as indicating that these parents do not care. We also know that culture plays a major role in the extent and manner to which parents get involved with their children's schooling. Certain types of family involvement, such as attending parent-teacher conferences, are more common in mainstream American culture than among other cultures (Garcia-Coll & Marks, 2009).

One of the most important student characteristics impacting parent involvement is the age of the child. Parent involvement decreases significantly during the middle and high school years (Eccles & Harold, 1996). This decline in involvement may stem from parents' beliefs that they lack the skills to assist with more challenging subjects. It may also reflect parents' beliefs that their involvement in schoolwork is less important in adolescence because their children are becoming more autonomous. However, these beliefs are inaccurate, as parent involvement in adolescence continues to be an important predictor of student engagement and academic achievement (Hill et al., 2004).

It is also important to consider the beliefs and attitudes of school personnel towards parent involvement. Prior research has shown that parents have higher rates of involvement when they feel like the school is making an effort to involve them (Epstein, 2001). Many administrators and teachers see the value of family-school cooperation and actively encourage greater involvement. However, it is also true that some teachers and administrators who have been discouraged by unsuccessful attempts to involve families in the past believe that the effort to involve parents is not worth it. Unfortunately, in some schools personnel actively discourage parent involvement. This is especially true in low-income and racially or ethnically diverse neighborhoods where parents are often seen as part of the problem rather than part of the solution (Eccles & Harold, 1996).

Table 3.2   Barriers to Parent Involvement

Parent Characteristics
• Low income
• Low parent education
• African American and Hispanic
• Non-native English speaker
• Cultural beliefs
• Work schedules
• Lack of transportation options
• Lack of child care
• Low parent confidence
• Low parent efficacy
• Parent attitude toward school
• Limited parent history of involvement
Child Characteristics
• Age
• Academic achievement
• Low motivation
School Characteristics
• Limited opportunities for parent involvement
• Large schools
• Level (middle or high school)
• Physical structure
• Teachers' and administrators' beliefs regarding parent involvement

STOP AND REFLECT

1. What are your beliefs regarding parent involvement in your classroom? How are you communicating these beliefs to parents?

2. Have you encountered students with controlling parents in your classroom? What can you do to more effectively work with these parents?

3. Using Table 3.2, what are some barriers to parent involvement in your classroom?

   a. What can you do to address these barriers?

   b. What can your school do to break down those barriers school-wide?

In the following section, Melissa describes how her school uses home visits as a way to connect with parents across language and socioeconomic lines.

ENGAGEMENT IN PRACTICE: CONNECTING WITH PARENTS THROUGH HOME VISITS

Melissa: At the Integrated Day Charter School in Norwich, Connecticut, the school year begins long before Labor Day. Teachers begin the school year with home visits to students and their families. These informal visits allow the team of parent, student, and teacher to ask questions, allay fears, and set the groundwork for a positive relationship in the future. Recognizing the value of parent involvement, our teachers attempt to cross cultural, language, and socioeconomic barriers in order to strengthen learning early on. Phone numbers are exchanged, opportunities for future parent involvement are shared, and students feel comfortable enough to open up in their own environments. It is not unusual to share food, get a tour of the students' home, and view recently read books. This first interaction with families creates a foundation upon which families and teachers can build all year.

Increasing Parent Involvement in the Classroom

It is clear from the research that parent involvement is a critical factor in children's engagement and achievement. Research also suggests that parents want to be more involved in their children's

Table 3.3   Strategies for Increasing Parent Involvement

1. *Create a welcoming environment for parents.* Parents are more likely to be involved if they feel welcome in the school and classroom. Solicit parent feedback on the type of environment they would feel most welcome in. Try to develop a personal rapport with parents and encourage them to visit the school, work with their child at home, or help out in the classroom if their schedule permits.

2. *Communicate frequently with parents.* Prior research shows that communication plays a critical role in parent involvement. Teachers should develop a home-to-school and school-to-home communication method(s) that works best with the population they serve. Possible methods include mail, phone, e-mail, Web sites, newsletters, and face-to-face meetings. Initial contact should be positive in nature. It is also critical to provide access to materials in other languages for non-English-speaking families.

3. *Offer opportunities for parents to volunteer.* Provide a variety of ways that parents can be involved in school-related activities, including volunteering in the classroom, chaperoning field trips, and assisting on curriculum activities at home.

4. *Offer events that encourage families to come to school.* Studies suggest that parents would be more involved in school if they had more resources and information on how to support their children. In addition to conferences, open houses, and school-wide events, schools should offer parent workshops on strategies for working with their child in different subject areas. Events should be scheduled at different times during the day, during evening hours, and on weekends to accommodate diverse schedules.

5. *Provide resources to help parents help their child with homework.* Teachers should assign homework in a way that both encourages and supports family involvement. For example, teachers can give an assignment that requires children to ask parents questions or do an activity with them. Teachers should also provide information to parents on the skills required for students at that grade level. Finally, it is important to provide parents with a way to monitor children's homework and track their progress.

6. *Provide resources to support learning at home.* Teachers can also play a role in helping parents to set up an intellectually rich home environment that encourages learning. Teachers can provide suggestions on informal learning activities that use materials in the home environment to stimulate children's interest. Teachers should also encourage literacy by asking parents to read to their child regularly or listen to their child read at home.

7. *Offer opportunities for parents to provide input and be involved in decision making for school.* The ultimate form of parent involvement is to give parents some input into decisions about the school. This may occur through committee work, fund-raising, or serving on school boards. Although this type of parent representation is not possible at all schools, teachers can solicit parent input on curriculum, field trips, and other decisions at the school.

education and want information and help from teachers and schools in making this possible. Table 3.3 lists some practical strategies for increasing involvement in the classroom.

STOP, REFLECT, AND TRY

1. Use Table 3.3: to evaluate the strategies you use to increase parent involvement in your classrooms.

   a. In which areas of parent involvement are you consistently strong throughout the academic year?

   b. What do you see as the two most important potential areas for improvement?

2. Integrate one of the strategies for increasing parent involvement in your classroom. Record the different ways in which parents respond and the ways that your students respond to the parent involvement.

In the following *Engagement in Practice* sections, Michele describes strategies used in her classroom and at her school to increase parent involvement. First, she outlines how she uses student-parent-teacher journals to improve communication with parents. Next, she describes how her school provides information and resources to parents.

ENGAGEMENT IN PRACTICE: STUDENT–PARENT–TEACHER JOURNALS

Michele: One strategy my grade-level team uses to communicate with parents is a student-parent-teacher journal, or SPT journal. This is a notebook that goes between home and school every day. Students mainly write at the end of the day a few times a week to share what they've learned, to write to a prompt from the teacher as a reflection, or to reinforce and review learning. (e.g., "What

(Continued)

(Continued)

type of poetry did you learn this week? Share one poem that you wrote with your family at home.") Sometimes the teacher assigns an assignment in the journal that involves doing an activity or sharing knowledge with family members at home. Parents are encouraged to write back to students or comment on their journal entries. Parents can also write to the teacher if they have any questions or need to share information. The teacher uses it to communicate with the parents if they need to give specific updates on behavior, academics, or simply want to share something great that happened in the week. It is a great three-way communication method and especially useful for working with parents who want to be involved with what is going on at the school.

ENGAGEMENT IN PRACTICE: CURRICULUM, FAMILY LITERACY, AND MATH AND SCIENCE NIGHTS

Michele: In the first month of the school year, my school has a Curriculum Night for all parents and guardians to attend. Teachers share information about the overall grade level curriculum, expectations, homework and grading policies, and classroom and communication procedures for the year. These information sessions are held in the classrooms and are repeated a few times throughout the night so families with multiple children at the school can learn about each child's grade. There are also information tables set up for extracurricular and after-school programming.

My school also does a Family Literacy Night during the year so family can learn more about reading and writing activities we do in school and what they can do to help their children at home. Teachers plan and facilitate various activities for the Literacy Night, such as interactive games, shared writing projects, reader's theater, and learning about various reading strategies. Teachers can prepare handouts with information and resources for parents regarding literacy activities, and families can take any projects or games that they create so they can continue to use them at home.

Previously, I worked with a school in the Philippines that had a Family Math and Science Workshop. For one night, teachers prepared various interactive math and science games, experiments, and activities in learning stations that students and their families visited. Families were able to explore bubbles, do chemical experiments with colors, build pyramids and other structures with sticks and clay, and apply math through cooking activities such as measuring. Families left at the end of the night with more knowledge about the kinds of learning that were happening in their children's classrooms and the ways they could use everyday objects around them to explore math and science concepts.

CHAPTER SUMMARY

The goal of Chapter 3 was to help teachers reflect on how two out-of-school contexts—extracurricular activities and families—impact engagement in the classroom. The reality is that students spend a greater percentage of their time outside of school than they do inside the classroom, and involvement in these contexts can either positively or negatively influence their level of engagement. First, research-based evidence on the benefits of extracurricular participation for academic outcomes was outlined. This research was presented to counter the myth that extracurricular activities are just extras and that involvement detracts from academics. Although low-income youths benefit most from participation, they also are less likely to participate than their more advantaged counterparts. These findings suggest that through both individual teachers and school-wide efforts, extracurricular activities should be made more available to students, especially those most at risk. Next, research comparing engagement in school and in out-of-school contexts was presented. Self-determination theory was outlined as a potential theory for explaining why out-of-school contexts tend to be more engaging places. This theory provides a framework for teachers to consider how well contexts support students' need for autonomy, competence, and relatedness. In the last section of the chapter, different types of parent involvement and barriers to parent involvement were presented. Teachers are the critical participants in parent involvement in the classroom. Therefore, the chapter concluded with practical strategies for increasing parent involvement that can be implemented at any age level.

TEXT-TO-PRACTICE EXERCISES

TPE 3.1: **Survey student involvement outside of school.** Survey your students about their involvement in activities outside of the school. Ask them what they do with their after-school time. Where do they have the most fun? When are they most bored? Where are they most challenged?

TPE 3.2: **Compare engagement in and out of the classroom.** Using self-determination theory as a framework (see Figure 3.1), compare your classroom to a structured out-of-school context (e.g., extracurricular activities, an after-school or community-based program). How does each context support students' need for relatedness, autonomy, and competence? What aspects of out-of-school contexts could you incorporate in your classroom?

TPE 3.3: **Survey parents about involvement.** Survey parents in your classroom about their level of parent involvement. What do they perceive as barriers to involvement? What resources would help them to be more involved?

KEY TERMS AND CONCEPTS

Autonomy-supportive parenting: Occurs when parents value and use techniques that encourage independent problem solving, choice, and behavior.

Classroom structure: The amount of information in the context about what strategies are effective in achieving school success.

Controlling parenting: Occurs when parents externally regulate children's behaviors and offer limited opportunities for choice and problem solving.

Experience sampling methods: A methodological technique in which youths carry beepers and report on what they are doing and how they are feeling when they are randomly beeped.

Initiative: The capacity for devoting effort over time to achieving a goal.

Parental efficacy: Parents' confidence in their intellectual abilities and in their ability to help their child with schoolwork.

Self-determination theory: A motivational theory designed to explain the relation between context and engagement. This theory assumes that individuals will have higher engagement in contexts that support their need for relatedness, autonomy, and competence.

RESEARCH-BASED RESOURCES

Books and Reports to Read

Davis, C., & Yang, C. (2005). *Parents and teachers working together.* Turner Falls, MA: Northeast Foundation for Children.

Epstein, J. L. (2001). *School, family, and community partnerships: Preparing educators and improving schools.* Boulder, CO: Westview Press.

Epstein, J. L., Coates, L., Salinas, K. C., Sanders, M. G., & Simon, B. S. (1997). *School, family, and community partnerships: Your handbook for action.* Thousand Oaks, CA: Corwin Press.

Garcia-Coll, C., & Marks, A. K. (2009). *Immigrant stories: Ethnicity and academics in middle childhood.* Oxford, UK: Oxford University Press.

Mahoney, J. L., Larson, R. W., & Eccles, J. S. (Eds.) (2005). *Organized activities as contexts of development: Extracurricular activities, after-school and community programs.* Mahwah, NJ: Lawrence Erlbaum.

Web Sites to Visit

1. **Education.com** (www.education.com). This site provides resources for teachers on increasing parent involvement in their classrooms.

2. **U.S. Department of Education** (www.ed.gov/parents/landing.jhtml). This site from the U.S. Department of Education provides resources for parents so they can help their child to succeed in school.

3. **Parent Involvement Matters** (www.parentinvolvementmatters .org). This advocacy organization provides resources for increasing parent involvement and strengthening family/school/community partnerships.

4. **Everyday Engagement for Families** (www.everydayengage ment4families.com). This site includes resources and professional development activities to help educators strengthen their relationships with families.

5. **Read Write Think** (www.readwritethink.org/parent-afterschool-resources). Read Write Think is an international reading association. Its site includes resources to help parents support their children's literacy inside and outside of school.

6. **Harvard Family Research Project** (www.hfrp.org/family-involvement). The Harvard Family Research project does research on family involvement and out-of-school time. The site includes information on effective ways to increase family involvement. www.hfrp.org/out-of-school-time. The Harvard Family Research project site also includes resources and publications about out-of-school time.

7. **National Institute of Out-of-School Time** (www.niost.org). The National Institute of Out-of-School Time at Wellesley College does research on out-of-school time. It also consults with school districts and individual programs to improve the quality of after-school programs.

8. **Self-Determination Theory** (www.selfdeterminationtheory .org). This site includes a description of self-determination theory, publications related to the theory, and copies of measures.

CHAPTER FOUR

MYTH 4: Hands-On Is Minds-On

How to Create More Engaging Classroom Tasks That Result in Deep Learning

How do I initially motivate my students to want to learn? How do I sustain this interest and translate it into deeper learning? How do I get my students to really understand what they are doing rather than just focusing on finishing the assignment or passing the test? These are difficult questions that have been at the heart of educational research over the past several decades. It is clear that to answer these questions teachers will need to attend to both the motivational and cognitive features of classroom tasks.

In the classroom students perform a variety of tasks, including listening to the teacher, answering questions, filling out worksheets, solving problems, reading texts, completing projects, and writing for a variety of purposes. The characteristics of these tasks shape student motivation, direct students' attention to particular aspects of the content, and specify ways of processing information (Blumenfeld, Kempler, & Krajcik, 2006), all of which affect learning.

In many classrooms the motivational features of the task take precedence. Many teachers focus on creating fun and interesting activities but pay less attention to the cognitive dimensions.

Although it is important to capture a student's attention, it is incorrect to assume that just because a student is having fun that deep learning will occur. The reality is that the features of the task that initially promote motivation often only serve as a "hook" and do not hold the student's interest (Mitchell, 1993). Moreover, even if motivation is sustained, there is no guarantee that this motivation will translate into deeper learning.

Teachers play a critical role in sustaining motivation and translating it into higher-quality cognitive engagement. In this chapter, research on both the motivational and cognitive features of tasks related to higher engagement is presented. Practical strategies for making tasks more motivating *and* cognitively engaging are emphasized.

DESIGNING CLASSROOM TASKS FOR ENGAGEMENT

One reason why so many students are disengaged in school is that many classroom tasks are boring and offer limited opportunities for deeper conceptual understanding. A growing body of educational research is exploring how to make classroom tasks more interesting and cognitively engaging to students. Some of this research has focused on the task features that enhance **intrinsic motivation**, or what people do without external incentives (Ryan & Deci, 2000). Intrinsically motivating activities are those that individuals engage in for no reward other than interest and enjoyment. This research has identified challenge, variety, novelty, fantasy, choice, and meaningfulness as important dimensions of engaging tasks.

Challenge. Classroom tasks that are challenging but can be accomplished with reasonable effort promote engagement. There are several aspects of task challenge, including the level of difficulty of the task content, the procedures that are required to complete the task, and the social organization of the task (i.e., whether students work individually or with others) (Blumenfeld, 1992). If any of these aspects are too easy, students will not have the opportunities to be deeply invested and they may even disengage because they are bored. Conversely, if any of the aspects of a task are too difficult, students may give up because it is too hard.

The benefits of moderate task difficulty are supported by motivational theories. According to Csikszentmihalyi's (1991) flow theory, individuals experience **flow** when there is a match between task challenge and skill level. Individuals in flow merge action and awareness, lose sense of time, and have strong task concentration. Task challenge also relates to self-determination theory (See Figure 3.1, Chapter 3). An adequate level of task challenge can support students' perceptions of competence, or how good they are at an activity. According to self-determination theory, engagement is higher in a context that supports students' need for competence.

Selecting appropriately challenging tasks can be difficult for educators. Prior research has shown a poor match between the tasks teachers choose and students' skill levels (Blumenfeld, 1992). In addition, teachers that emphasize **performance goals**, or how their students are doing relative to their peers, may discourage their students from taking risks in the classroom. In a performance-orientated classroom, the emphasis is on demonstrating that one has done better than his or her peers. In these environments, learning is only viewed as a way to achieve a desired goal, the emphasis is often on achieving success with little effort, and failure-avoiding patterns of motivation are common. This type of learning environment is especially problematic for students like Benjamin and Beatrice, profiled at the beginning of Chapter 1, who are motivated primarily by grades and by not making mistakes. Instead, to encourage students to select challenging tasks, teachers should emphasize **mastery goals**, or learning and understanding the material (Ames, 1992). In mastery-oriented environments, students are focused on developing new skills and trying to understand their work, and the emphasis is on effort rather than how they are doing relative to their peers. Mastery goals have been found to increase the time students spend on tasks and their persistence in the face of difficulty (Linnebrink & Fredricks, 2008).

Variety. Doing the same thing every day gets old fast, and students, like everyone else, thrive on variety. Many teachers use predictable and unvarying formats. Although this predictability does provide some structure for students, the lack of variety has negative implications for student motivation. Prior research has shown that task diversity is related to higher interest (i.e., emotional engagement) and effort directed at learning content (i.e., cognitive engagement) (Ames, 1992). Task diversity also has emerged as an important feature in qualitative studies of engaging classrooms (Blumenfeld, Puro, & Mergendoller, 1992). This research shows that even minor changes in instructional format can have a significant effect on student engagement. Teachers can maintain students' engagement by using a variety of instructional formats such as whole-class instruction, small-group work, pairings, individual seatwork, class debates, contests, games, movies, and presentations.

Fantasy. Researchers also have examined the characteristics of computer games to understand why they are so intrinsically motivating and compelling to so many children and youths. Novelty, curiosity, control, and fantasy have been identified as key factors that help to explain why these games are so engaging (Malone & Lepper, 1987). These dimensions can also be applied to school tasks. Teachers can make tasks more engaging by incorporating aspects of fantasy, such as role-playing and the opportunity to create imaginary characters, locations, or objects, and game-like features, such as rules and goals, competition, and challenge. Teachers also can introduce mystery through some element of surprise, suspense, or uncertainty about the outcome. Furthermore, teachers can elicit curiosity by presenting information and asking questions that reveal discrepancies in students' understanding.

However, although the use of these strategies will likely increase short-term attention, one concern is that they may actually detract from learning and motivation in the long term (Blumenfeld, 1992). Students may get so hooked on the novel aspects of the task that they fail to focus on the problem to be solved. Prior research has shown that too many "bells and whistles" can actually deflect from content and may confuse students (Blumenfeld et al., 1991). Unless tasks are carefully designed, variety may heighten emotional engagement at the expense of cognitive engagement.

Choice. As outlined in self-determination theory (See Chapter 3, Figure 3.1), some degree of autonomy can enhance student engagement. Students need to be able to make some decisions about the types of task they work on and have some flexibility in how they complete these tasks. Students who are given the opportunity to make choices have been found to show higher levels of persistence, enjoyment, intrinsic motivation, and learning (Cordova & Lepper, 1996). Table 4.1 lists some strategies for increasing opportunities for choice in the classroom.

Table 4.1   Strategies for Increasing Choice in the Classroom
1. *Choice over what to study.* Students can help to generate a list of readings or topic areas to investigate in the class. Offer students choices about what to read and to write about for assignments.
2. *Choice over how to complete tasks.* Students can choose among several different assignments. For more complex assignments, students can choose how to approach the problem, what steps to follow, and what resources to use.
3. *Choice about when to complete assignments.* Students are given options about when to complete assignments. For example, during the course of a lesson, teachers can give students a choice of completing three out of five assignments.
4. *Choice over rules and consequences for misbehavior.* Students can help to generate class rules and the consequences for not following these rules.

Meaningfulness. Even if tasks in the classroom are diverse and challenging, it does not necessarily mean that they are meaningful to students. Although there are a few students like Fiona and Franco who are intrinsically motivated by learning and easily become interested, the reality is that for many students the tasks in school have little interest or value to them. Educators can increase the meaningfulness of tasks by drawing on students' prior knowledge and experiences, connecting tasks to real-world situations, and highlighting the importance of tasks for future course selection and career options. For example, one way to engage a student like Ryan is to incorporate his interest in sports, computers, and building into lessons. Prior research shows that students are more likely to learn and remember information when it is linked to their prior knowledge and experiences (Willingham, 2009). Table 4.2 outlines some practical strategies for making school tasks more meaningful and personally relevant to students.

Table 4.2   Practical Strategies for Increasing Personal
Meaningfulness of Tasks

- Survey students about how they and their families spend time outside of school.

- Incorporate aspects of students' interests and cultural practices into lessons.

- Offer students opportunities to ask questions, express opinions, and respond personally to the content in some way. Take advantage of students' comments and questions to provide additional information and elaboration on a topic.

- Connect instruction to popular movies, music, and television shows.

- Connect instruction to real-world challenges in students' communities. Have students document the problems in their school or local community and develop practical solutions to solve these problems.

- Provide opportunities for students to participate in real-world tasks that are similar to tasks experts would engage in. For example, students in science can model the work of scientists by asking questions, developing hypotheses, designing experiments, and collecting data to answer their questions.

- Highlight the relevance of school tasks for future courses and careers.

- Incorporate field trips that relate to course content.

- Invite speakers who work in the field being studied to come and talk to the class.

- Offer explanations for why students are doing a task.

- Emphasize the intrinsic aspects of learning (i.e., learning for the sake of learning) over extrinsic factors such as grades or external incentives.

- Integrate music, drama, and the visual arts into lessons.

In the following *Engagement in Practice* section, Melissa describes the concept of a Higher Order Thinking School (HOTS), which is an educational reform model in Connecticut that uses the arts to make learning more meaningful to students and help them to develop critical-thinking skills.

ENGAGEMENT IN PRACTICE: HIGHER ORDER THINKING SCHOOLS (HOTS)

Melissa: My school is a Higher Order Thinking School (HOTS). This is an educational reform model in Connecticut that helps students to develop critical-thinking abilities, independent judgment, and creative problem-solving skills. The goal of this reform is to integrate the arts into all subject areas so that students are able to communicate their ideas and learning in creative ways. There are opportunities for teacher-artist collaborators at each school, with the goal of artists and teachers to jointly design arts-integrated experiences that align with state and district standards.

This reform model offers extensive opportunities for choice, fantasy, and variety. Students are encouraged to use the arts to synthesize relationships between ideas. For example, when practicing grammar, I asked my students to study a painting of a rail yard. They looked for nouns, adjectives, verbs, and adverbs. After they looked at the painting in this way, I asked them questions about what happened just before this scene and just after. From there the students found synonyms for their word bank and wrote stories about the paintings. Each story was unique! In this way, students approach a dry subject—grammar—through the arts.

Another example of the HOTS approach was experienced by our upper elementary school students. While studying a science unit on light, they worked with a HOTS actor. Together they explored light through a social justice theme. Who has light and who does not? What kind of impact does that have? The students, their teachers, and the artist in residence created shadow plays of their new learning. Paper puppets were displayed from an overhead projector behind a large white screen. Combined with the living shadows of the students themselves, the larger school community experienced the work of these classes through performance art.

Using these strategies, teachers can make tasks more meaningful to students. However, the reality is that even with these changes, some of what students need to do in school will likely still be uninteresting to them (e.g., homework, standardized tests). In these situations, teachers will need to reframe the tasks to help students see a potentially uninteresting activity as a personally meaningful one. To do this, teachers need to understand students' goals, interests, and needs and link school tasks to these interests and goals (Assor, Kaplan, & Roth, 2002). Teachers should provide students with explanations for why they are doing a task (e.g., "The reason I am asking you to do this is because . . ."), and frame lessons around intrinsic versus extrinsic goals (e.g., "Learning these words provides an opportunity to grow your skill as a writer") (Reeve & Halusic, 2009).

Teachers can also increase the personal relevance of tasks for students by presenting these potentially less interesting tasks within the context of more meaningful work. For example, it will be more interesting for students to explore punctuation in a book that they have chosen to read than in a worksheet on semicolons. Writing letters to community members as part of the research process also will be more meaningful than practicing writing a formal letter to an imaginary recipient. Charting their own progress (quiz scores, work completion, or other data) on a graph also is a more meaningful way to teach numeracy skills than a math worksheet.

The reality of our assessment culture has put pressure on many teachers to spend some of their class time getting students ready for standardized tests. For the majority of students, this is not a meaningful task. Test preparation is often tedious, and a common response from students is to do as little as they can to complete the activity. In the following *Engagement in Practice* section, Michele outlines how she has reframed preparation for standardized testing in the context of a more meaningful literacy activity. She also discusses how she provides students with explanations for why they should do a task that most perceive as uninteresting or unimportant.

ENGAGEMENT IN PRACTICE: STANDARDIZED TESTING PREPARATION

Michele: In my urban public school district, the state standardized test is a big deal. Although no teacher wants to "teach to the test," the reality is that testing has become so prevalent in our schools that teachers are expected to spend some time familiarizing students with the testing format and including it in our classroom practice. One aspect of the standardized tests is a reading response component where students are required to read a passage and write an essay response to a question about this passage. Often my fourth-grade students find the test passages uninteresting. Many write as quickly as possible to just get it over with, while others panic because they don't know where to begin. Over the past few years, I have changed my approach to this response practice by incorporating it into the part of my instruction that includes writing literary essays. This has turned out to be a great fit as we write literary essays to get to the meaning and deeper understanding of a text. Standardized-testing prompts ask similar questions, such as to explain the main idea or theme, or to describe how a character changes. However, unlike the test response, I can offer more choices when we write literary essays. Students can choose the books and texts they want to write about. As students become more familiar with the literary essay genre, I can introduce reading response practice that is more structured like the tests. By this time, students see it as more of a project that they know how to approach because they have the skills to break it down into manageable steps. It is also easier than the literary essays we write in class because the test passage is much shorter with less text to analyze.

Many of my fourth graders question why they have to answer questions and read passages that don't interest them. I also explain how this helps them become better at critically reading and writing, which will help them in high school, college, and even their jobs. When I introduce my class to a practice test question, I always remind them that their job is to convince the reader of what they are trying to share through their response. I tell them that the people who read their responses are often teachers, so they should pretend they are writing to me! I have found that students are less stressed and more confident about their response part of the test, and they actually get great satisfaction out of analyzing texts to prove their points.

STOP, REFLECT, AND TRY

1. How would you characterize the level of task challenge in your classroom? How do you support students who either find the tasks too challenging or too easy?

(Continued)

(Continued)

2. In what ways do you incorporate student interests into your lessons? What are additional ways you can make tasks more meaningful and personally relevant to students?

3. Which of the strategies outlined in Table 4.2 do you currently use in your classroom? Which could you add? Track how students respond to these changes.

4. What types of opportunities do you have for students to make choices in your classroom in terms of the following:

   a. Content

   b. Form

   c. Timing

   d. Procedures

   e. Rules

COGNITIVE COMPONENTS OF THE TASK

In addition to the motivational features of the task, it is important to consider the cognitive dimensions. Tasks differ in the demands they make on students in terms of comprehension, strategy use, procedural skill, and cognitive processes (Doyle, 1983; Henningson & Stein, 1997; Marx & Walsh, 1988). For example, in one class, students might be required to apply an algorithm to answer several well-structured problems. In another class, students might be required to apply a mathematical procedure to solve a real-world problem. The cognitive demands inherent in these two classrooms tasks are very different. For the first task, there is only one way to solve the problem. In contrast, in the second task, the problem is more complex and there are multiple ways to arrive at a solution.

Table 4.3 outlines four different types of academic tasks that emphasize different procedural and cognitive skills. Many classroom tasks emphasize memorization, applying formulas and procedures, and search-and-match strategies (i.e., searching text for words and passages and applying a particular formula). Tasks such as those in the Common Core and Next Generation Science

Standards involve higher-order cognitive processes that emphasize comprehension, interpretations, application of knowledge or skills to new situations, and synthesis of information. To help students to meet these standards, teachers will need to include more comprehension and opinion tasks (see Table 4.3).

Students do both memory and comprehension tasks in school. For example, in literacy domains, memory tasks direct attention to the surface aspects of text and reproduction of words, while comprehension tasks direct attention to the conceptual structure and meaning of text. There is also an important distinction between procedural and comprehension tasks. Procedural tasks are accomplished by using a standard set of algorithms. This involves the development of a highly automatic thought process in which the procedure is applied to similar tasks in an automatic fashion.

Table 4.3 Types of Academic Tasks

Type of Task	Definition	Example	Skills
Memory tasks	Recognize or reproduce knowledge previously encountered	Memorizing spelling words	Memorization Recall
Procedural tasks	Apply a standardized routine or formula to answer a question	Additional and subtraction drills	Memorization Recall
Comprehension	Draw inferences about information or procedures, apply previously learned procedures to new situations, select appropriate procedures to solve new problems	Make predictions about chemical reaction, devise alternative formula for squaring a number	Interpret Analyze Evaluate Synthesize
Opinion	State a preference	Value clarification exercises, select favorite short story	Evaluate Justification

Source: Adapted from Doyle, 1983.

In contrast, comprehension tasks require that students know why a procedure works and when to use it.

Some research has contrasted open-ended and closed-ended tasks (Turner, 1995), which have different cognitive demands. **Open-ended tasks** allow students to select information and make decisions about how to use this information to answer a question or solve a problem that has multiple processes or possible answers. These problems are sometimes described as "ill-structured" because there is no one set procedure that guarantees a correct solution. In contrast, **close-ended tasks** require that students use specific information to come up with a predetermined solution. Examples of close-ended tasks include multiple choice tests, true/false tests, fill-in-the-blank tests, and problems that can be solved without showing process.

Using open-ended tasks in the classroom is associated with higher student engagement. Turner (1995) compared motivation and strategy use in young children doing open-ended and closed-ended literacy tasks. During open-ended tasks, children used more reading strategies, persisted longer, and controlled attention better than did children engaging in close-ended literacy tasks.

There are several reasons why open-ended tasks are more engaging. First, students have more opportunities to contribute and express their ideas because there are many possible solutions to a problem. This gives students the opportunity to take ownership and develop a unique answer, which supports their need for autonomy (see Chapter 3 for more discussion of self-determination theory). Another reason that these types of problems are more engaging is that students are often asked to show their work, explain their answers, and explain the methods they used to arrive at these answers. This can help support their need for competence (See Chapter 3 for more discussion of self-determination theory).

STOP AND REFLECT

1. How would you characterize the types of tasks students do in your classroom?

2. What types of close-ended tasks do you typically include in the classroom?

3. How often do your students have the opportunity to do open-ended tasks in your classroom? What types of open-ended tasks do you include?

4. How do students respond to both the close- and open-ended tasks in your classroom behaviorally, emotionally, and cognitively?

Bloom's Taxonomy offers one perspective for classifying academic tasks according to their degree of cognitive complexity. This taxonomy was originally developed in 1956 to reflect objectives in three domains—cognitive, affective, and psychomotor—and was recently updated to reflect twenty-first-century students and teachers (Anderson & Krathwohl, 2001). In this revised taxonomy, there are six cognitive processes that go from the simplest behavior to the most cognitively complex behavior. Table 4.4 outlines these six processes and gives examples of tasks for each. Using Bloom's Taxonomy can help teachers to develop more cognitively engaging tasks that require students to use more complex cognitive processes.

Table 4.4   Bloom's Taxonomy of the Cognitive Domain

Category	Question	Terms
Remembering	Can student recall or remember information?	Define, list, duplicate, memorize, repeat
Understanding	Can student explain ideas?	Describe, discuss, identify, report, translate, explain
Applying	Can student use information in a new way?	Demonstrate, illustrate, solve, use, interpret
Analyzing	Can student distinguish between the different parts?	Compare, contrast, differentiate, distinguish
Evaluating	Can student justify a decision?	Argue, defend, support, evaluate
Creating	Can student create a new product or point of view?	Assemble, create, formulate, construct, design

AUTHENTIC TASKS

As outlined in Chapter 2, the traditional tasks in many schools are close-ended tasks that bear little resemblance to how learning happens in other settings. In many classrooms, tasks focus on recall and repetition of abstract and decontextualized knowledge. Students are given few opportunities to represent their knowledge in other ways, to solve open-ended and real-world problems, and to create **artifacts** that are shared with their peers (Blumenfeld et al., 1991). The prevalence of low-level and close-ended tasks contributes to students' disengagement and lack of understanding of content.

To counteract problems of low motivation and disengagement, educators have focused on designing **authentic tasks** that are situated in meaningful contexts, are cognitively complex, and reflect how learning happens outside of the classroom. Although these types of tasks are not yet the norm in most classrooms, research from both motivation and cognitive psychology demonstrate their benefits for engagement and learning (Bransford, Brown, & Cocking, 1999; Fredricks et al., 2004).

One of the key features of authentic tasks is that they have intrinsic value or meaning to students beyond just achieving success in school. In these instructional environments, students often work together collaboratively to solve real-world problems, they

Table 4.5   Five Standards of Authentic Instruction

Standard	Description	Instructional Strategies
Higher-order thinking	Students manipulate information and ideas in a way that transforms their understanding.	Open-ended problems with unpredictable outcomes
Depth of knowledge	Knowledge is deep when it concerns the central idea of a topic. Students develop arguments, solve problems, and construct explanations.	Covering fewer topics in a systematic way
Connectedness to world	Value and meaning beyond the instructional context	1. Students address real-world problems. 2. Students use personal experience as a context for applying knowledge.

Standard	Description	Instructional Strategies
Substantive conversation	Conversation and interaction focused on learning and understanding content	1. Sharing of ideas in exchanges that are not scripted or entirely controlled 2. Dialogue builds on each student's ideas to improve collective understanding.
Social support for student achievement	High teacher expectations, respect, and inclusion of all students in the learning process	1. Teachers convey the importance of taking academic risks and impart that a climate of mutual respect contributes to learning. 2. Teachers solicit and welcome contributions from all students.

Source: Adapted from Newmann & Wehlage, 1993.

use technology-based tools, and they are guided by teachers who scaffold instruction. These tasks incorporate significant subject matter, mirror the situations in which the knowledge is likely to be used, and employ assessments that require demonstration of understanding rather than just taking a test (Newmann, 1992; Newmann & Wehlage, 1993). An authentic task also requires that students develop some artifact that is shared with one's peers in a public venue. What constitutes an artifact will vary depending on the discipline.

STOP, REFLECT, AND TRY

1. In what ways do you incorporate students' interests into your lessons? What are additional ways you can make tasks more meaningful and personally relevant to students?

2. How often do students have opportunities to work on authentic tasks?

(Continued)

(Continued)

In which subject areas?

3. How do students respond to authentic instruction models behaviorally, emotionally, motivationally, and cognitively?

4. Choose a lesson you will teach in the next week. How could you make this lesson more authentic? Observe how your students respond to your adaptation.

AUTHENTIC INSTRUCTIONAL MODELS

Project-based learning is an instructional approach that incorporates authentic learning tasks and can be used in a variety of subject areas. These instructional environments are characterized by 1) a driving question that is meaningful to the learner and anchored in a real-world context, 2) student-conducted investigations that result in the development of artifacts or products, and 3) the use of cognitive tools, particularly technology, to represent ideas. Project-based instructional approaches can increase engagement because students are involved in solving authentic problems, working with their peers, and creating artifacts. They also have the potential to enhance learning and cognitive engagement because students need to formulate plans and track and evaluate their progress (Blumenfeld et al., 1991). As students engage in these tasks, they develop research and inquiry skills, communication and presentation skills, organization and time-management skills, group participation and leadership skills, and critical-thinking skills. They also learn how to apply these skills and knowledge to real-world contexts. In the following sections, Melissa and Ellen describe how they use versions of project-based learning in their classrooms.

ENGAGEMENT IN PRACTICE: PERSONAL RESEARCH

Melissa: Tasks become more meaningful when students can apply what they have learned to a topic or question that is of personal interest to them. In my school, individualized research is used as one way to engage students in a deep-learning experience. Students are encouraged to ask questions about their world, current events, or subjects that interest them. After identifying a topic, the process of extended research begins. Students are taught to investigate questions, critically evaluate resources, gather information to answer their questions, and create a presentation for their peers and larger community showcasing what they have learned and where they could go next in this research. Students are encouraged to write letters to "experts" on the topics, which helps to connect their work to the real world and can help to reveal potential career opportunities. My role is to integrate their skills and required curriculum into the process.

A seventh-grade student pursued the topic of beekeeping and why the honeybee population has been diminishing. He drafted questions about the topic and then found a local beekeeper. He was able to visit local hives and learn about the care, maintenance, and handling of bees firsthand. This hands-on experience was fun, but, more importantly, it was linked to the reading and research he was doing on the topic. On presentation day, he came to class in character with full beekeeper's garb. He brought a small hive, honey samples, and the tools needed to keep bees. He presented his findings orally with visual aids such as graphs, photographs, and manuals. He also published a research report. His peers were enthralled and engaged. In this way, the student learned and he also created a learning experience for his peers.

ENGAGEMENT IN PRACTICE: PROJECT-BASED LEARNING

Ellen: Last year, in order to provide students with background information pertaining to mythology, I lectured them on the Greek deities. Although I knew that it was a boring way to present what

(Continued)

(Continued)

could be very interesting material, I wasn't sure how else to go about teaching it. After the lesson, I thought that it was a fairly successful approach; however, upon grading the assessment, I found that it was much less favorable than I had hoped. This year, I implemented project-based learning to teach students the same information. In project-based learning, the teacher's role is to set students up for success by designing the learning tools and rubrics but then to step back and let students construct knowledge on their own. Before beginning the unit, I worked intensively to design all the tools necessary to help students achieve success. I created a worksheet that I used to introduce students to the unit. It outlined my expectations, including the objectives and standards that I wanted them to master over the course of the activity. I also created a research outline that would help them sort and compile information as they used MacBooks and iPads to identify reliable resources and data. In addition to the introduction and outline, I also created a rubric so that both students and I would know exactly what needed to be done in order to earn the highest possible grade. My original objective for the unit was quite basic. I wanted students to be able to identify the twelve Olympian gods and goddesses and to describe their characteristics and list their domains. In order to accomplish these objectives, I assigned a couple of students to each Greek god or goddess. Students used computers to research characteristics and traits of their assigned subject. The research guide that I prepared for them required them to identify traits and defining characteristics of their god or goddess. Once students had completed their research, they wrote a journal entry from the perspective of their subject, and, through the narrative, they indirectly presented their findings to their classmates in our school museum in front of the statue depicting their god or goddess. Their classmates listened carefully and took notes on a master grid. I held students accountable for this information by assuring them that their assimilation of it would be assessed. Throughout the presentations, I stood in the back and observed. I watched as my students took complete control of the activity. They were engaged as both presenters and members of the audience.

Unlike my lecture the previous year, I didn't have to redirect anyone because they knew that they were responsible for informing themselves and that the information that they were presenting and learning would appear on their upcoming assessment. As presenters, they knew that if they didn't give their classmates sufficient information, they would not only be hurting themselves but they would also be failing their classmates by not providing them with enough information to pass the test. Students held each other accountable by asking questions at the conclusion of each presentation if their classmate neglected to touch upon a required piece of information. It was amazing to watch students avidly taking notes as their classmates presented, without being prodded by me. It was also equally exciting to see them raise their hands to be called upon by their classmates rather than me. I knew that the project was a complete success even before the summative assessment because as I observed, I saw that every single student in every single class was actively engaged.

Expeditionary learning. Expeditionary learning is a school reform model that is organized around project-based learning principles. Expeditionary learning (EL) grew out of Outward Bound, an adventure program known for wilderness expeditions. Instruction is organized around learning expeditions, or interdisciplinary investigations that result in significant products, public presentations, and portfolios that are shared with audiences beyond the classroom. Conceptually, learning expeditions are similar to wilderness expeditions in that they involve fieldwork, service, teamwork, and building a connection to the world outside of the classroom (Thomas, 2000). Research shows that schools that have implemented expeditionary learning have higher achievement, higher attendance, and a more positive school culture (Thomas, 2000). Currently, there are over 165 expeditionary schools that serve over 45,000 elementary, middle, and high school students across the nation. The expeditionary learning network provides support for EL schools (www.elsschools.org).

Project-based science. Project-based science, developed by Joe Krajcik and his colleagues at the University of Michigan, is another example of a project-based instructional approach (Krajcik, Blumenfeld, Marx, & Soloway, 1994). The five key dimensions of project-based science classrooms are 1) a driving question, 2) investigations, 3) artifacts, 4) collaboration, and 5) technology. Students in project-based science classrooms do the following:

- Ask questions
- Refine questions
- Make predictions
- Design experiments
- Collect and analyze data
- Draw conclusions
- Communicate ideas and findings to others
- Create artifacts

Students in project-based science classrooms tend to choose to investigate questions that relate to their own personal health and wellness, to the environment, to their communities, and to current events. Some examples of project-based science questions are 1) What's in our water?, 2) Why do I look the way I do?, 3) What makes me stay on a skateboard?, and 4) Where are there poisons in our lives? (www.umich.edu/~pbsgroup/whatPBS .html)

Authentic literacy. Authentic instruction also has been applied to literacy activities. Many students enjoy reading and writing outside of school but find the traditional literacy tasks in school boring and disconnected from meaningful literacy activities. **Authentic literacy** is defined as the reading and writing of real-life texts for real-life purposes. Some examples of authentic literacy tasks include reading newspapers, science brochures, informational books, Web sites, song lyrics, and magazines. Duke, Purcell-Gates, Hall, and Tower (2006) offer two criteria for determining the authenticity of literacy activities: 1) the text is read or written outside of learning to read or write, and 2) the purpose for which the text is read or written is the same as that for which it is used outside of the classroom. In the following *Engagement in Practice* section, Ellen describes how authentic literacy is integrated at her school.

ENGAGEMENT IN PRACTICE: INCORPORATING AUTHENTIC LITERACY

Ellen: Students are given twenty minutes each day to read anything that interests them. They are encouraged to not read academic texts. Copies of the daily newspaper are available so that students have opportunities to catch up on national, state-wide, and local news. Many teachers will go out of their way to bring materials that interest students. I have given students everything from basketball magazines to articles on the history of hip-hop dance.

Concept-Oriented Reading Instruction, or CORI, which was developed by John Guthrie and his colleagues at University of Maryland, is an example of an authentic instructional literacy model that was designed to increase students' engagement in reading (Guthrie, Wigfield, & Perencevich, 2004). The CORI program is designed to foster reading engagement and comprehension by teaching reading strategies, scientific concepts, and inquiry skills and by supporting the development of student intrinsic motivation to read (www.corilearning.com). Students read and write trade and other authentic texts for the purpose of learning something that interests them and communicating it to others. Students in CORI classrooms have been found to have higher reading comprehension, reading strategy use, and reading motivation (Wigfield et al., 2008).

In the following *Engagement in Practice* section, Michele outlines how she has increased authentic literacy in the classroom by having her fourth graders create nonfiction books and share their creations with their peers.

ENGAGEMENT IN PRACTICE: CREATING NONFICTION BOOKS

Michele: When my fourth-grade class studies nonfiction, I give them the opportunity to make their own nonfiction books that we can use in the classroom. This really motivates them to learn what

(Continued)

(Continued)

goes into making a nonfiction book. As a class, we brainstorm and review the different types of nonfiction text features that help organize information and write them on a poster, with one illustration of each feature. Then I set up baskets filled with various nonfiction books around the room and the students go on a scavenger hunt in pairs to find and mark the different features with labeled sticky notes. I keep all these books on hand so we can go back and reference the marked pages when we make our nonfiction books.

The students make nonfiction books about a topic we are studying in class, usually related to science or social studies. For example, one year while we were studying interactions between land and water, students created books teaching about land and water formations, erosion, and the water cycle. Students work in groups and each individual is assigned to complete one or two pages of the book. They use headings, diagrams and labels, illustrations with captions, different types of print to emphasize key words, and maps and graphs to present their information. Students take great care in working on these books because they know we will include them in our classroom library, along with all the other nonfiction books. Anyone can refer back to these books as resources, as well as read them during independent reading time. They really enjoy seeing each other's work and being "published" nonfiction writers in our classroom.

Thematic instruction. Another strategy to make instruction more authentic is to use **thematic instruction,** an instructional approach that is based on the idea that students learn best when instruction is organized around a larger theme that is used to teach specific concepts (Kovalik, 1994). Instruction that is organized around main ideas facilitates student comprehension and understanding. The key is to choose themes that relate to students' lives outside of the classroom. Teachers can involve students in selecting themes, brainstorming and prioritizing issues for study, planning classroom activities, and making connections among different concepts and these larger themes. In the following section, Ellen outlines how she used thematic instruction in her English classes.

**ENGAGEMENT IN PRACTICE:
THEMATIC INSTRUCTION**

Ellen: To teach *Great Expectations* this past year, I used thematic instruction. I paired each chapter or group of chapters with a unique topic, such as nature versus nurture, views of women, the author's perception of the rich and poor, and the author's perception of good versus evil. As we read, students searched the text for examples to illustrate the topic. I recorded these examples in graphic organizers on the board as the students recorded them in their notes. Once we had collected enough information, we tried to identify a pattern and worked together to come up with a generalization or a theme. Themes included: one's surroundings and company influence their behavior; women are evil, abusive, and manipulative; being good gets you nowhere; and money is power. Rather than reading the text as an archaic story that bears no relevance to contemporary life, this process allowed students to read the text as a time capsule that serves to perpetuate the social norm. This process made the reading experience much more meaningful and, therefore, made the text much more engaging. After using this technique, I saw that the average test grade for *Great Expectations* was much higher than that of the previous unit. The failure rate also dropped to nearly 1 percent.

MOTIVATIONAL AND COGNITIVE CHALLENGES WITH AUTHENTIC INSTRUCTION

Although authentic instruction has been found to be more engaging for students, these instructional models present additional challenges for both students and teachers. One of the challenges is that this type of instruction requires a shift from a teacher-directed to a student-centered instructional environment. In teacher-directed instructional environments, the teacher is in control and shapes learning primarily through direct instruction methods. Students in these environments are passive recipients of teachers' knowledge. In contrast, in child-centered instructional environments, the focus is on the student as a learner and the teacher plays a more facilitative role. As a result, in these environments, students need to be active learners and assume greater responsibility for their own learning. This is going to be more challenging for students like Rachel, profiled at the beginning of Chapter 1, who lack the self-confidence and skills to take greater ownership in their own learning.

Sharing power can be difficult for teachers. Authentic instructional environments require a shift from the model where the teacher is the authority figure to a model where teachers and students are partners in the learning process. One mistake that some teachers make is assuming that active learning means relinquishing the teacher's management responsibilities for structure and control. Such abandonment can result in chaos, with students feeling frustrated and unclear about what they need to do to achieve success. Teachers still need to set up the conditions and play an active role in organizing the learning experience while assuming the role of a coach, facilitator, and manager.

The small-group component of more authentic instructional environments also presents additional challenges. Students vary in their social skills, ability to engage in productive discussions, and ability to stay on-task during group work. Some students have the social skills to work productively with their peers to solve problems, while students like Ryan will need more support, guidance, and monitoring from the teacher to have successful group interactions. There are also concerns that some group members will engage in **social loafing** and not contribute adequately to group work. Social loafing is the tendency of some individuals to exert less effort on a task when they work in a group then when they work individually. Strategies for successful group work are presented in Chapter 6.

Authentic instructional environments include tasks that are procedurally complex and cognitively challenging. Critique, reflection, and revision of work are central components of these instructional environments. There are individual differences in how well students respond to critique and cognitively challenging work. One concern is that some students like Beatrice, who was described at the beginning of Chapter 1 as wanting to avoid failure, may stop when they feel like they have done enough work and have difficulty with critique and revisions. It is critical that teachers help students to see that errors are a natural part of this type of learning rather than indicative of failure. Another concern is that some students like Benjamin will focus on grades and completing the work with minimal effort at the expense of learning goals and conceptual understanding (Blumenfeld et al., 2006). If teachers emphasize competition, rote procedures, and behavioral management, then students are more likely to perceive tasks as busy work and focus on simply completing the task rather than engaging deeply in the content.

One of the challenges in these authentic instructional environments is that some students are resistant to tasks with high cognitive demands because it is less clear what they should do or how they should do it. When faced with challenge and task ambiguity, these students may pressure teachers to simplify the tasks. There is evidence that teachers respond to this pressure from students by implementing cognitively complex tasks in a way that reduces student thought (Blumenfeld, 1992).

Another concern is that students will focus so much on procedures that the content and opportunities for deeper learning get lost. A case study of middle-level students in their first experience with project-based science offers evidence to support this concern. In these classrooms students focused more on procedural issues and completing their work than on science content or deeper conceptual understanding (Krajcik et al., 1998). Similarly, in mathematics, Henningsen and Stein (1997) examined the ways that classroom-based factors shape students' engagement with cognitively complex tasks. They identified several features of mathematics tasks that were related to declines in cognitive engagement, which may readily be applied to other content areas. Table 4.6 describes each of these five task features.

Table 4.6 Task Characteristics Related to Decline in Cognitive Engagement

1. *Reduction in cognitive complexity of tasks.* Cognitively complex tasks were often viewed as ambiguous and risky by teachers and students. As a result, teachers often tried to reduce complexity and simplify these tasks. This resulted in lower thinking, effort, and reasoning by students.

2. *Shift away from meaning and understanding to a focus on accuracy and completion of answers.* Some teachers focused on the solution at the expense of process and understanding.

(Continued)

Table 4.6   (Continued)

3. *Inadequate time for tasks.* Teachers who provided too little time for a task had students who emphasized procedural thinking over grappling with content. Teachers who provided too much time without adequate supports for students who were having difficulty also had students with lower cognitive engagement.
4. *Inappropriateness of task for particular group of students.* Some students had low motivation and lacked the prior knowledge to be successful at the task.
5. *Lack of accountability for high-level products and processes.* In some classrooms, students were not expected to justify their methods and explanations and were given the impressions that these tasks did not "count." In these cases, students did not engage deeply in these tasks and only focused on the work that counted.

STOP AND REFLECT

1. How have you tried (or might you try) to implement authentic instructional models in your classroom? How did (might) your students react to these instructional models?

2. Which of the challenges described in the last section did you encounter or would you expect to encounter when trying to incorporate authentic instructional models?

3. What strategies did (could) you use to address each of these challenges?

Cognitive Strategy Use

Students need to be able to plan, set goals, organize, and self-monitor while working on cognitively complex tasks. **Self-regulated learning** refers to self-generated thoughts, feelings, and behaviors that are directed towards achieving goals (Zimmerman, 2002). Examples of self-regulatory strategies include:

- Self-evaluation
- Organization and transformation
- Goal setting and planning

- Information seeking
- Record keeping
- Self-monitoring
- Environmental structuring
- Giving self-consequences
- Rehearsing and memorizing
- Seeking social assistance from parents, peers, or other adults
- Reviewing

Students need a variety of cognitive and self-regulatory strategies to work on cognitively complex tasks. They also need strategies to integrate and connect information with previous knowledge. Research has shown that students have greater comprehension, achievement, and performance when they use elaboration and organization strategies as opposed to shallow processing and rehearsal strategies (Greene & Miller, 1996). Some examples of elaboration strategies for complex tasks include summarizing material to be learned, creating analogies, explaining the ideas in the material to someone else, and asking and answering questions. Examples of organizational strategies for complex tasks include outlining material and identifying connections among ideas.

One of the challenges with implementing cognitively complex tasks is that some students lack these cognitive and self-regulatory strategies. Moreover, even when students possess these strategies, they may not know when and how to use them to foster conceptual understanding. Strategy use also depends on motivation and control (Paris & Paris, 2001). Prior research has shown that strategy use can be taught both explicitly through instruction, directed reflection, and metacognitive discussions, and indirectly through modeling and through tasks that require reflective analysis of learning (Paris & Paris, 2001).

STRATEGIES FOR IMPLEMENTING COGNITIVELY COMPLEX TASKS

There are several strategies that teachers can use to support students' engagement in cognitively complex tasks. Table 4.7 outlines some practical strategies for maintaining student engagement in these tasks. For example, teachers can support cognitive engagement 1) by providing appropriate amounts of time to explore ideas and make connections, 2) by selecting tasks that build on students' prior knowledge, and 3) by emphasizing explanations, meaning, and understanding over the recall of specific information or application of specific procedures (Doyle, 1988; Stein, Grover, & Henningsen, 1996).

Instructional scaffolding. Teacher **scaffolding** can help students to understand and to make connections between ideas, which is especially important in cognitively complex learning.

Table 4.7   Practical Strategies for Implementing Cognitively Complex Tasks

1. *Provide appropriate amount of time for tasks.* Teachers should provide enough time for students to explore ideas and make connections. It is important that teachers emphasize thoughtful inquiry over the speed and quantity of tasks.

2. *Select tasks that build on students' prior knowledge.* Teachers should select tasks that are at an appropriate difficulty level so that students can utilize relevant prior knowledge.

3. *Emphasize meaning and understanding.* Teachers should provide the message that explanations and justifications are as much a part of learning as are correct answers. Teachers should minimize ability and performance-related learning and should emphasize mastery learning and understanding.

4. *Model high-level thinking and reasoning.* Teachers and peers can model high-level thinking and reasoning by providing examples of meaningful explanations and appropriate justifications.

5. *Press for student understanding.* Teachers should press students for justifications, explanations, and meaning through questioning, comments, and feedback.

6. *Draw conceptual connections.* Teachers should make explicit connections between the concepts students are learning and what they already know and understand.

7. *Diagnose problems and provide feedback.* Teachers should break larger projects into smaller tasks and periodically assess students' progress. This will help teachers to diagnose problems and provide feedback.

8. *Encourage students to self-question and self-monitor.* Teachers should encourage students to engage in self-questioning and self-monitoring as they are work on a task. Self-questioning can increase metacognitive skills by encouraging students to monitor their own thinking.

Scaffolding occurs when either a teacher or a more able peer provides assistance and guidance that enables a student to complete a task that would be impossible to do without the support. Teachers and peers can also support students' higher-level thinking by explicitly modeling such thinking strategies. Finally, teachers should encourage students to engage in self-monitoring or self-questioning as they progress through a task.

In the next two *Engagement in Practice* sections, Melissa and Michele discuss how they use instructional scaffolding to teach reading strategies in their classrooms.

ENGAGEMENT IN PRACTICE: USING JOURNALING TO SCAFFOLD READING STRATEGIES

Melissa: Students can practice reflecting upon their own reading strategies through journaling with the teacher. My middle school students periodically write letters to me about the books they are reading. They may also write letters to each other to mix up the format. The following questions are a few that might frame a student's response:

1. From whose point of view is the story told?

2. Whose point of view is missing?

3. What events or characters can you relate to and why?

4. What motivates the character(s)? How do you know?

5. Who is the intended audience?

6. What other questions do you have as you read this book?

7. Why is the setting important to the plot?

8. How does the author use dialogue to move the story along?

9. Analyze the author's style. How does he/she organize the parts of the book?

10. Why did you choose this book?

(Continued)

(Continued)

I am able to write back to students in response to their higher-order thinking by asking them more questions to guide them as they read. The journal is a safe and confidential tool in which students can write things they may not ask in a class discussion. This strategy is great for scaffolding learning—it helps less confident readers "practice" responding before we have class discussions. I also post letters to my class about the books I am reading as well. In this way, I am presenting an ongoing model of the strategies they are learning.

ENGAGEMENT IN PRACTICE: ANALYZING AND SYNTHESIZING WHAT WE READ

Michele: My fourth graders learn and practice various reading strategies throughout the year, using a variety of tasks. For example, we often read magazine articles. In order to understand the material better and think more critically about the topic, I want them to do more than just summarize and explain what they have read. I realized these types of texts work well in preparing class debates, and it's a great opportunity for students to work in different groupings. For these debates, I choose a variety of articles on the same topic so students can gather as much information as possible and see various perspectives. I always make sure the topic is interesting and relates to them. For example, one time we debated the pros and cons of standardized testing. Individuals or pairs are assigned different articles so that when they come together in groups, they can share what they've read with others and learn from each other. In their reading, analysis, and evidence collecting, they practice the strategies that I have modeled and that we have practiced before. I actually assign students to different sides of the debate, whether they agree or not. Some of the students are reluctant at first if they don't agree with the side, but because of all the work that goes into preparing and all the evidence they are able to collect to support their side, all the students are invested by the time we get to debating. They have outlines and notes to keep the discussion going. I have been quite impressed by how eloquent many are. They are experts at this point, and confident in presenting each side and backing up their assertions. Not only that, we all have a deeper understanding of the texts we have read and of the overall topic.

CHAPTER SUMMARY

Chapter 4 described ways to make classroom tasks more motivationally *and* cognitively engaging to students. A key principle in this chapter is that motivation is necessary, but it is not sufficient for full engagement in learning. Teachers often focus on motivational dimensions such as making tasks fun or hands-on and pay less attention to the cognitive dimensions that are necessary to translate this motivation into sustained cognitive engagement. Research-based strategies from the intrinsic motivation literature that incorporated the dimensions of novelty, challenge, choice, fantasy, and meaningfulness were presented. Task features that increase motivation include adequate challenge, opportunities to make choices, and some connection to students' lives outside the classroom. Next, differences in the cognitive dimensions of academic tasks were reviewed. Engagement is higher in classrooms with open-ended tasks that have multiple possible solutions and require students to use higher cognitive level processes to evaluate and create knowledge. Unfortunately, many of the tasks in schools are close-ended tasks with one right answer that require lower-level cognitive skills such as recall and repetition.

Authentic tasks that are situated in meaningful contexts and reflect how learning happens outside of the classroom were outlined as a model for creating an instructional environment that incorporates both motivational and cognitive dimensions. Examples of authentic instructional environments in math, science, and literacy, such as project-based science, authentic literacy, and thematic instruction, were presented. Although the use of authentic tasks is associated with a variety of motivation and cognitive benefits, it is much more difficult to implement this type of instruction in the classroom. Some of the instructional, group, and individual challenges with incorporating authentic instruction in the classroom were discussed. For example, because authentic instructional tasks are ambiguous and cognitively complex, a common response by teachers is to reduce the complexity and simplify the tasks. Unfortunately, this only serves to lower the cognitive demands for students. The chapter concluded with practical strategies for implementing cognitively complex tasks in the classroom. Teachers play a critical role in scaffolding and modeling higher-level thinking and reasoning.

TEXT-TO-PRACTICE EXERCISES

TPE 4.1: **Rate Intrinsic Value of Tasks:** For two typical days, rate all of the tasks students are given on a scale from 1 to 5 (1 = "none"; 5 = "high") in the following areas:

1. Task value

2. Opportunities for choice

3. Active student role

4. Peer interaction allowed

5. Novel/different type of task

6. Level of challenge

7. Opportunities for creative problem solving

8. Directly related to students' personal experience

TPE 4.2: **Rate Instruction on Level of Authenticity:** Using Table 4.5, evaluate a lesson on the five standards for authentic instruction on a scale from 1 to 5.

1. Higher-order thinking (1 = "lower-order thinking only"; 5 = "higher-order thinking is central")

2. Depth of knowledge (1 = "knowledge is shallow"; 5 = "knowledge is deep")

3. Connected to world beyond classroom (1 = "no connection"; 5 = "connected")

4. Substantive conversation (1 = "no substantive conversation"; 5 = "high-level substantive conversation")

5. Social support for student achievement (1 = "negative social support"; 5 = "positive social support")

TPE 4.3: **Interview Students About Tasks in the Classroom**: Interview a few students about the tasks in the classroom. Below are possible questions:

1. Which tasks do you find most interesting in the classroom? Why?

2. Which tasks did you find least interesting? Why?

3. Do you feel challenged in the classroom? Why or why not?

4. Do you feel like you have the skills to do the work?

5. In what ways do you have opportunities to be creative?

TPE 4.4: **Develop a Sample Lesson**: Develop a sample lesson with cognitively complex tasks. Describe the cognitive and self-regulatory skills that students will need to be successful at this lesson. Answer the following questions:

1. Did I provide appropriate amounts of time?

2. Does the task build on students' prior knowledge?

3. Is the task situated in real-world contexts?

4. Does the task reflect subject matter?

5. Did I offer opportunities for students to demonstrate their knowledge in different ways?

KEY TERMS AND CONCEPTS

Artifact: Product that students create in an authentic instructional environment and share with their peers.

Authentic literacy: The reading and writing of real-life texts for real-life purposes.

Authentic tasks: Tasks that are situated in meaningful and real-world contexts, are cognitively complex, and reflect how learning happens outside of the classroom.

Bloom's Taxonomy: Classification of learning objectives into three domains: cognitive, affective, and psychomotor. This taxonomy was originally developed in 1956 and was recently updated to reflect twenty-first-century students and teachers.

Close-ended tasks: Tasks that have one correct answer. Multiple choice tests, true/false tests, fill-in-the blank tests, and tasks where students do not show their work are examples of close-ended tasks.

Expeditionary learning: A school reform model that is organized around learning expeditions in which students do original interdisciplinary research and produce high-quality products for audiences beyond the classroom.

Flow: A mental state where an individual is completely emerged in an activity for its own sake. Individuals in flow lose sense of time and consciousness and experience strong concentration and focused attention.

Intrinsic motivation: Being motivated by an internal interest or enjoyment in the task as opposed to being motivated by external factors.

Mastery goals: Students who hold mastery goals focus on understanding or mastering the task. These students are interested in self-improvement and tend to compare their current performance to their prior performance.

Open-ended tasks: Tasks that have multiple possible solutions or several ways to reach the correct answer.

Performance goals: Students who hold performance goals focus on demonstrating their ability relative to others. These students are interested in competition, demonstrating their relative competence, and outperforming others.

Project-based learning: An instructional approach that is organized around a driving question. Students investigate this question through collaboration over an extended period of time. They use technology and the project culminates in a public presentation, product, or performance.

Project-based science: An inquiry-based instructional approach that was developed at the University of Michigan for use in science classrooms. The five key dimensions of project-based science classrooms are 1) a driving question, 2) investigations, 3) artifacts, 4) collaboration, and 5) technology.

Scaffolding: A teacher or a more able peer provides assistance, support, and modeling so that a student can complete a task that he or she would not be able to complete alone.

Self-regulated learning: Process by which learners attempt to monitor and control their own learning.

Social loafing: The tendency for an individual to exert less effort on a task in group work then he or she would do individually.

Thematic instruction: Instruction organized around larger themes that are used to teach content.

RESEARCH-BASED RESOURCES

Books and Reports to Read

Berger, R. (2003). *An ethics of excellence: Building a culture of craftsmanship with students.* Portsmouth, NH: Heinemann.

Bransford, J. D., Brown, A. L., & Cocking, R. R. (1999). *How people learn: Brain, mind, experience, and school.* Washington, DC: National Academy Press.

Cooke, S. L. (2013). *The synergistic relationship between student empowerment and creativity in the middle school classroom.* Retrieved from ProQuest database.

Csikszentmihalyi, M. (1991). *Flow: The psychology of optimal experience.* New York: HarperPerennial.

Daniels, H., & Harvey, S. (2009). *Comprehension and collaboration: Inquiry circles in action.* Portsmouth, NH: Heinemann.

Daniels, S., & Zeleman, S. (2004). *Subjects matter: Every teacher's guide to content area reading.* Portsmouth, NH: Heinemann.

Denton, P. (2005). *Learning through academic choice.* Turner Falls, MA: Northeast Center for Children.

Guthrie, J. T., Wigfield, A., & Perencevich, K. C. (Eds.). (2004). *Motivating reading comprehension: Concept-oriented reading instruction.* Mahwah, NJ: Lawrence Erlbaum.

Harvey, S. (1998). *Nonfiction matters: Reading, writing, and research for grades 3–8.* Markham, Ontario: Stenhouse Publishers.

Harvey, S., & Goudvis, A. (2000). *Strategies that work: Teaching comprehension for understanding and engagement.* Markham, Ontario: Stenhouse Publishers.

Hattie, J. (2012). *Visible learning for teachers: Maximizing impact on learning.* New York, NY: Routledge.

Keene, E. O., & Zimmerman, S. (2007). *Mosaic of thought: The power of strategy instruction* (2nd ed.). Portsmouth, NH: Heinemann.

Kovalik, S. (1994). *Integrated thematic instruction: The model.* Kent, WA: Susan Kovalik & Associates.

Lewison, M., Leland, C., Harste, J., & Christensen, L. (2007). *Creating critical classrooms: K-8 reading and writing with an edge.* New York, NY: Routledge.

Marzano, R. J., & Kendall, G. S. (2008). *Designing and assessing educational objectives: Applying the new taxonomy.* Thousand Oaks, CA: Corwin Press.

Newmann (1992). *Student engagement and achievement in American secondary schools.* New York, NY: Teachers College Press.

Reichel, A. G. (2010). *Expect more: Children can do remarkable things.* Bloomington, IN: Authorhouse.

Sousa, D., & Pilecki, T. (2013). *Stem to steam: Using brain-compatible strategies to integrate the arts.* Thousand Oaks, CA: Corwin Press.

Strachota, B. (1996). *On their side: Helping children take charge of their learning.* Turner Falls, MA: Northeast Foundation for Children.

Thomas, J. W. (2000). *A review of project-based learning.* Retrieved on 10/22/13 from www.bobpearlman.org/BestPractices/PBL_Research.pdf.

Web Sites to Visit

1. **Edutopia.com** (www.edutopia.com). This site offers educational resources on project-based learning, including profiles of schools that have incorporated project-based learning models.

2. **Concept-Oriented Reading Instruction** (www.corilearning.com). This site includes resources related to concept-oriented reading instruction, which was developed at the University of Maryland. Information on research studies, professional development, and copies of measures are included on the site.

3. **Project-Based Science** (www.umich.edu/~pbsgroup). This site includes information on project-based science, which was developed at the University of Michigan. Project-based planning software is available on the site.

4. **Expeditionary Learning** (www.elschools.org). This site includes resources about the expeditionary learning model. It offers examples of lessons, research results, and professional development opportunities.

5. **Buck Institute for Education: Project Based Learning for the 21st Century** (www.bie.org). This site includes resources on project-based learning, including planning forms, assessment rubrics, and research articles.

6. **Jason Learning** (www.jasonproject.org). This is a non-profit organization that connects students to real scientists and researchers in order to provide authentic learning experiences. Curricular resources and information on professional development is included on the site.

7. **Facing History and Ourselves** (www.facing.org). This site includes resources for educators to help them teach civic responsibility, social justice, and tolerance. Sample lessons and units, videos, and information on professional development are available on the site.

8. **Read Write Think** (www.readwritethink.org). Read Write Think is an international reading association. Literacy resources, lesson plans, and information on professional development are available on this site.

9. **Teach Unicef** (www.teachunicef.org). This site includes interdisciplinary global education resources for K-12 teachers in social studies, science, math, English/language arts, and foreign languages. Lesson plans, stories, and multimedia are available on the site.

CHAPTER FIVE

MYTH 5: Focus on Content: Don't Make It Personal

How Relationships Matter for Student Engagement

S trong and supportive relationships between teachers and students are fundamental to students' engagement and healthy development. Students who perceive their teacher as supportive and caring are more likely to develop positive attitudes towards school, take intellectual risks, and persist in the face of difficulty. It is particularly important to build quality relationships with students who are at risk for school failure. Prior research shows that a supportive relationship with a teacher can distinguish at-risk students who succeed in school from those who do not (Pianta, Steinberg, & Rollins, 1995). Unfortunately, many students, especially those who are academically at risk, are not experiencing these types of relationships with their teachers. Furthermore, there is evidence that these poor relationships with teachers are actually contributing to student disengagement over time.

One misconception held by many teachers, especially those who teach the middle and secondary levels, is that their primary role is to teach content knowledge and skills and that developing relationships with their students is important but not essential for learning. Many teachers struggle with balancing the time and emotional effort that is required to develop high-quality teacher-student relationships with their instructional demands and academic responsibilities. Although some teachers see relationships and instruction as competing demands, the reality is that to fully engage students, teachers need to attend to both the academic and interpersonal dimensions. If teachers only focus on academics and fail to acknowledge the interpersonal dimensions, students will be more likely to disengage emotionally and will be more apprehensive about making mistakes. In contrast, if teachers focus on only providing emotional support and fail to attend to the academic dimensions of the classroom, students will be less cognitively engaged and experience less academic success.

Previous research illustrates the benefits of both a socially supportive and an intellectually challenging environment for behavioral, emotional, and cognitive engagement (Fredricks et al., 2004). In this chapter, research on the effects of both interpersonal and academic supports on student engagement is presented. Practical strategies for improving student-teacher relations, especially among those students who are most challenging, are outlined.

STOP AND REFLECT

1. What are your top five responsibilities in your role as a classroom teacher?

2. How do you balance the time required to meet academic demands with the time required to develop relations with your students?

3. How can you develop meaningful and beneficial student-teacher relations while still holding students accountable for their academic progress?

4. How do you develop relations with your students? Are these relations initiated by you or the students?

5. Which students do you have the most difficulty engaging? How would you describe your relations with these students?

TEACHER SUPPORT AND STUDENT ENGAGEMENT AND ACHIEVEMENT

A growing body of research shows that positive teacher-student relations are associated with indicators of behavioral, emotional, and cognitive engagement and with achievement outcomes (e.g., Birch & Ladd, 1997; Hamre & Pianta, 2001; Fredricks et al., 2004; Ryan & Patrick, 2001; Wang & Eccles, 2012). Having close and caring relationships with teachers has been found to be especially important to the engagement of low-income and African American and Hispanic youths (Garcia-Reid, Reid, & Peterson, 2005). Teacher support has been shown to be predictive of higher levels of the following:

- Student participation
- Self-directedness
- On-task behavior
- Cooperative behavior
- Effort
- Attendance
- Enjoyment of school
- Interest
- Value
- School satisfaction
- Social skills
- Critical-thinking skills
- Self-regulation
- Standardized test scores
- Grades

The outcomes listed above are those that every teacher wants and that every teacher observes in successful students. Apparent in this list of outcomes are behaviors that demonstrate how teacher-student relations are also a key aspect of successful classroom management. Many behavioral problems in school are the result of a breakdown in teacher-student relationships. Students who have developed positive relationships with their teachers are more likely to comply with classroom norms, which in turn should reduce their probability of disruptive behavior (Birch & Ladd, 1997). In a meta-analysis of over 100 studies, Marzano, Marzano, and Pickering (2003) found that teachers who had high-quality relations with their students had 31 percent fewer behavioral problems. The quality of early teacher-student relations also has long-term consequences. Students who had more conflict with teachers in kindergarten were found to have lower academic achievement and more behavioral problems in the eighth grade (Hamre & Pianta, 2001).

The need for high-quality student-teacher relations continues as students get older and is particularly important in helping them to manage school stressors. One such stressor is the transition from elementary to middle school. Students show declines in motivation, engagement, self-esteem, and academic performance over the transition to middle school (Wigfield, Brynes, & Eccles, 2006). Positive relationships with teachers can help to buffer some of these declines. Students who perceive greater teacher support in middle and high school have higher engagement, higher achievement, and lower risk behavior (Gregory & Weinstein, 2004; Resnick et al., 1997; Wentzel, 1998).

Unfortunately, research also has shown the negative consequences of lack of teacher support. Klem and Connell (2004) found that elementary school students with low levels of teacher support were twice as likely as the average student to report being disengaged from school (Klem & Connell, 2004). Students like Ryan, described at the beginning of Chapter 1 as aggressive, bored, and confused, often fail to develop positive relationships with their teachers. As a result, these students are more likely to perceive school as an unwelcoming and alienating place. Failure to develop positive connections with teachers puts students at a greater risk for disengagement and the possibility of dropping out (Croninger & Lee, 2001).

For many teachers, their teacher education program and professional development focused on student learning. The knowledge and skills for building teacher-student relations were assumed but were not an explicit part of their preparation or continuing education. This puts many teachers at risk of developing positive relationships with only a few students—most likely those students who already have strong interpersonal and academic skills. The following sections provide a brief background of the essential qualities of teacher-student relations that are based in both theory and research.

ESSENTIAL CHARACTERISTICS OF MEANINGFUL TEACHER–STUDENT RELATIONS

According to **attachment theory**, early child-caregiver interactions provide a context for the development of a secure attachment relationship, which in turn provides the child with a sense of security and a basis for exploration. Attachment theory also can be used to explain why teacher-child relations are important for student engagement (Pianta, 1999). Teachers that provide emotional support and a consistently safe environment are more likely to have students that develop a secure teacher-student attachment relationship. As a result, these students will be more likely to take risks and explore their environment because they trust that their teacher will be there to respond to any difficulties they experience in the classroom.

STOP, REFLECT, AND TRY

1. Identify the teachers in your school, grade-level team, or department who have developed the most trust with students.

    a. How is student engagement (behavioral, emotional, and cognitive) different in their classrooms?

    b. What strategies have they used to develop trust?

    c. Apply what you believe to be a trust-building strategy in your classroom. Observe how students respond.

2. What is your role as a teacher when students have not experienced positive teacher-student relations? How do you identify these students? How do you respond?

Self-determination theory (see Chapter 3) is another theoretical perspective that can be used to explain the effects of teacher-student relations on student engagement. According to this theory, students come to the classroom with three psychological needs: relatedness, autonomy, and competence

(Connell & Wellborn, 1991). Positive teacher-student relations can help students to meet these needs. Teachers who develop a personal and caring relationship with their students can help them to meet their need for relatedness. Teachers who offer students opportunities to make decisions can help support students' need for autonomy. Finally, teachers who provide clear expectations for students and feedback on their performance can help students to meet their need for competence. The following sections explore strategies for supporting these three needs in every classroom.

BUILDING RELATEDNESS IN THE CLASSROOM

Although researchers have defined teacher support in slightly different ways, the definitions all tend to involve characteristics such as caring, friendliness, understanding, dedication, and dependability (Ryan & Patrick, 2001). In the early years, positive teacher-student relations help students to adapt to both the academic and social environment. Through these relationships children develop social skills and emotional understanding that they can use in their relationships with their peers. Children who form close relationships with their teachers have been found to get along better with their peers (Hamre & Pianta, 2006). During adolescence, relationships with teachers serve a somewhat different function. Middle school and high school teachers can provide students with emotional and social support, which can in turn strengthen students' connection to school. Teachers in the secondary school years also can serve as role models, help students with problem solving, and provide information and strategies that support academic performance.

Professional caring. One way that teachers support students' need for relatedness is through **pedagogical caring**. Nel Nodding (1988) argues that developing caring relationships is necessary for meeting the academic objectives of schooling. Students who perceive that their teacher cares about them are more likely to engage in content, comply with classroom norms, and be secure enough to take intellectual risks. Teachers can show students that they care about them by supporting their social and emotional needs. Teachers can do this by truly listening to students, showing them mutual respect, getting to know them as individuals, and understanding each of their unique strengths and challenges.

It is important to remember that caring has an instructional dimension. Caring does not mean that teachers should allow students who are experiencing challenges to make excuses for failing to complete work or not participating in discussions. Caring teachers dedicate the time and effort to make sure students are meeting academic demands. Teachers also demonstrate caring through their choice of what and how they teach. Table 5.1 outlines characteristics that adolescents used to describe a caring teacher (Wentzel, 1997).

Table 5.1 Characteristics of Middle School Teachers "Who Cared"

1. Models a Caring Attitude Toward Work
• Makes a special effort
• Teaches in a unique way
• Makes class interesting
2. Democratic Interaction Styles
• Listens well
• Asks questions
• Pays attention
• Is equitable
• Models respect
3. Develops Individualized Expectations
• Focuses on students' unique skills
• Appreciates individuality
4. Provides Constructive Feedback
• Checks work carefully
• Offers constructive praise

STOP AND REFLECT

1. What characteristics would you add to Table 5.1 to characterize a caring and supportive teacher?

2. What characteristics in Table 5.1 would students use to characterize you as their teacher? Which aspects are less evident in your instruction?

3. What messages are you communicating to students through your choice of content, classroom norms, and individual interactions with students?

4. What are additional ways you could demonstrate caring to your students?

Professional sensitivity. Another way teachers support students' need for relatedness is through **teacher sensitivity**, or the level of a teacher's attunement and responsiveness in the classroom. Highly sensitive teachers notice subtle cues from students and respond in ways that help to alleviate problems. For example, sensitive teachers notice changes in students' emotions and behaviors and when they are having difficulty with an assignment. These teachers then make adjustments to their instruction to better support their students' needs.

Teachers who express positive emotions in the classroom and model enthusiasm towards learning can also support students' need for relatedness. In a series of observational studies, Julie Turner and her colleagues (Turner et al., 1998; Turner et al., 2002) found that teachers who were rated by observers as exhibiting positive emotions more frequently had students who reported higher math motivation, higher math involvement, and lower use of avoidance strategies. As part of their positive emotional displays, these teachers modeled their personal interest in mathematics and used enthusiasm and humor to reduce student anxiety during challenging work.

Finally, teachers can support students' need for relatedness by sharing some of their own personal experiences. Davis (2006) found that students felt they had the most motivating relationships with teachers who shared information about their own experiences in school, their own personal difficulties with learning, and their families. This can help to make teachers seem more personable and relatable to their students. However, one challenge that teachers face is determining what information is appropriate to share and where to set boundaries.

STOP AND REFLECT

1. What aspects of your personal experiences do you feel comfortable sharing with students in order to support their need for relatedness?

2. How can you connect your personal experiences to course content in ways that would help students relate their experiences to yours?

3. Which aspects of personal experiences do you feel uncomfortable sharing or believe are inappropriate to share? Should all shared experiences be related in school?

In the following *Engagement in Practice* section, Michele describes how she has shared her interests and personal experiences with her students.

ENGAGEMENT IN PRACTICE: SHARING PERSONAL EXPERIENCES

Michele: In my classroom we use the Writing Workshop model, and every student has a writer's notebook that they use for recording ideas, practicing skills, and writing. I keep my own writer's notebook as well, and this provides a great opportunity for me to share my own interests and personal experiences with my students. When I teach a writing lesson, I have usually prepared an example in my notebook that involves something that recently happened to me, thoughts I've

(Continued)

(Continued)

had on my mind, or a childhood story. They especially love hearing the stories about when I was in fourth grade and the stories I share about my brother and me. I originally started my own writer's notebook so I could model using it for students, but I've found that it also allows students to get to know me through my writing, just as I get to know them through theirs. I also see that their writing becomes more personal to them and less about what they think they should write. They begin to enjoy the process more, take more risks in their writing, and are more willing to share with each other and listen respectfully when we read aloud from our pieces.

Table 5.2 outlines a variety of practical strategies for supporting students' need for relatedness in the classroom that are based on the research on teacher-student relations.

Table 5.2 Practical Strategies for Supporting Students' Need for Relatedness

1. *Get to know students in your classroom.* Teachers should try to learn as much as possible about students' interests and backgrounds outside of school. Asking a student how his or her weekend was is a simple way to learn about a student's life. Teachers can use information on students' interests to create opportunities in the classroom that match these interests. Furthermore, having a greater understanding of students' unique lived experiences can help teachers to build stronger emotional connections to students.

2. *Demonstrate positive emotions in the classroom.* Students watch teachers for cues on how to respond to the classroom. It is important to model positive behaviors and emotions in the classroom. Videotaping lessons is one way teachers can become more aware of any negative feelings they may be projecting towards students.

3. *Be responsive and respectful of students' needs.* Teachers can demonstrate caring by listening to and respecting students' concerns. Weekly teacher-student meetings and class discussions are one way for students to voice their concerns. Teachers should also pay attention to how individual students are behaving and feeling and provide additional support to students who appear to be having difficulty.

4. *Be aware of both the explicit and implicit messages you are giving students.* Teachers demonstrate caring through their individual interactions and messages they provide to students. In addition, teachers implicitly provide messages about what they care about through what and how they choose to teach.

5. *Reflect on your individual relationships with students in your classroom, especially those that have not been positive or close.* Think about what you say and how you act towards difficult students. Reflect on why you may have a difficult relationship with this student and how you view these interactions. Obtain support from other professionals at the school (e.g., special education teachers, school psychologists, and social workers) when needed.

STOP, REFLECT, AND TRY

1. Do you believe that all students need to feel that they belong in every classroom?
2. Are there some students that you have difficulty connecting with? Why? What could you do to improve these relationships?
3. How do you know whether you have "connected" or not with all students in the ways that you intend?

In the following *Engagement in Practice* section, Melissa describes how she uses a teacher report card to get feedback on how well she is meeting her students' need for relatedness.

ENGAGEMENT IN PRACTICE: TEACHER REPORT CARD

Melissa: After my students bring home their report cards each term, I ask them to complete one for me. This is the best way for me to understand the needs of my students and their perceptions of our experience together. The teacher report card may be filled out anonymously if desired. The questions use a Likert scale and address topics such as classroom management, fairness, enthusiasm, and

(Continued)

(Continued)

respect. Students also rate my ability to give clear directions, use language they understand, give valuable feedback, and rate their interest in the variety of activities I assign. There are questions that directly assess whether or not they feel cared about in class. This feedback is very important to me. As a result of the report cards, I have improved my feedback on student writing and am more cognizant of the language I use in class. In addition, I have asked a peer to observe my teaching and to tally how often I call on boys or girls and different ethnic groups to make sure I treat students fairly.

BEING AN AUTONOMY-SUPPORTIVE TEACHER

Teachers differ in the extent to which they support students' need for autonomy. Researchers have differentiated the instructional behaviors of **autonomy-supportive teachers** from those with a more controlling teaching style (Reeve & Halusic, 2009; Reeve & Jang, 2006). Table 5.3 outlines some differences between autonomy-supportive and controlling teachers. Autonomy-supportive teachers use non-controlling and informational language, allow students to work in their own ways, encourage students to take greater responsibility for their own learning, and give students opportunities to have input and make decisions (Reeve & Jang, 2006). In contrast, **controlling teachers** pressure students to act in a certain way by using external incentives, controlling statements, directives, and commands. In these situations, students are motivated by external factors and pressuring language rather than by their own internal motivation.

Table 5.3   Autonomy-Supportive Versus Controlling Teaching Practices

Autonomy-Supportive Teachers	Controlling Teachers
Arrange learning opportunities and materials so students manipulate objects and have conversations rather than watch and listen	Keep possession of and monopolize learning materials

Autonomy-Supportive Teachers	Controlling Teachers
Ask students what they want	Physically exhibit worked-out solutions and answers before students have time to work them out independently
Give students time to work in their own way	Tell student the answer instead of allowing them the opportunity to discover it
Communicate a clear acknowledgement of students' perspectives	Utter directives and commands
Provide opportunities for students to talk	Use controlling language as a way of directing students' work
Are responsive to students' questions and comments	Use should/ought to sentences
Praise signs of improvement and mastery	Use praise as a contingent reward
Provide rationales for why a particular course of action may be useful	
Encourage persistence and mastery	

STOP AND REFLECT

1. Using Table 5.3, describe what teachers might say or do that would send either autonomy-supportive or controlling messages to students?

2. Using Table 5.3, how you would characterize your teaching style? Would you characterize yourself as more autonomy supportive or controlling or a hybrid of both? Reflect on your own beliefs about classroom management and how they shape your teaching style.

3. What are one or two changes you could make to your instruction to be more autonomy supportive? Implement these changes in the classroom. How do students react?

In the following section, Michele describes how she uses autonomy-supportive practices in her classroom to establish rules and consequences for behavior.

ENGAGEMENT IN PRACTICE: AUTONOMY-SUPPORTIVE PRACTICES (ESTABLISHING CLASSROOM RULES AND CONSEQUENCES FOR BEHAVIOR)

Michele: At the start of every school year, my students and I establish rules for the classroom together. Before we discuss rule-making, we've already talked about the personal goals for the year and what we are looking forward to as fourth graders. When we begin the discussion of rules, I ask them questions like, "How can we make sure that everyone achieves their goals this year?," and "What does our classroom need to look like, sound like, and feel like in order for us to all do our best and enjoy fourth grade?" The discussion leads to students coming up with the rules we want in our classroom. I generally encompass all the brainstormed rules under three main areas. Examples from one year include 1) respect others, 2) respect ourselves, and 3) respect our learning environment. Along with the rules, we also discuss consequences. After reading about the Responsive Classroom approach, I began using the Apology of Action with my students. The guiding statement we use to understand and remember this is, "You break it, you fix it." We have a discussion and activity to share potential conflicts that might happen in school and come up with ways that we can "fix" the situation, whether it involves fixing physical messes or making relationships better. The Apology of Action has really helped my students take ownership of solving problems in the classroom. I have to provide a lot of modeling and guidance at the beginning of the year, but as time passes, they are better able to come up with possible solutions when they report to me with a problem.

Many teachers assume that they need to use controlling behaviors to get students to behave appropriately and to adhere to their agendas. However, several empirical studies show that students with autonomy-supportive teachers experience greater autonomy, higher classroom engagement, more favorable psychological well-being, deeper conceptual understanding, and higher academic achievement than do students in controlling classrooms (Reeve, Jang, Carrell, Jeon, & Barch, 2004). One concern that many teachers have with adopting autonomy-supportive practices is that they will be giving up control in their classrooms and will be perceived by students as permissive. However, increasing student autonomy does not mean that students should be allowed to do whatever they please. Instead, choices should be given within the context of structured opportunities. Contrary to many teachers' counterarguments, prior research shows that autonomy-supportive teachers actually provide *more*, not less, classroom structure as compared to their controlling counterparts (Jang, Reeve, Ryan, & Kim, 2009).

Giving students some choice over what to study can be a powerful way to engage them. In the following *Engagement in Practice* sections, Melissa describes how her school uses self-selected student research and student-led conferences to support students' need for autonomy.

ENGAGEMENT IN PRACTICE: SELF-SELECTED STUDENT RESEARCH

Melissa: Self-selected student research, or personal research, is a process of questioning, investigating, planning, and sharing new learning. In middle school, students have researched topics from the effects of the media on teenage girls to comparing world religions. Students are autonomous, their topics often address issues that are important and relevant to them, and each project is differentiated. At each level of competency, students present what they learn to their peers. These student-driven projects occur three times a year. For one of these cycles, the middle school students host a Research Night and invite parents and the greater community to visit the school and engage in questions and comments with the researchers. Students are motivated to learn about something they have chosen and they respond positively to feedback from their peers. All students make their own decisions about how to represent their learning.

ENGAGEMENT IN PRACTICE: STUDENT-LED CONFERENCES

Melissa: About a decade ago, our school made an intentional shift from conferences with parents about student achievement and goal-setting directed by teachers to conferences in which students take the lead. All students keep their work for the marking period in a portfolio. A few weeks before conference time, students are asked to review the collection and choose several samples from each academic area. At least one sample must show something that they are proud of and another sample must show something they continue to work on within that subject. These are then marked with cover sheets on which the learner explains why he or she has chosen the piece and what it exemplifies. Once the work has been chosen, the students practice with a peer. Their peers are instructed in how to ask questions and offer feedback to improve the plan for the real conference day. On conference day, the room may have three to four students and their families all sharing at once. The average time is thirty minutes, which is much longer than a typical teacher-led conference. The teacher's role is to circulate and facilitate from afar—the students run the show! At the end of the conference, each student completes a sheet with academic and social goals. It is also an opportunity for students to ask their parents for what they need. I have heard children ask for a quiet place to study, more time at the library, and even ask their parents to get them to school on time.

The results have been amazing. The fragmented and short conferences have been replaced with longer and more meaningful exchanges. The accountability has shifted from teachers to students, which has resulted in improved motivation and self-confidence, as well as organization and speaking skills. The conferences are well attended. We also offer parents the opportunity to meet privately if they have other concerns. This practice shift allows our students to be actively involved in the evaluation process. As a result, they become more reflective and motivated. They see what they are capable of and learn how to set reasonable goals for future growth.

SUPPORTING STUDENTS'
NEED FOR COMPETENCE

Students' need for competence is supported in classrooms that they experience as optimal in structure for being successful (Skinner & Belmont, 1993). **Classroom structure** refers to the amount of information in the context about how students can effectively achieve desired outcomes. In classrooms that are optimal in structure, both the expectations and consequences of behavior are clear to students. Teachers can provide structure by giving students a clear sense of how their actions are related to classroom outcomes. For example, one question students often ask is, "If I do my homework (behavior), will I do better on the exam (outcome)?" Teachers can help students answer this question by clearly communicating what students need to do to be successful and providing specific feedback to students on how they are doing and how they can perform at higher levels.

The verbal messages teachers provide to students also impact how students feel about their abilities and the likelihood that they will be able to achieve desired outcomes. Teachers often assume that they need to give students messages about being smart for them to be confident and successful learners. Carol Dweck (1999) has shown that this type of praise often backfires. When teachers praise students for ability, the students are more likely to worry about how smart they look. As a consequence, these students are less likely to take intellectual risks. Benjamin, who was described as avoiding challenges at the beginning of Chapter 1, is an example of a student who would be particularly sensitive to this type of praise. Students like Benjamin get so invested in the label of being smart that they focus more on keeping this label than on learning. Rather than praising Benjamin for his grade (product), pointing out how much he has improved or praising his efforts on challenging work would be more effective in promoting competence.

How teachers respond to students' incorrect responses also sends important messages to students about their ability. Some students like Beatrice, who was introduced in Chapter 1 as the type of student who will comply but avoids challenging tasks because she is afraid to make mistakes, need different types of teacher support. Teachers need to encourage students like Beatrice to take risks in the classroom and view mistakes as a way to check for understanding rather than as an indicator of ability. This does not mean teachers should not praise students, but it does mean that they need to think about what, when, and how they are praising students.

Brophy (1981) outlined guidelines for providing effective and ineffective praise in the classroom (see Table 5.4). Effective praise relies on describing student behavior and not judging it. When teachers praise students for hard work and effort ("You must have worked very hard!"), students are more likely to persist in the face of failure, seek challenges, and focus on learning. This type of praise affirms students' efforts and strategy use as opposed to praise that focuses on their abilities and accomplishments. Teacher praise requires that teachers know their students well because praise for something that was not truly accomplished will not be effective.

Table 5.4   Guidelines for Effective and Ineffective Praise

Effective Praise	Ineffective Praise
• Is delivered contingently	• Is delivered randomly and unsystematically
• Specifies the particulars of the accomplishment	• Is restricted to global positive reactions
• Shows spontaneity, variety, and other signs of credibility; suggests clear attention to students' accomplishments	• Shows a bland uniformity, which suggests a conditioned response made with minimal attention
• Rewards attention of specific performance criteria (which can include effort criteria)	• Rewards mere participation without consideration of performance processes or outcomes
• Provides information to students about their competence or the value of their accomplishments	• Provides no information at all or gives students information about their status
• Orients students to a better appreciation of their own task-related behavior and thinking about problem solving	• Orients students to comparing themselves with others and competing

Effective Praise	Ineffective Praise
• Uses students' own prior accomplishments as the context for describing students' present accomplishments	• Uses the accomplishments of peers as the context for describing students' present accomplishments
• Is given in recognition of noteworthy effort or success at difficult (for this student) tasks	• Is given without regard for the effort expended or the meaning of this accomplishment (for this student)
• Attributes success to effort and ability, implying that similar successes can be expected in the future	• Attributes success to ability alone or to external factors such as luck or easy task
• Fosters endogenous attributions (students believe that they enjoy the task and/or they want to develop task-relevant skills)	• Fosters exogenous attributions (students believe they expend effort on a task for external reasons—to please the teacher, win a competition or reward, etc.)
• Focuses students' attention on their own task-relevant behavior	• Focuses students' attention on the teacher as an external authority figure who is manipulating them
• Fosters appreciation of and desirable attributions about task-relevant behavior after the process is completed	• Intrudes into the ongoing process, distracting attention from task-relevant behaviour

Source: Brophy (1981). Used with permission.

STOP AND REFLECT

1. How would you characterize the level of structure in your classroom? Do students know what they need to do to be successful? If they do, how do they know this? If not, how could you make your expectations clearer to students?

2. Using Table 5.4, how would you characterize the types of praise you provide to students? What do you typically say? What changes could you make to praise more effectively in the classroom?

HOW TEACHERS SUPPORT COGNITIVE ENGAGEMENT

Classrooms vary in their demands for cognitive engagement. Some teachers emphasize higher-order thinking, while others focus primarily on following procedures or directions. To promote cognitive engagement, teachers need to give students the opportunity to synthesize, represent, demonstrate, and apply their knowledge in a variety of ways rather than just arrive at the right answer. This has become even more important as the norms and expectations for learning are changing in K-12 education. Key aspects of the Common Core Standards and Next Generation Standards are higher-level thinking skills. For students to be successful in these classrooms, teachers need to emphasize understanding and learning as opposed to just getting the right answer.

Academic press is one concept that has been used to explain how teachers provide different demands for learning in the classroom. Teachers who **press for understanding** provide challenging tasks, articulate high standards, and expect high effort. Teachers expect students to explain their work, do not allow students to get away with doing easy work, and give students harder problems once they have mastered a concept. Teachers who press students for understanding are implicitly communicating the message that students can master content (Middleton & Midgley, 2002). In contrast, teachers who **press for performance** emphasize the end product and competition with peers. Teachers who press toward performance are giving students the message that they are competing with other students and that following procedures and completing work are more important than understanding.

Table 5.5 outlines items from the academic press for understanding scale (Middleton & Midgley, 2002). This scale was developed for math but can be applied to other domains. All items are on a 1-to-5 Likert scale, with higher numbers demonstrating higher academic press.

In a qualitative study of science classrooms, Blumenfeld and colleagues (1992) found that teacher press, support, evaluation, and opportunities for learning were characteristics of classrooms where students reported high levels of cognitive engagement.

Table 5.5   Academic Press Scale

1. As I answer a question in math class, the teacher often asks me to explain why I think it is the right answer.	
Not at all true (1)	Very true (5)
2. When I show I can do a problem in math, the teacher gives me harder problems to think about.	
Not at all true (1)	Very true (5)
3. In math class, the teacher doesn't allow me to get away with doing easy work.	
Not at all true (1)	Very true (5)
4. In math class, the teacher presses me to do thoughtful work.	
Not at all true (1)	Very true (5)
5. In math class, the teacher gives me work that really makes me think.	
Not at all true (1)	Very true (5)

Source: Middleton & Midgley (2002).

Table 5.6 outlines characteristics of teachers in these classrooms and provides strategies for how teachers can press for understanding.

Table 5.6   Characteristics of Teachers in High Cognitive Engagement Classrooms

- Made explicit connections between new information and things students had learned previously
- Guided students' thinking when posing higher-level questions
- Asked students to summarize, make comparisons between related concepts, and apply the information they learned
- Required students to explain and justify their answers
- Prompted or reframed questions
- Probed students when their understanding was unclear
- Monitored for comprehension rather than procedural correctness during activities

(Continued)

Table 5.6   (Continued)

• Added questions requiring written explanation of results or alternative representations of information in the forms of diagrams or charts
• Modeled thinking, suggested strategies, and problem solved with students when students had difficulty instead of providing right answer
• Reduced procedural complexity of tasks by demonstrating procedures, highlighting problems, providing examples, and allowing for planning time

In the following *Engagement in Practice* section, Melissa describes how she supports cognitive engagement in a literacy lesson.

ENGAGEMENT IN PRACTICE: SUPPORT COGNITIVE ENGAGEMENT IN LITERACY ACTIVITIES

Melissa: In my class students read a variety of novels dealing with dystopian societies. The books were at a variety of reading levels to address the needs of the varied ability in my classes. The students met together to discuss the reading and journal responses. They worked on their comprehension of the text in a collaborative manner with each other and also through letters to me in their journals. To guide my classes to higher cognitive engagement, I assigned a final project that involved making explicit connections to previous knowledge as well as comparing what they had read in their novels to real-life situations. For example, after reading about the effects of excessive consumerism and media domination in one book, students researched the companies who own most of the media in our culture, the possible effects of that control, and strategies to become more critical about what they watch and the messages they are being sent. Another group read about a corrupt government that prohibited aid from reaching its needy citizens. This group researched how this scenario continues today in places around the world and compared events in the book to similar situations in Somalia. A third group read about a dystopian government that used a "game" to control its citizens. The readers identified and explored the reality TV phenomenon today and why our culture is drawn to the different themes of survival, competition, and exploitation. The fourth group was asked to analyze the moral hierarchy of a community of young boys in their novel and how that hierarchy helped or hindered these characters as they attempted to reach their goals. They were then asked to decide as a group upon their own hierarchy of social values and write explanations for why they chose as they did. Through these higher-level assignments, students found deeper meaning in the books they read and made connections that even exceeded my expectations. Each project had a clear rubric, which was explained prior to the work. This assessment was far more meaningful than a standard book test.

BARRIERS TO DEVELOPING HIGH-QUALITY RELATIONSHIPS

Developing high-quality relationships with students can be challenging. The quality of these relationships is impacted by structural, teacher, and student factors. One barrier is the limited opportunities many teachers have for both interpersonal and academic interactions with their students. Most teachers believe it is much easier for elementary teachers to develop more positive teacher-student relations. However, a recent large-scale observation study of 2,500 elementary school classrooms showed that the nature and quality of teacher-student interactions in many classrooms is lacking. Elementary students typically had limited opportunities to interact with their teachers, and in most cases these exchanges were compliance driven. Most instructional interactions focused on a task that required a discrete answer rather than on interactions related to analysis, reasoning, or problem solving (Pianta et al., 2007).

Research on the experience of students in many middle and high schools paints a similar picture of poor-quality interactions with teachers. Relationships between teachers and students become less personal, more evaluative, and more competitive during the middle school years (Lynch & Cicchetti, 1997). The impersonal and evaluative nature of middle schools fails to support adolescents' increasing need for relatedness. In addition, many middle schools emphasize managing and controlling student behavior over supporting students' need for autonomy. Jacquelynne Eccles and her colleagues (1993) suggest there is a **developmental mismatch** between students' needs and the context of many middle schools. This developmental mismatch helps to explain the decline in students' motivation and engagement during this period.

Other research has examined the characteristics that distinguish high-quality teacher-student interactions. Surprisingly, a teacher's experience and education has been shown to have little relation to quality of relationships with students (Hamre & Pianta, 2006). In contrast, teachers' beliefs and their perceptions of students play an important role in shaping the quality of student-teacher relations. One important teacher belief is **teacher efficacy**, or a teacher's belief that he or she can have a positive influence on student learning. Teachers with high self-efficacy are more likely to interact with students in a way that increases student engagement (Midgley, Feldlaufer, & Eccles, 1989). Finally, the quality of teacher-student interactions is often related to characteristics of the child (see Chapter 3 more discussion of teacher-student relations). Teachers tend to respond more positively to academically motivated and socially competent students and more negatively to students who they view as unmotivated, disruptive, or interpersonally disconnected (Stuhlman & Pianta, 2002).

BUILDING RELATIONSHIPS WITH DIFFICULT STUDENTS

Why do teachers often respond to disengaged students with less support and warmth? It is more challenging to foster high-quality relationships with at-risk students like Ryan and Rachel, the disengaged students from Chapter 1. Developing relationships involves emotional work, which can be difficult, especially for a beginning teacher. Prior research suggests that many teachers approach these relationships from a cost-benefit perspective and struggle with whether the time, energy, and emotional investment required for developing relationships with more challenging students is worth it (Davis, 2006). Unfortunately, there is also evidence that those students who would benefit most from positive relationships with their teachers are also those that are least likely to get this support (Baker, Grant, & Morlock, 2008).

The link between teacher-student relations and engagement is reciprocal over time (Skinner & Pitzer, 2012). High-quality relations with a teacher serve to bolster a student's perceptions of competence, autonomy, and relatedness, which in turn elicits further teacher support. Students like Fiona and Franco, the fully engaged students in Chapter 1, are more likely to have more positive interactions with their teachers, which serves to further increase their engagement over time. In contrast, unsupportive interactions between a teacher and student makes it more likely that the student will perceive himself or herself as unwelcome, incompetent, and pressured. In turn, these negative self-perceptions lead to further withdrawal of support from the teacher. Ryan has developed a poor relationship with his teacher and has begun to feel alienated from the school context. The lack of support he receives from his teacher leads to further disengagement. Findings from several research studies suggest that these individual differences in engagement are magnified over time, with highly engaged youth getting more engaged over time and less engaged youth becoming more disengaged over time.

How can teachers break this cycle of unsupportive teacher-student relations? A teacher's immediate response to a difficult student is to assume that the student is purposely trying to defy or manipulate. However, it is important to remember that students' (mis)behavior and disengagement often reflect other factors rather than a purposeful intent. It is possible that the student is trying to protect his or her self-beliefs. It is also possible that the student is trying to get some attention because he or she lacks a supportive or caring adult relationship. It is important for teachers to change the way that they view their relationships with disengaged students. Teachers often view relationships with difficult students in terms of a deficit perspective (i.e., something about the student that is unchangeable) rather than seeing disengagement as an opportunity to intervene and cultivate a stronger relationship.

In the following *Engagement in Practice* section, Michele describes strategies she uses in her classroom to build relationships with difficult students.

ENGAGEMENT IN PRACTICE: BUILDING RELATIONSHIPS WITH ALL STUDENTS

Michele: I have noticed that most of my challenging students tend to fall into two groups: those who attempt to get my attention through negative behavior and those who seem to not want anything to do with me and tend to be unresponsive. I try to do what I can each day in the classroom to engage and include these students, but I've discovered two ways that have helped me to reach out a little more and given them the positive attention they may need. The first is through lunches with the teacher. Each week of the school year, I feature a different student, and on the Friday of that week, the featured student gets to have lunch with me and two classmates that he or she chooses to invite. We eat together in the classroom and just chat. It really helps me to get to know my students better and spend more one-on-one time together. I have also found that including two other classmates helps my more socially awkward students to feel more comfortable and practice building friendships. I know that lunch is a valuable time for teachers since we have very little free time during the day, but doing these lunches once a week has really helped to strengthen my relationships with students.

The second way I've reached out to challenging students is through writing. One year I had a very challenging student who had difficult home and life experiences and was emotionally insecure. She had a hard time getting along with classmates and repeatedly got in trouble for talking back, defiance, and inappropriate behavior. Academically, she wanted to do well, but whenever something became challenging, she immediately gave up or had a meltdown, convinced she was stupid. I realized she craved my attention and needed me to spend more time with her because she was seeking a positive adult relationship. So aside from the work she did with our school counselor, I gave her a journal and asked her to start writing down things she wanted to say to me and get off of her chest. Instead of shouting things out in class and interrupting lessons by trying to get my attention, I wanted her to write things down. The journal was also a place for her to let me know when she was angry or disagreed with me about something. During breaks and at the end of the day, I would read her journal and respond to her. If she needed me to see something she could place the journal on my table. It didn't work perfectly, but it made a difference. She felt like she was being heard, and I could listen to her without taking away from the rest of the class.

Pianta (1999) developed a teacher-relationship interview that teachers can use to reflect on their relationships with individual students. Table 5.7 includes some sample questions from this interview.

Although it is challenging, teachers should not give up too quickly on efforts to develop positive relations with difficult students. Research shows that more difficult students benefit even more from developing positive relations than their more easygoing peers (Baker et al., 2008; Meehan, Hughes, & Cavell, 2003). The reality is that positive teacher-student relations can help to support students who are at risk for disengagement and school failure.

Table 5.7   Sample Questions From the Teacher-Relationship Interview

1. Choose three words that tell about your relationship with _____ (*child's name*). For each word tell me about a specific experience or time that describes that word.

2. Tell me about a specific time when you and _____ (*child's name*) clicked. How did you feel? How do you think the child felt?

3. Now, think about a time when you weren't clicking. How did that feel? How do you think the child felt?

4. Tell me about a time recently when _____ (*child's name*) misbehaved? What happened? Why? How were the two of you feeling? Is this the way things typically work out?

5. Tell me about a time when _____ (*child's name*) was upset and came to you. What happened? Why? How were the two of you feeling? Is this the way things typically work out?

Source: Pianta (1999).

There is also evidence that greater conflict or disconnection between students and teachers can actually heighten the risk (Hamre & Pianta, 2006). It is clear that when teachers evaluate whether the benefits are worth the time investment to develop higher-quality relationships, the answer is a resounding yes. There are substantial benefits for student engagement, achievement, and healthy development, while the cost of not trying to improve these relationships will lead to even greater disengagement over time.

STOP AND REFLECT

1. Have you found that the time and energy required to develop relationships with more challenging students was worth the effort?

   a. When did this happen?

   b. How did the student respond?

   c. What did you learn?

2. Think about a student with whom you have had a difficult relationship.

   a. How do you feel about this student right now?

   b. How did you react to signs of disengagement from this student?

   c. What would you do differently?

   d. How will you respond to future signs of difficult teacher-student relationships?

CONNECTING WITH DIVERSE STUDENTS

One of the challenges many teachers face is connecting with students of diverse backgrounds. Teachers report that they enjoy interacting with those students that reflect some aspects of themselves (Davis, 2006; Davis, Summers, & Miller, 2012). However, the reality is that the background of many teachers does not reflect the demographic reality of their students. Many educators are white, middle-class women, while an increasing number of students are African American, Asian, and Hispanic children and children who live in low-income families. Unfortunately, there is evidence of a mismatch between ethnically diverse students and white teachers' communication styles and interactions, which can often result in higher conflict in the classroom (Delpit, 1995). This misalignment may help to explain the finding that African American youths, particularly boys, are disciplined more frequently and harshly than students in other racial or ethnic groups (Ferguson, 2000).

One reason for the higher level of conflict in diverse class-rooms is that many teachers hold lower expectations for their African American, Hispanic, and low-income students. (Review Table 5.4 for messages of low expectations.) Ennis (1996) found that many teachers perceived low-income students as disinter-ested in learning, and, as a consequence, were more likely to use pedagogies that treated these students as passive participants in learning. These differential expectations have negative conse-quences for students' engagement and achievement. Prior research has linked perceptions of teachers' racial/ethnic stereo-types and discrimination to lower grades, competence, and value beliefs (Eccles, Wong, & Peck, 2006).

The concept of **cultural synchronization** has been used to explain the ways in which conflict occurs in relationships between "minority" (e.g., African American and Hispanic) students and "majority" (i.e., white) teachers as a result of a misalignment between values and interaction patterns (Irving, 1990; Monroe & Obidah, 2004). For example, Wubbels, den Brok, Veldman, and van Tartick (2006) found that white teachers were more likely to mis-interpret the intention and actions of their racially and ethnically diverse students. These teachers were more likely to view their multi-cultural classrooms as emotionally charged and perceive their stu-dents' interpersonal messages as personally offending or threatening.

A common response by teachers to the perception that stu-dents are being disrespectful is to try to assert control (reflect back on Table 5.3). However, a controlling response usually backfires, with students further disengaging from the classroom. Instead, to create greater cultural synchronization, teachers need to be mind-ful of their own perceptions of students, be ready to explore their own prejudices, and take ownership for any misinterpretations of student behavior. This requires that they talk with students and understand different cultural frames of reference.

To develop relationships with diverse students, many teachers will need to change their approach to instruction and curriculum. **Culturally responsive teaching** involves purposely responding to the needs of culturally and ethnically diverse students in the classroom through instructional processes and the use of culturally relevant curriculum (Brown, 2004). Rather than viewing students from a deficit perspective, teachers should view ethnically and culturally diverse students' experiences as valuable assets that can be incorporated in the classroom. Table 5.8 outlines the characteristics of culturally responsive teachers (Brown, 2004; Gay, 2002; Wubbels et al., 2006).

Table 5.8   Characteristics of Culturally Responsive Teachers

Develops Culturally Diverse Knowledge Base

- Understands the cultural characteristics and contributions of different ethnic groups
- Understands ethnic groups' cultural values, traditions, communications, and learning styles
- Is mindful of one's own perceptions and prejudices of students

Incorporates Culturally Relevant and Diverse Curricular Content

- Includes curriculum that reflect a wide range of ethnic individuals and groups
- Includes a wide range of images in the classroom that cut across time, age, gender, place, social class, and ethnic group
- Contextualizes issues across race, ethnicity, class, and gender
- Includes multiple types of knowledge and diverse perspectives
- Develops a curriculum that empowers students to be involved in their school and community

Develops Personal Relationships With Diverse Students

- Shows respect for and interest in students' personal backgrounds
- Uses knowledge of students' lives to design instruction that builds on what they are already know
- Communicates individually with students about non-academic matters
- Develops relationships based on mutual respect and reciprocity

Demonstrates Cultural Caring and Builds a Learning Community
• Helps students feel safe and secure
• Builds communities of learners in which the welfare of the group takes precedence over that of the individual
• Builds effective cross-cultural communication
Monitors and Manages Student Behavior
• Provides clear social and behavioral expectations
• Deals immediately with inappropriate behaviors to prevent escalating conflicts
• Negotiates without giving in while at the same time honoring students' perspectives

STOP, REFLECT, AND TRY

1. What obstacles have you experienced in developing relationships with students whose backgrounds are different from yours?

2. Using Table 5.8, evaluate the extent to which your curriculum and instruction is culturally responsive. In which areas is your instruction most responsive? Least responsive?

3. What changes could you make to better meet the needs of diverse groups of students?

4. Choose one area of culturally responsive instruction and incorporate it into your next lesson. Collect data on student interactions and responses. How did students respond?

In the following *Engagement in Practices* sections, Ellen and Melissa describe strategies they have used to create more culturally responsive classrooms.

ENGAGEMENT IN PRACTICE: CULTURALLY RESPONSIVE INSTRUCTION

Ellen: When making presentations, I use pictures to illustrate concepts. Because I am white, I almost always chose pictures of white people. I didn't realize this pattern until one of my students pointed it out to me. Now I am careful to use pictures that are more inclusive. I also try to make my lessons as critical as possible. Rather than using a multicultural approach, we try to break down power relations in class. For example, when teaching the *Odyssey*, we talk about otherness, racism, and sexism. It is very engaging and usually leads to some very heated discussions.

ENGAGEMENT IN PRACTICE: INVENTORY RESOURCES IN THE CLASSROOM

Melissa: Each year I inventory the books available in my language arts classroom. Not only do I want a range of genres, I want to make sure the texts present a wide range of cultures. I look at the diversity of authors, the range of diversity amongst the protagonists, the subject matter, and the social justice themes. I try to supplement the collection with secondhand books or new ones as the budget allows. Sometimes I will keep a set of books that I deem not culturally responsive or that presents a sanitized version of historical events to use for a critical discussion with students.

In the past, I have also asked my students to sort and categorize all the titles in our classroom library. All the books are pulled from the shelves. Groups of students take a pile of books and discuss genres, themes, and authors and check publication dates. They explore cultural and social themes and illustrators and usually end up with a few titles they want to add to their own reading lists. This process leads to great discussions about books. At the end, students decide their own categories and create book baskets. The result is the same; the books have been inventoried. But now my students know what's there and what isn't. They can make suggestions for new books to add to the library.

CHAPTER SUMMARY

Chapter 5 began with an overview of the research linking quality teacher-student relationships to engagement and achievement outcomes. The goal of this chapter was to counter the myth that teaching content is more important than developing relationships with students. New theoretical frameworks such as attachment theory and previously discussed theories such as self-determination theory were presented as theoretical perspectives that can be used to explain the positive link between teacher support and engagement. Both theories emphasize the need for relationships and relatedness in classrooms, specifically in student-teacher relations. Next, research-based strategies for how teachers can support students' need for relatedness, autonomy, and competence—the three basic needs in self-determination theory—were presented. The chapter concluded with a discussion of barriers to building high-quality relationships. Practical strategies for building relationships with difficult students and strategies to connect to a diverse group of students were outlined. The reality is that few students can optimally engage in classroom learning without a meaningful teacher-student relationship and that teachers must carefully reflect upon and change their interactions and instructional practices as part of an ethic of care and of culturally responsive practice.

TEXT-TO-PRACTICE EXERCISES

The following exercises are meant for self-study or use in a professional learning community. Reflecting upon these activities and discussing them with colleagues is important. More important, however, is to use these exercises as springboards for improving teaching practice.

TPE 5.1: **Interview students about teacher-student relationships.** Interview a few students about their perceptions of a caring and supportive teacher. The following are possible questions:

    a. What makes a good teacher?

    b. How does a teacher demonstrate that he or she cares about students?

    c. How do teachers provide support/trust/safety in the classroom?

In lieu of interviews, a class project can be assigned at the beginning of the school year or semester.

TPE: 5.2: **Evaluate effectiveness of teacher praise.** The following scenarios illustrate different ways teachers might provide praise in the classroom. Using Table 5.4, describe what the teacher did that was effective and/or ineffective in providing praise.

Scenario 1: As Mrs. Smith hands back reading tests to her seventh-grade students, she stops to speak to some students who put forth a particularly strong effort on the assignment. She tells one student, "Katie, I just wanted to let you know that I really recognized all of the hard work that you put into this assignment. It was a very difficult assignment and I could tell that you tried your best and noticed great improvement from your last assignment. I especially appreciate how you integrated the quotations so carefully into your own language. It makes your writing so much stronger because the quotes are being used to back up your points. This is something you should continue doing on all of your papers!"

Scenario 2: Mrs. Jones is a fifth-grade teacher. On all of her tests, she writes "Good job!" and draws a smiley face if the assignment is completed. Maria is a very strong student in the class. Mrs. Jones shows the other students how much Maria wrote and tells them that she likes Maria's paper because of its length. Mrs. Jones also has a points program. When the students complete their homework, they get a point. When everyone in the class gets ten points, the whole class gets a reward.

Scenario 3: Mr. Gonzalez assigned his high school students a project about fairness in school. He asked the students to collaborate on writing a letter to the local school board telling its members what they thought was unfair about schooling. He gave each student credit for participation in the exercise. He had the students compare their letters to each other to see which letter was the most effective. He then gave each group comments about their letters in which he praised their efforts and gave them specific feedback on how they did in relation to a rubric he had developed.

Scenario 4: Mr. Johnson has weekly conferences with his elementary-age students. He reviews the students' work for the week and tells the students what they have done well and what they need to improve on. He then helps the students make goals for the next week.

When a student has clearly demonstrated strong effort to reach his or her goals, Mr. Johnson offers praise to the student and rewards him or her for the effort. Each student has a chart to measure how many weeks their goal is reached. When the students reach their goals, they note it on the chart. The charts are publicly displayed.

TPE: 5.3: **Evaluate instructional features that support cognitive engagement.** Which aspect of Table 5.6 would characterize your classroom? How does it vary by subject area and lesson? What changes could you make to your instruction to incorporate more of the features of a high cognitive engagement classroom?

TPE: 5.4: **Reflect on your relationships with students.** Think about students who you have had both positive and negative relationships with. Answer the questions in Table 5.7 about these students. Using information in this chapter, describe strategies you could use to improve these relationships.

TPE: 5.5: **Develop a culturally responsive lesson.** Using information in Table 5.8, develop and teach a culturally responsive lesson. How did diverse students respond to this lesson?

KEY TERMS AND CONCEPTS

Academic press: Efforts by teachers to push students towards different learning goals.

Attachment theory: Theoretical perspective on the relationship between child and caregiver that develops as a consequence of early patterns of interactions.

Autonomy-supportive teachers: Teachers who value students' perspectives. These teachers use non-controlling language, allow students to work in their own ways, encourage students to take greater responsibility for their own learning, and give students opportunities to provide input and make decisions.

Classroom structure: Classroom structure refers to the amount of information in the context concerning what strategies are effective to achieving school success, while lack of structure refers to students' experience of confusion about expectations and consequences.

Controlling teachers: Controlling teachers insist on a right way of thinking, feeling, or behaving. These teachers pressure students to act in a certain way by using external incentives, controlling statements, directives, and commands.

Cultural synchronization: Alignment between "majority" (white) teachers and "minority" (e.g., African American and Hispanic) students' values and interactions; lack of alignment leads to conflict.

Culturally responsive teaching: Pedagogy that recognizes the importance of including students' cultural references in all aspects of learning.

Developmental mismatch: Mismatch between students' development needs and the characteristics of schools. This concept has been most often applied to the middle school years.

Pedagogical caring: Demonstrating caring to students through both social and academic support in the classroom.

Press for performance: Occurs when teachers emphasize that the outcomes of work are more important than the process of learning.

Press for understanding: Occurs when teachers emphasize understanding and learning, which provides students the message that they believe that students can learn.

Teacher self-efficacy: A teacher's belief in his or her capacity to influence children.

Teacher sensitivity: Level of attunement and responsiveness to students' behavioral and emotional needs.

RESEARCH-BASED RESOURCES

Books and Reports to Read

Armento, B. J., Irvine, J. J., Jones, J. C., Frasher, R. S., & Causey, V. E. (2000). *Culturally responsive teaching: Lesson planning for elementary and middle school grades.* New York, NY: McGraw-Hill.

Austin, T. (1994). *Changing the view: Student-led parent conferences.* Portsmouth, NH: Heinemann.

Boynton, M., & Boynton, C. (2005). *The educator's guide to preventing and solving discipline problems.* Alexandria, VA: Association for Supervision and Curriculum Development.

Cruz, G., Jordan, S., Melendez, J., Ostrowski, S., & Purves, A. (1997). *Beyond the culture tours: Studies in teaching and learning with culturally diverse texts.* Mahwah, NJ: Lawrence Erlbaum.

Davis, H. A., Summers, J. J., & Miller, L. M. (2012). *An interpersonal approach to classroom management: Strategies for improving classroom engagement.* Thousand Oaks, CA: Corwin.

Delpit, L. (1995). *Other people's children: Cultural conflict in the classroom.* New York, NY: New Press.

Ferguson, A. (2000). *Bad boys: Public schools in the making of black masculinity.* Ann Arbor: University of Michigan Press.

Hollins, E. R., & Oliver, E. I. (1999). *Pathways to success in school: Culturally responsive teaching.* Mahwah, NJ: Lawrence Erlbaum.

Irving, J. J. (1990). *Black students and school failure: Policies, practices, and prescriptions.* New York: Praeger.

Marzano, R. J., Marzano, J. S., & Pickering, D. J. (2003). *Classroom management that works: Research-based strategies for every teacher.* Alexandra, VA: ASCD.

Pianta, R. C. (1999). *Enhancing relationships between children and teachers.* Washington, DC: American Psychological Association.

Sleeter, C. E., & Cornbleth, C. (2011). *Teaching with vision: Culturally responsive teaching in standards-based classrooms.* New York, NY: Teachers College Press.

Vatterott, C. (1999). *Academic success through empowering students.* Westerville, OH: National Middle School Association.

Vitto, J. M. (2003). *Relationship-driven classroom management: Strategies that promote student motivation.* Thousand Oaks, CA: Corwin.

Web Sites to Visit

1. **Edutopia.com** (www.edutopia.org). This site has resources for educators on how to develop stronger teacher-student relationships.

2. **Connecting with Students** (www.connectingwithstudents .org/intro.html). This site is an online community and training tool to help educators connect with every student in their classroom.

3. **My Teaching Partner** (www.mtpsecondary.net). This site provides information on My Teaching Partner, an individual

professional development program designed to help teachers improve their relationships with their students.

4. **Teaching Tolerance** (www.tolerance.org). This site is a project of the Southern Poverty Law Center and includes classroom resources for culturally relevant instruction. Sample culturally relevant instruction related to social activism, civic responsibility, and human rights is available on the site.

5. **Measures of Teacher-Student Relationships** (www .curry.virginia.edu/academics/directory/robert-c.-pianta/ measures). This site, developed by Robert Pianta, includes copies of survey and observational measures to assess the quality of teacher-student relationships.

6. **Responsive Classroom** (www.responsiveclassroom.org). This site provides information on the Responsive Classroom model, an instructional approach in the elementary school grades that is designed to help students develop social and emotional competencies.

7. **Origins** (www.originsonline.org). This site includes resources related to the Responsive Classroom model for elementary schools and Developmental Designs, an intervention to teach social, emotional, and academic skills during the middle school years.

8. **Collaboration for Academic, Social, and Emotional Learning (CASEL)** (www.casel.org). This site includes resources on social and emotional learning in schools, including activities, research, and professional development opportunities.

9. **Zinn Education Project** (www.zinnedproject.org). This site uses the work of Howard Zinn and provides resources for teachers emphasizing the role of working people, women, people of color, and organized social movements in shaping history.

10. **Sample Teacher Report Cards** (www.dalat.org/pdf/pd/ TeacherEvaluation%201.doc). This link is a sample teacher report card.

C H A P T E R   S I X

MYTH 6:
Socializing With
Peers Detracts
From Student
Engagement

*How to Create a Peer Context
That Supports Engagement*

S chools and classrooms are inherently social places. Prior research demonstrates that students' social and academic lives are intertwined. Peers can provide companionship, emotional support, and validation, and they can help with solving academic problems. Students who have positive relationships with their peers have been found to have higher levels of engagement, motivation, and achievement (Wentzel, 2009). In contrast, students who are rejected by their peers have poorer academic and behavioral outcomes over time (Ladd, 2005).

However, despite the evidence regarding the importance of peer support for a range of positive outcomes, a common concern expressed by some teachers is that having their students spend time socializing with their peers is not productive and can actually discourage students from being engaged in their work. For some teachers the goal is to create a quiet classroom where students are working individually on tasks without the distraction of peers. One concern is that having students interact with their peers will mean giving up some control because interactions will be less predictable. In turn, this "loss of control" will increase the chance that discipline problems will arise, especially in cases where students are easily distracted or where their behavior distracts peers. Although there are situations in which peer and social experiences discourage engagement (e.g., a class clown drawing attention), the research overwhelmingly supports the positive links between positive peer experiences and higher engagement (Wentzel, 2009).

The focus on isolated student work stems in part from our assessment-driven educational system in which academic preparation for standardized tests has become the priority. In this context, many teachers feel that addressing the social dimensions of the classroom and developing a sense of community are less essential aspects of their roles and instructional time. This narrowing focus on academic content without peer interaction has made it difficult for some students to develop the social skills necessary to be successful in today's society and may be contributing to the sense of isolation and alienation that many students feel. In addition, although students spend all day in school with their peers, the structure of many classrooms offers few opportunities for interaction with peers during the school day. The teacher-directed and individualized instructional practices that dominate many classrooms have made it difficult for students to develop strong relationships with their peers.

The goal of this chapter is to debunk some of the myths about peer support and the benefits of quiet classrooms and limited student interactions. First, the research on the links between peer support and friendship and engagement and learning are presented. Next, information on cooperative and collaborative learning models is outlined to show how peers can support learning and engagement. The challenges that result with group work, as well as practical research-based strategies for creating more effective and productive groups, are discussed. Finally, research on the importance of building community in the classroom is outlined, along with practical strategies for enhancing classroom community that can be readily implemented in any classroom.

WHY ARE PEER RELATIONSHIPS IMPORTANT?

Most students have **social goals** in regards to their relations with their peers that they pursue at the same time as academic goals. Some of these social goals include developing friendships and being accepted by their peers (Ryan & Shim, 2008). Having positive relationships with friends and feeling socially supported at school can increase students' interest in school. Social support from peers is especially critical during early adolescence when youths have a greater need for relatedness. Unfortunately, the middle school years are often when teachers try to control social interactions even more than in the elementary school years.

One way that researchers have examined the effects of peers on engagement is to examine the concept of **peer acceptance**, or how much a student is liked or disliked by the other students in the class. Students who are accepted by their peers tend to be cooperative, friendly, and sociable (Rubin, Bukowski, & Parker, 2006). An extensive body of research has linked students' perceptions of peer acceptance in both elementary and secondary schools to a range of positive academic outcomes (Buhs & Ladd, 2001; Wentzel, 2009). For example, researchers have found that being accepted by ones' peers is associated with the following positive outcomes:

- Interest in school
- School enjoyment
- Positive attitudes toward school
- Academic competence
- School involvement
- Higher standardized test scores
- Higher grades
- Lower-risk behavior

In contrast, the experience of **peer rejection**, or being actively disliked by one's peers, can lead to lower engagement and increases the probability of dropping out of school (Ladd, Herald-Brown, & Kochel, 2009). Rejected children have been found to have higher disengagement in both structured activities in the classroom and in unstructured activities outside of the classroom such as recess or playground periods (Asher, Rose, & Gabriel, 2001). These children are often the last to be chosen by peers for group work. Peer rejection increases students' perceptions that they are less competent both socially and academically, which in turn decreases participation in classroom activities. Over time, peer rejection can lead to increased disruptive behavior in school and poor academic outcomes (see Chapter 3 for more discussion of peer rejection).

FRIENDSHIPS

Other research has examined the consequences of friendship on social and academic adjustment. Friendships exist between pairs of children or youths and occur only as long as both participants choose to be in the relationship (Ladd et al., 2009). Simply having a friend at school has been related to a range of positive social, psychological, and academic outcomes (Berndt & Keefe, 1995; Ladd, 1990; Wentzel & Caldwell, 1997; Wentzel, Barry, & Caldwell, 2004). For example, Wentzel and Caldwell (1997) found that having friends in middle school was related to higher grades, higher test scores, and more prosocial behavior.

Friends provide a variety of types of support that help students adjust to school. Friends can offer emotional support through validation, encouragement, and caring. Students who perceive that their friends are emotionally supportive tend to be engaged in school. In addition, students who have developed positive relationships with their classmates are more likely to enjoy a safe environment and are less likely to be the targets of peer-directed violence (Wentzel, 2005). Conversely, students who do not believe that their friends care about them are at risk for disengagement (Buhs, Ladd, & Herald, 2006). Friends also can influence engagement by providing informational support such as help on homework or advice regarding personal problems with family and other friends (Altermatt, 2007; Wentzel, Baker, & Russell, 2009). For example, Altermatt (2007) found that interactions with peers can help middle school students cope with academic failures.

STOP AND REFLECT

Identify highly engaged (e.g., Franco, Fiona) and disengaged (e.g., Rachel, Ryan) students in a class by making a list with the following headings:

Always highly engaged   Often disengaged   Neither

1. For each student in the "highly engaged" column, answer the following questions:
   a. What is the student like when engaged?
   b. Who are the student's friends? How do you know?
   c. Is the student accepted by his or her peers? How do you know?

2. For each student in the "highly disengaged" column:
   a. What is the student like when disengaged?
   b. Who are the student's friends? How do you know?
   c. Is the student accepted by his or her peers? How do you know?

3. For each student in the "neither" column:
   a. Do you know this student as well as the students in the other two columns? What could you do to get to know him or her better?
   b. Does he or she have friends in either the "highly engaged" or "often disengaged" columns?

TEACHERS' BELIEFS AND INSTRUCTIONAL PRACTICES

Teachers influence peer relations (i.e., peer acceptance and rejection) and friendships through their beliefs and instructional practices. Prior research suggests that teachers prefer students like Fiona and Franco who are compliant and conform to school rules rather than students like Ryan and Rachel who are aggressive, disruptive, or disengaged (Fredricks et al., 2004). Through both verbal and nonverbal interactions, teachers send messages to their classes about which students they really like having in their classroom and which students are more difficult. Students tend to be aware of these teacher preferences and either accept or reject other students based on these behavioral expectations.

The instructional approach that a teacher chooses to use in the classroom can also influence peer relations. Students have more friends, have closer friendships, and are less likely to experience peer rejection when teachers use **student-centered learning practices** (e.g., involving students in decision making, offering opportunities for students to interact). In contrast, students have fewer positive social outcomes in classrooms characterized by **teacher-directed methods** (e.g., lectures, direct instruction) where the teacher is primarily in control (Donohue, Perry, & Weinstein, 2003). In student-centered classrooms, teachers encourage students to talk to each other about assignments, work in small groups, and move around the classroom when working on activities. Finally, the physical arrangement of desks in the class can have implications for peer relations. In the traditional classroom, students are seated in rows and their focus is entirely on the teacher. This provides limited opportunities for peer interaction. In contrast, seating students at small tables or in groups of desks is more conducive to small group work and will increase opportunities for students to interact with their peers.

STOP AND REFLECT

1. Identify three instructional strategies you use that positively impact the level of peer acceptance in the classroom.

2. Identify three instructional strategies you use that may negatively impact the level of peer acceptance and actually increase public rejection in the classroom.

3. Think about opportunities you provide for students to interact with their peers and then answer the following questions:

   a. How often do you provide these opportunities?

   b. Why do you provide them?

   c. How do students respond?

4. Describe one way that you could increase opportunities for peer interactions. In what situations would you make this change?

HOW DO PEERS SOCIALIZE ENGAGEMENT?

There are a variety of ways that peers socialize engagement and achievement. One way is through modeling, or observing how other students perform a particular behavior. For example, a student can observe a friend's commitment to school and listen to his or her views on the value of school for the future. Individuals also can watch how their peers respond to a difficult problem to see whether they persist and cope with difficulty or experience negative affect and give up. Previous research has shown that students who viewed their friends as having high academic goals behaved in ways to promote their own academic achievement (Wenztel, Filisetti, & Looney, 2007).

Peers may also influence engagement by either reinforcing a positive academic orientation or by reinforcing negative academic values and beliefs. The notion of peer pressure has received considerable attention in both the popular media and research literatures. We often assume that peer pressure is negative. Research suggests that peer pressure is much more complex and varies in intensity and consistency by the age of the child and depending on whether or not peers endorse academically oriented values (Brown & Larson, 2009). On the one hand, there is some evidence that early adolescents are more likely than younger students to downplay their effort at schoolwork in front of peers than in front of teachers (Juvonen & Murdock, 1995). However, other studies suggest that the peer group has a limited effect on adolescents' school-related beliefs and behaviors (Berndt & Keefe, 1995). Finally, some research suggests that many peers exert positive pressure by encouraging their friends to study and put forth effort in school (Ryan & Deci, 2000). In other words, peers probably have all of these influences at different times and in different situations.

Peers may also influence engagement because of the characteristics of the students who choose to be friends. Students tend to self-select themselves into groups that have similar motivation and engagement levels. Highly engaged students like Fiona and Franco are more likely to choose friends who also are involved in and have positive attitudes towards school. In contrast, students who are at risk for disengaging from school are more likely to choose friends who have shared similar negative school experiences. Students like Rachel and Ryan who do not conform to school rules or dislike school are less likely to receive support from their peers. In turn, the lack of peer support results in these students having fewer social and academic opportunities over time. Researchers have found that hanging out with friends who are highly engaged promotes engagement over time, whereas hanging out with peers who are disengaged and low achieving can dampen engagement over time (Kindermann, 2007).

STOP AND REFLECT

1. Identify six ways peers socialize engagement in your classroom—three ways with their actions and three ways with their words.

2. Give at least three examples of when you have seen evidence of peer pressure in your classroom. When was it positive? When was it negative?

3. Return to the chart you created earlier classifying students as highly engaged or disengaged. Are your highly engaged students friends with each other? Do the disengaged students hang out together? Identify ways you could encourage these students to interact with each other in class.

Benefits of Peers for Cognitive Engagement and Learning

In addition to having social and emotional benefits, peers can support cognitive engagement and learning. According to cognitive theories of development, working with others exposes individuals to differing views, which in turn forces them to coordinate or restructure their own views (Rogoff, 1998). Piaget and Vygotsky offer two different theoretical perspectives for why interactions with peers may offer opportunities for cognitive engagement and learning. According to Piaget, peers support cognitive development because interactions tend to be symmetric and equalitarian (Gauvain & Perez, 2007). A more equitable power structure makes it easier for peers to debate and share ideas and makes it more likely that cooperation and joint decision making can occur. In contrast, Vygostsky (1978) places great emphasis on asymmetric peer relations and social interactions. He assumes that peers contribute to learning when an older and more competent individual provides assistance to his or her less able peers within their **zone of proximal development**, or range of tasks they can do with help. In this way, peers can scaffold learning while offering social, emotional, and motivational support.

There is evidence to support both theoretical perspectives. Prior research has linked active discussion, problem solving, and elaboration among peers with advances in cognitive complexities (Gauvain & Perez, 2007). Peers can influence cognitive development and engagement by doing the following:

- Providing feedback
- Debating ideas
- Asking questions
- Asking for justifications
- Providing elaborations
- Sharing strategies for solving problems
- Offering suggestions, explanations, and elaborations
- Redefining a problem in a way that is more accessible

COOPERATIVE LEARNING AND COLLABORATIVE INSTRUCTION

There are two different models of how peers can work together in the classroom to support engagement and learning: cooperative learning models and collaborative models. These two models differ in the level of structure and amount of teacher control.

Cooperative learning is a common instructional technique that teachers use to organize students into small groups. In these environments, students work together to solve a structured problem with the teacher still maintaining control. There are a variety of ways that cooperative learning can be integrated in the classroom. Some of these techniques are informal and can take as little as a few minutes to implement. Others are more structured activities that occur over the course of a whole lesson. In addition, there are some formalized **cooperative learning models** that have been developed by researchers and applied to a variety of different classroom situations.

Cooperative models are the most successful when they are an integral feature of the classroom. However, the reality is that in many classrooms, teachers spend the majority of the day talking and only do peer-grouping activities as a special or extra part of the day that is separate from the larger classroom structure. Table 6.1

Table 6.1   Sample Cooperative Learning Models

Informal Models
Think/share models. These are informal cooperative learning activities that usually last a few minutes. Students explain to a partner(s) something related to the lesson and/or share their response to a question or prompt. Students can switch partners and share their response with another classmate.
Group check/check and coach. After working individually on a topic, students work together in groups to review a list of questions to check for understanding.
Learning together model. Students work together in small groups on a group assignment sheet. A single product is turned in, and the group members receive rewards together.
Formal Models
Reciprocal Teaching (Palinscar & Brown, 1984). An instructional strategy where students work in small groups to lead a discussion of a reading text. Students focus on four structured reading strategies: summarizing, questioning, clarifying, and predicting. Once students have learned the strategies, they take turns assuming the role of a teacher in leading a dialogue about what has been read.
Student, Teams, Achievement, Division (STAD) (Slavin, 1994). A cooperative learning model with teams that usually consist of four members who are mixed in gender, ability, and ethnicity. The teacher presents the lesson, and pupils work in teams to ensure that all members have mastered the objective. Pupils then take individual tests on the material, and scores are averaged for teams and compared with past scores. Teams are rewarded for meeting certain criteria. The STAD method is most appropriate for teaching well-defined objectives with single right answers, such as mathematical computations and applications, language usage and mechanics, geography and map skills, and science facts and concepts.
Jigsaw (www.jigsaw.org). The class is divided into several teams, with each team preparing separate but related topics. The class is then re-divided into mixed groups, with one member of each team in each group. Each person in the group teaches the rest of the group what he/she knows and then helps the rest of the group pull all of the pieces together to complete the task. Research on the jigsaw technique has shown that it reduces racial conflict, reduces prejudice and negative stereotypes, and improves motivation.

outlines both informal cooperative learning techniques and formal models (Jolliffe, 2007; Slavin, 1994).

Collaborative learning models differ from cooperative models in that students examine a significant question or develop a meaningful project. The authentic learning models outlined in Chapter 4 are examples of collaborative learning approaches. In these environments, tasks tend to be open-ended, students are given greater input in decision making, and the teacher's role is more that of a facilitator. Generating knowledge is the focus, and students work in groups to pose and answer questions or define problems with no predetermined answer. The small groups gather evidence or data, interpret findings, and draw conclusions. The ultimate goal is to create artifacts that emphasize understanding and are shared with the larger class or community.

The Open Classroom Model, developed by Barbara Rogoff and her colleagues in an elementary school in Salt Lake City (Rogoff, Turkanis, & Bartlett, 2001), is another example of a collaborative learning model. The goal of this classroom model is to create a community of learners. The model is based on several assumptions (Rogoff, 1994):

- Adults serve as leaders and facilitators.
- Emphasis is on the process of learning rather than the outcomes.
- Learning through collaboration is central to learning as a community.
- Activities build on children's prior interests, needs, and prior understanding.
- Evaluation of student progress is ongoing and occurs by working with the students and observing and following conversations of their learning.

Prior research has shown many social, academic, motivational, and engagement benefits of both cooperative and collaborative learning models (Cohen, 1994; Slavin, 1991b; Slavin, 1996) including the following:

- Reduced status differences in classroom
- Positive interactions of students from different ethnic backgrounds
- Higher self-esteem

- Higher intrinsic motivation
- Positive attitudes towards school
- Greater acceptance of others
- Feelings of belonging
- Greater persistence
- Greater conceptual understanding
- Higher achievement

SOCIAL CHALLENGES WITH GROUP WORK

Although the effectiveness of cooperative and collaborative learning models has been well documented, there also are many potential pitfalls with group work. Just putting students together in groups does not mean it will be productive. We can all remember times when we were put in groups that did not collaborate effectively, where there was little guidance on what to do, and when one or two individuals ended up doing the majority of the work. In the next section, we outline some of the potential problems that may arise with group work and some potential research-based strategies for addressing each of these issues.

Productive group work assumes that students have the social skills to engage in discussion and sustain participation. Unfortunately, the reality is that some students do not have these skills. For effective group work, students need to be able to 1) get to know and trust their peers, 2) communication accurately and unambiguously, 3) accept and support each other, and 4) resolve conflicts constructively (Johnson, Johnson, & Holubec, 1994). A list of social skills that can help students accomplish these goals is outlined in Table 6.2. These skills may need to be explicitly taught, modeled, and continually reinforced in group work.

There are several other social issues that can make group work challenging. One is that students have individual differences in their responses to collaboration, with some students preferring to work alone rather than with their peers (Blumenfeld et al., 2006). It is important for teachers to acknowledge these individual differences and provide a range of opportunities in the classroom for both collaborative and individual work. Another concern is the peer status differences that may result if students who are weaker academically or who have difficulty with social

Table 6.2 Social Skills for Effective Group Work

- Listening
- Taking turns
- Acknowledging when others have spoken
- Following through on commitments
- Considering different perspectives
- Giving and receiving constructive feedback
- Allowing others to voice opinions and assume responsibility
- Using active listening
- Avoiding hurtful statements
- Stating views without being defensive
- Being able to manage conflict
- Accepting group's decisions
- Disagreeing respectfully
- Staying on task
- Self-reflection

skills make it more difficult to engage in productive group work. An additional problem is **social loafing**, a situation in which some group members exert less effort because they rely on the other group members to do the work. This problem is exacerbated when the accountability structure does not take into account individual contributions to group work. Finally, some students may struggle to manage their behavior and sustain participation, especially in collaborative learning models in which the group work and tasks occur over longer periods of time.

KEY STRATEGIES FOR SUPPORTING COOPERATION AND COLLABORATION

Clear objectives. Although there are challenges inherent in group work, extensive research exists on strategies that have been found to make group work more productive. Productive group work requires scaffolding, monitoring, and support from teachers. Cooperative grouping is most successful when teachers set up clear instructional objectives and guidelines regarding the social skills and behavior that are appropriate during group work (Johnson et al., 1994). Teachers should assess academic progress and the use of interpersonal skills and intervene when necessary to clarify goals and suggest more specific social skills to use.

Modeling. It is also important to model effective interactions and explain the type of talk that you expect to hear from students. For example, teachers should model how to give suggestions and provide explanations within a group. Prior research has shown that students follow teachers' models during group work. For example, Webb, Nemer, and Ing (2006) found that students rarely offered specific help to students because it was rarely exhibited by teachers. Instead, they told the other students the answer without any explanation on how to arrive at it. In the following *Engagement in Practice* section, Michele describes how she models group interactions in **literature circles**, a collaborative and student-centered reading strategy.

ENGAGEMENT IN PRACTICE: MODELING GROUP INTERACTIONS IN LITERATURE CIRCLES

Michele: Guided reading groups are a regular part of our classroom reading time, but over the course of the year, I move the students towards literature circles. Unlike the guided reading format, students have more opportunities to choose the texts they read and the groups they are in and ultimately take responsibility for leading and determining what they will discuss in their literature circles. I assign individual roles that rotate each time the group meets, and each student is responsible for preparing a small assignment for his or her role, but the actual meeting and discussion is more open-ended and can go in different directions. Students who are comfortable with more structure can share what they have prepared in their role, but there are many students who only spend a brief amount of time sharing their individual work and instead want to talk more about their questions and thoughts on the book.

Over the years, I've found that the most important part of literature circles is the preparation and modeling that I do to help them to be comfortable and independent. We always do the first literature circle together as a class, with everyone reading the same book. As we read through the book and become more comfortable with the roles and norms we've established for working in literature circles, the students can branch off into smaller groups and practice discussing what they've read. After each meeting, we spend a few minutes reflecting on how it went, sharing with the whole class on what went well and what was challenging. From the beginning and through the whole time we do literature circles, I always share experiences I've had as a member of books clubs outside of the school. This really helps when I model things such as how I mark things in my book, prepare questions for book club meetings, share opinions, and agree or disagree respectfully with others. Once we've completed the first book all together, I find that students are more comfortable jumping right into their own literature circles and they are more purposeful in their work together.

Interdependence and grouping of students. One question teachers need to decide is how to group students. This decision will vary depending on the age of the students, the students' familiarity with group work, the students' social skills, and the amount of time allotted for the activity. Johnson and his colleagues, who are leaders in research on cooperative grouping (1994), do not recommend letting students select their own groups because it results in more homogenous groups of students by ability, race, and gender. Research suggests that heterogeneous grouping results in greater depth of understanding and quality of reasoning because students consider a wider range of perspectives and give and receive explanations more frequently (Johnson et al., 1994).

The easiest way to assign students to groups is randomly. Another possibility is to assign students different roles in the group so that each individual can make a clear contribution to the group. Some examples of different roles that are included in group work are the leader, observer, resource gatherer, time keeper, and presenter. Assigning roles can help to foster interdependence among students. Finally, Johnson and his colleagues (1994) present another strategy for grouping that supports students who are having social difficulties in the classroom. They suggest that teachers should ask students to list three of the classmates with whom they would like to work with. From these lists, teachers can identify students who no one wants to work with and create groups that include skillful and supportive students around each of these isolated students.

Tasks and interaction. Cooperative and collaborative learning are not just about getting students together into groups. The design of the task is also critical to productive group work. Tasks need to be designed so that participation of every member is necessary to complete the task and structured in such a way that students have to interact. One possibility is to have teachers assign tasks so that each individual has a unique piece of information that is essential for completing the task. This is a central aspect of the **jigsaw method** (see Table 6.1). It is also important to design meaningful tasks where individuals need to work together and discuss ideas. This is more likely to occur with open-ended tasks that require problem solving and several possible solutions than with closed-end tasks where students complete worksheets that emphasize lower-level skills and recall (Blumenfeld et al., 2006). In the following *Engagement in Practice* section, Michele describes how she uses small groups to have students teach each other.

ENGAGEMENT IN PRACTICE: TEACHING EACH OTHER

Michele: Usually at the end of a science or social studies unit, my students work on a culminating project showing what they have learned or allowing them to pursue a topic further. I like to plan some group projects, either in pairs or larger groups, so students have the opportunity to work together and share ideas. The final part of the project is to present their learning to the rest of the class through a presentation in which they are the "teachers." They are very motivated and become quite creative when they know that their peers are the audience, as opposed to just completing an assignment for me. I guide them through the process and help them to prepare and practice their presentations. I also structure many of the projects in a way that makes it easier for the students to interact with the audience and teach them, rather than simply talking at them. I do this by using technology such as PowerPoint or video, integrating art and drama, or using a game format. Each student is also held accountable by requiring that they each have a role or take on a certain part of the project so I can see what their individual contribution is. These projects are great ways to come together and review what we've learned as well as gain a new understanding from what each group teaches us.

A common response to group work is to divide the assignment up among different group members but not to have a mechanism to come back and talk together about the ideas. To facilitate interactions, tasks should emphasize larger learning goals rather than discrete knowledge. This will make it less likely that students will divide up tasks into discrete activities that do not require them to integrate the findings together. For true collaboration, individuals need to have a mechanism to discuss ideas and promote positive face-to-face interactions.

Accountability. Another important dimension of productive group work is the accountability system. This can be based entirely on individual performances, can be a single group grade for all members, or can include both individual and group assessments. We advocate an accountability system that includes assessments for both individual and group members. Only assigning individual grades provides little incentive for students to work together to solve a task. On the other hand, only assigning a group grade increases the likelihood of social loafing and the potential of poor interpersonal relations because of blaming low achievers for low grades (Blumenfeld et al., 2006).

There are several ways to structure individual accountability, including 1) individual tests for each student, 2) calling on students randomly to present the group's work, 3) observing and recording the frequency with which each member contributes, 4) assigning one student the role of checker, and 5) having students teach what they learned to someone else (Johnson et al., 1994). It is also important that teachers establish timelines for both individual and group completion of the assignment and provide evaluations of individual and group progress throughout and at the completion of the task.

In order to enhance accountability, some have advocated the use of competition and group rewards (Slavin, 1996). Student, Teams, Achievement, and Development (STAD) (see Table 6.1) is an example of one cooperative learning model that uses competition and group rewards to motivate students (Slavin, 1994). There is debate in the literature about the use of group rewards in cooperative learning models (Blumenfeld et al., 2006; Kohn, 1991; Slavin, 1991a). On one hand, Slavin (1991a) argues that group rewards are necessary to create peer norms that favor achievement and increase the likelihood that students will actively explain ideas rather than just giving the others in their group the answer. On the other hand, one risk with group rewards is that students will focus more on winning than on the inherent value of learning (Blumenfeld et al., 2006). The use of group rewards and competition has been found to work best with structured and closed-ended tasks. This approach has tended to be less effective at promoting motivation when tasks are ill-structured and complex (Cohen, 1994).

In the following *Engagement in Practice* section, Ellen outlines how she groups students and holds them accountable during literature circles.

ENGAGEMENT IN PRACTICE: GROUP ACCOUNTABILITY

Ellen: My second unit is a study of the novel. To execute this unit, students participate in literature circles. Prior to choosing groups, I give students a book talk in which I advertise the book offerings and highlight the important characteristics of each book. This exercise not only engages students with the unit content but it also helps me to group students by interest, reading level, and student compatibility. After the book talk, students write down their top three choices on book selection sheets. I use the data from the sheets to group students. On the first day of the unit, I distribute the books and all of the unit information, including due dates, role sheets, a unit overview, and assessments. We spend an entire period discussing the logistics. Then, groups complete their first assignment, which is to fill out a calendar that they refer to each class to make sure that they are progressing at a rate that will enable them to finish the reading, activities, and assessments by the completion of the unit. They must decide how many pages they should read each class period in order to complete the reading on time. They also must decide on what days each group member will complete each role to prevent overlapping from occurring. Students assess their group members on a scale of 1–3 each day to hold each other accountable for preparation and participation. I do the same as I circulate the classroom to balance out any biases. The first day of the unit is challenging because most students aren't used to the freedom that the unit provides; however, soon thereafter, as long as the chemistry is right, groups benefit greatly from the experience.

Persistence. Finally, group work requires perseverance from both teachers and students. Even with the best-laid plan and the most explicit guidelines and assessment rubrics, students may find cooperative or collaborative work very difficult. This is especially true at the beginning of group work. It is important to let them fall, make their own revisions, and get back up. With practice, groups become more effective at working together. The following two *Engagement in Practice* sections illustrate the evolution of group processes. In the first section, Ellen describes how changing the guidelines and division of tasks improved group processes. In the second section, Melissa describes how one group learned to work more effectively over time.

ENGAGEMENT IN PRACTICE: OUTLINING GUIDELINES AND TASK INTERDEPENDENCE

Ellen: Group work is most effective when students are actively engaged in the task at hand. My first attempt was a disaster because I asked five students to produce a product that required only the hands and attention of one student to create. That attempt resulted in poking, paper fights, and shouting, while about a fifth of the class worked hard to accomplish the assigned task. My second attempt was much more successful for several reasons. First, I clearly outlined group-work guidelines. Then, rather than giving the entire group one task to accomplish, I gave each group member a unique but important task to work on. After a few minutes, students swapped roles and continued working. This provided each member of the group with a chance to work on each task at least once. I told students that their grades depended on the ability to accomplish the task at hand. Unlike my last attempt, I was pleasantly surprised by students' focus. Almost everyone was focused on their task, not because their academic standing with me was at risk, but because their social standing with their peers was. They were holding each other accountable for completing the tasks. By the time they had finished, they had an excellent understanding of content, and they realized that group work can be beneficial and empowering. Although this collaborative lesson was unintended, it was actually more valuable than understanding content. By being active participants in student-centered group work, these students realized they don't necessarily need a teacher to create knowledge and to dictate which knowledge is valuable, they can do it with each other.

ENGAGEMENT IN PRACTICE: GROUPS WORKING MORE EFFECTIVELY OVER TIME

Melissa: During a unit on screenplays, my multi-age classes of seventh- and eighth-grade students had multiple tasks: they read plays cooperatively, watched old *Twilight Zone* episodes, and, as an assessment, they wrote and produced mini-plays. As the classes became more skilled with writing plays for the screen and analyzing the craft, I asked them to produce a short film. Students brainstormed topics that interested them, such as bullying, drugs, popularity, zombies, and science fiction. Based on their interests, they chose their own working groups. Each group was provided explicit rubrics for the writing of the plays, the division of labor, and the expectations for collaborative work. Periodically during the assessment, students were asked to self-assess and to assess the other members of their group on their participation, problem-solving skills, and other social skills necessary for group work (see Table 6.2). I assessed the groups' work periodically as well. Students were engaged because they selected their own teams, they chose their own issues to write about, and they cast their own characters as well as assigned other roles such as editor, musical director, and photographer.

The group that stands out to me was made up of four powerful personalities. They took twice as long to make a decision as other groups and argued loudly about roles. My role as a facilitator was not to solve these problems for them but to make them aware of where they were in the process and where they needed to be in two weeks. Their progress was slow for four days. What happened next was amazing. The group decided that they spoke over one another far too much and were wasting precious time. They wanted to complete the task because they had chosen the topic. They began to use a "talking stick" in their group to guide their discussions and everyone had to take a turn. Then they voted on decisions to make sure most were in agreement. I continued to assess their group and let them know they had made remarkable changes since the beginning of the lesson. These periodic check-ins provided students with feedback on their process. The filming began and I witnessed ongoing problem solving, civil discussion, and compromise and laughter. One student, who rarely completes any homework, took the film home and edited it, overlaying it with visual effects and music. There were moments that I wanted to split the group up to

(Continued)

(Continued)

complete an alternative individual assessment, but in the long run, this group's outcome far exceeded my expectations. The student who edited film at home ended up signing up for another filmmaking experience through our media class. Allowing these students the space to try things, to fail, to try again, and then succeed was critical. The quality of the film was adequate. However, the evolution of their collaborative skills was stellar and they presented their script and film to their peers as a cohesive foursome.

STOP AND REFLECT

1. Opportunity: How often do you do group work in the classroom? Which topics/lessons lend themselves best to group work? Which model do you use or adapt?

2. Social skills: What types of skills do your students need to learn and practice in order to work productively in groups (see Table 6.2)? How and when do you teach them these skills?

3. Tasks: How do you create tasks that require students be responsible for and dependent on each other?

4. Interdependence: How do you ensure that there is an equitable division of labor for each group?

5. Accountability: Do you use rewards to encourage productive group work? Why or why not? If so, what types of rewards do you use?

6. Persistence: How much time do you allow your students to work through their own problems before intervening?

7. Which of the previous six areas of group work is the most critical for you as a teacher? What important first step could you make to move toward more cooperative or collaborative experiences for your students?

CREATING CLASSROOM COMMUNITIES

Classroom communities are the broader contexts in which students interact with peers and find membership. Creating a classroom community can help students to foster positive relationships with their peers and develop social skills. **Classroom community** has been defined in a variety of ways in the literature, including as a sense of community, school belonging, school membership, school bonding, and school commitment (Osterman, 2000). What is common across these different conceptualizations is the idea that individuals feel emotionally connected to other students, feel they have a voice or role in activities, and feel that their need for relatedness is being met in the context (Battistich, Solomon, Watson, & Schaps, 1997; Osterman, 2000). In other words, they feel that the group is important to them, that they are important to the group, and that they will be cared for and supported (i.e., they are in a safe learning environment).

There are a variety of reasons it is important to build community in the classroom. First, building a classroom community enables teachers to address students' social, emotional, and cognitive skills. Second, a classroom community can teach students the values of respect and responsibility and how their behavior affects others. Finally, building community in the classroom is a critical foundation for social adjustment and academic achievement. Prior research has linked students' sense of community to a range of positive academic and school outcomes (Battistich, Schaps, & Wilson, 2004; Battistich et al., 1997), including the following:

- School enjoyment
- Peer acceptance
- Social adjustment
- Prosocial values
- Concern for others
- Conflict resolution skills
- Sense of autonomy
- Self-efficacy
- Lower disruptive behavior
- Lower drug and alcohol use
- Higher academic achievement

Caring School Communities, formerly called the Child Development Project (CDP), is an example of a comprehensive elementary school program that was designed to enhance children's sense of community (Watson & Battistich, 2006). Caring School Communities uses research-based practices to help schools become "caring communities of learners" by offering an environment of caring, supportive, and collaborative relationships. The benefits of such a school community may be particularly important for students who receive less of this type of support outside of school. (See www.devstu.org/caring-school-community for more information.) The key components of a caring school community include the following:

- Class meetings
- Cross-age buddies
- Activities that foster communication between school and home
- School-wide community-building activities that link parents, teachers, and other adults in the school

There are a variety of ways teachers can strengthen the sense of community in their classrooms. Table 6.3 describes these strategies.

Table 6.3   Practical Strategies for Building Community in the Classroom

- *Hold class meetings.* Regular class meetings can be used to talk about the importance of building community in the classroom and to give students practice in resolving social difficulties that will inevitably arise. These class meetings can also be used to plan special events.

- *Develop classroom norms regarding social behavior.* Developing norms for appropriate social behaviors in the classroom is important to establishing respect and civility in the classroom. Involving students in setting up these norms will help to increase students' sense of ownership. For example, students can provide feedback on the following questions:

  1. What is my ideal school like?

  2. How would you like to be treated by students and teachers?

  3. What can help make school a safe and happy place to learn?

- *Incorporate cooperative and collaborative games and activities.* Small-group activities can provide opportunities for students to practice making and sustaining relationships with other students.

- *Provide opportunities for students to get to know their classmates.* In a traditional classroom, students have few chances to get to know many of their classmates. Teachers should increase both the formal and informal opportunities for students to interact with and learn about all of the students in the classroom. Giving students opportunities to share their personal interests will help them to see both the similarities and differences between themselves and their classmates.

- *Emphasize mastery goals and reduce competition in the classroom.* Teachers should emphasize mastery goals, or individual effort and relative improvement, over performance goals, or how students are doing relative to their peers.

- *Incorporate activities to enhance social skills and prosocial values.* Teachers should use class meetings and discussions to enhance students' sensitivity to the needs and perspectives of others. Literature that includes themes related to friendship can also be a powerful way to discuss these ideas.

In the following *Engagement in Practice* sections, Ellen and Melissa describe strategies they have used to develop classroom communities. First, Ellen describes a strategy she uses to help students get to know each other better. Next, Melissa describes how she develops class norms regarding social behavior.

ENGAGEMENT IN PRACTICE: GETTING TO KNOW EACH OTHER BETTER

Ellen: Prior to reading a new story or starting a new unit, students independently fill out anticipation guides indicating whether they strongly agree, agree, disagree, or strongly disagree with several ethical and moral statements. In addition to indicating their stance, students also write down two points that illustrate it. Before class begins, I label the four corners of the room with these four choices. After students independently fill out their anticipation guide, we come together as a whole class. I read each statement aloud one by one. After I read a statement aloud, students find the corner that represents their stance. Once students

(Continued)

(Continued)

are settled, they take turns sharing the reason or reasons for their personal opinions with all of their peers. For instance, prior to reading *Romeo and Juliet,* one of the statements included on the anticipation guide was, "There are times when arranged marriage is appropriate." After reading the statement aloud in one of my classes, most students gravitated towards the corner of the room that was labeled "strongly disagree." One student, however, stood beneath the "strongly agree" sign. As he stood there, his class-mates jeered at him, wondering how any teenager could seriously agree with what seems to be such an unjust tradition. After the commotion subsided, the student enlightened his classmates, explaining to them that not only is arranged marriage an integral part of the Indian culture, but it is often viewed as a privilege that many Indian youths appreciate. On that day, not only did students get to know their classmate better, but they were also educated, by a classmate, about a different culture, helping to make them a bit more understanding and a bit less ignorant. Students and I always look forward to this activity because it develops a positive classroom culture and helps students to get to know one another much better.

ENGAGEMENT IN PRACTICE: DEVELOPING CLASSROOM NORMS

Melissa: Classroom meetings allow students to be heard, practice respectful use of language and listening, problem solve, and resolve social conflicts in class. My middle school students strug-gled with civil discourse at the beginning of the year. They talked over one another and made disparaging comments. It occurred to me that they did not know what it meant to listen and respond civilly. The political climate at the time was not serving as a positive model, and popular media also offered many rude and inappropriate examples of relating to people who hold dif-ferent opinions. Together we described what it means to discuss charged topics civilly. The students named what this would look like and sound like in our class. Students illustrated their ideas and came up with a list of guidelines for our class conversation. Their list follows:

- One person speaks at a time.
- All opinions are considered.
- No side conversations or whispering.
- Listen carefully and watch our body language.
- Discuss ideas, not people.
- Agree to disagree.

The guidelines created by students allowed us to have more constructive discourse. I consistently refer to them and so do my students. In this way, my students are self-directed and know they are in a safe environment where they are encouraged to share their opinions.

STOP, REFLECT, AND TRY

1. Draw a large circle on a blank sheet of paper and show how you balance the social dimensions of the classroom with the academic. Is it a 50–50 split? 20–80?

2. How would you describe the sense of community in your classroom? What aspects of Table 6.3 do you currently include in your classroom?

3. If you were to improve upon your classroom community, which *one* aspect of Table 6.3 would be most important to add to your instruction? Try this and observe your students' responses or ask them to evaluate the change in practice.

CHAPTER SUMMARY

Chapter 6 began with an overview of the research on the effects of peer acceptance, peer rejection, and friendship in order to counter the myth that peer interaction detracts from classroom engagement.

This chapter connected to the discussion of peer acceptance in Chapter 2, as well as to the importance of instructional strategies that provide for peer interaction described in Chapter 4. Research and theory also were used to counter the myth of quiet classrooms as being the best environments for learning. The research on the social and cognitive benefits of peer interaction was presented, and examples of both informal and formal cooperative and collaborative learning models were given. In addition, an overview of some of the challenges inherent in group work was provided. Research-based solutions to address these challenges and to advocate for more comprehensive and well-planned cooperative and collaborative models as part of regular classroom practice were outlined. The chapter concluded with a discussion of the importance of building community in the classroom and offered practical solutions for enhancing community. Classrooms that engage students with each other over time create powerful contexts for learning, socially, emotionally, and academically. A critical goal for every teacher is to enhance these opportunities for peer interactions in ways that engage students in meaningful learning.

TEXT-TO-PRACTICE EXERCISES

TPE: 6.1: **Complete a classroom sociogram.** A sociogram is a "mapping" of the friendships within a classroom. There are several ways to determine how connected students are to each other. Follow the instructions from Teaching Tolerance (www.tolerance .org/lesson/elementary-mapping-activity) or Robin Banerjee's Sociogram Tools (www.sussex.ac.uk/Users/robinb/socio.html). What did you learn about your students' relationships to each other? How can this information help you support more positive relationships in your classroom?

TPE 6.2: **Interview students about their friendships.** Interview students about their friendships. Ideally, choose students who vary in their social skills and level of peer acceptance. Possible questions include the following:

1. Who are your friends?

2. How are they similar or different from you?

3. How do they support you in school?

TPE: 6.3: **Develop a cooperative or collaborative learning lesson.** Using information in Chapter 6, develop a cooperative or collaborative learning lesson. How did students respond to this lesson? What challenges did you encounter? How did you address each of these challenges?

TPE: 6.4: **Develop strategies for productive group work.** The following table outlines several problems that may arise with group work in the classroom. For each challenge, develop a possible solution.

Challenge of Group Work	Possible Solutions
Some students have difficulty listening and offering constructive feedback to others.	
Some students dominate group work. Others engage in social loafing.	
Some students are disruptive and have difficulty managing their behavior in groups.	
Students divide up the task but just share answers and fail to come back to discuss and explain ideas.	

KEY TERMS AND CONCEPTS

Classroom community: Classrooms in which students feel emotionally connected to others, feel they have a voice or role in activities, and feel that their need for relatedness is being met.

Collaborative learning models: Opportunities for students to work in small groups on an open-ended problem with no clear answer; the teacher plays a more facilitative role.

Cooperative learning models: Opportunities for students to work in small groups on a structured task; the teacher retains control.

Jigsaw method: A method in which each individual has a unique piece of information that is essential for completing the task.

Literature circles: Small groups of students who read and discuss the same book. It is the student equivalent of an adult book club. This small-group activity provides opportunities for students to choose what they want to read and have some control over their learning.

Peer acceptance: Occurs when a student is generally well liked by peers; has a positive effect on engagement and on academic and social development.

Peer rejection: Occurs when a student is actively disliked by peers; has a negative effect on engagement and on academic and social development.

Social goals: Goals students try to accomplish with peers. Examples including making friends and fitting in.

Social loafing: Occurs when some group members exert less effort because they rely on other students to do the work.

Student-centered learning practices: Instructional approaches that put students' needs first, with the teacher playing more of a facilitative role. This pedagogy requires students to be active, responsible participants in their learning and make decisions about their learning.

Teacher-directed methods: An instructional approach where students complete activities designed by the teacher to achieve goals determined by the teacher. In these classrooms, teachers usually spend some time lecturing and then guide the students through problems step by step.

Zone of proximal development: Range of tasks that a student can do with the help of a more able peer or teacher.

RESEARCH-BASED RESOURCES

Book and Reports to Read

Aronson, E., & Patnos, S. (2011). *Cooperation in the classroom: The jigsaw method* (3rd ed.). London: Pinter & Martin.

Bierman, K. L. (2004). *Peer rejection: Developmental processes and intervention strategies.* New York, NY: Guilford Press.

Charney, R. (2002). *Teaching children to care: Classroom management for ethical and academic growth, K–8.* Turner Falls, MA: Northeast Foundation for Children.

Crowe, C. (2012). *How to bullyproof your classroom.* Turner Falls, MA: Northeast Foundation for Children.

Daniels, H. (2002). *Literature circles: Voice and choice in book clubs and reading groups.* Portland, ME: Stenhouse Publishers.

Daniels, H., & Harvey, S. (2009). *Comprehensive and collaboration: Inquiry circles in action.* Portsmouth, NH: Heinemann.

Daniels, H., & Stieneke, N. (2004). *Mini-lessons for literature circles.* Portsmouth, NH: Heinemann.

Davis, H. A., Summers, J. J., & Miller, L. M. (2012). *An interpersonal approach to classroom management: Strategies for improving classroom engagement.* Thousand Oaks, CA: Corwin.

Denton, P. (2007). *The power of our words: The teacher language that helps children learn.* Turner Falls, MA: Northeast Foundation for Children.

Denton, P., & Kriete, R. (2000). *The first six weeks of school.* Turner Falls, MA: Northeast Foundation for Children.

Gibbs, J. (2006). *Reaching all by creating tribes learning communities.* Windsor, CA: CenterSource Systems.

Kriete, R. (2002). *The morning meeting book.* Turner Falls, MA: Northeast Foundation for Children.

Johnson, D. W., Johnson, R. T., & Holubec, E. J. (1994). *The new circles of learning: Cooperation in the classroom and school.* Alexandria, VA: Association for Supervision and Curricular Development.

Jolliffe, W. (2007). *Cooperative learning in the classroom: Putting it into practice.* London: Paul Chapman.

Ladd, G. (2005). *Children's peer relations in school: A century of progress.* New Haven, CT: Yale University Press.

Rogoff, B., Turkanis, C. G., & Bartlett, L. (2001). *Learning together: Children and adults in a school community.* New York, NY: Oxford University Press.

Ryan, A., & Ladd, G. (Eds.) (2012). *Peer relations and adjustment at school.* Charlotte, NC: Information Age Publishing.

Slavin, R. E. (1994). *Using student team learning* (2nd ed.). Baltimore, MD: Johns Hopkins University, Center for Social Organization of Schools.

Web Sites to Visit

1. **Jigsaw Classroom** (www.jigsaw.org). This site includes resources related to the jigsaw classroom, a cooperative learning model developed by Elliot Aronson in the 1970s.

2. **Literature Circles Resource Center** (www.litcircles.org). This site includes resources about literature circles for both educators and students.

3. **Cooperative Learning Institute** (www.co-operation.org). This site developed by Johnson and Johnson includes research and professional development opportunities related to cooperative learning.

4. **Caring School Communities** (www.devstu.org/caring-school-community). This site provides resources related to the Caring School Community, formerly called the Child Development Project, an elementary school intervention program designed to increase classroom community.

5. **Scholastic** (www.scholastic.com/teachers/collection/creating-classroom-community). This site provides resources and lesson plans for teachers on how to create a classroom community.

6. **Center for Social and Character Development at Rutgers** (www.rucharacter.org). This site includes information on teaching to increase social and character development in schools. Lesson plans, research, and professional development opportunities related to character development are available.

CHAPTER SEVEN

MYTH 7: There's Only So Much a Teacher Can Do

How to Help Those Students
Still Struggling to Succeed

A s outlined in previous chapters, it is possible for educators to increase the level of engagement for all students in their classrooms by simultaneously making changes to the social and academic environment. Incorporating the research-based strategies presented in this book will help teachers create a more engaging and supportive environment. However, even after implementing these strategies, some teachers will still believe that it is not possible to engage all students. This belief is more common among educators in urban schools who teach students living in families and communities that are under-resourced and overstressed. Unfortunately, it is common for these teachers to become demoralized, have low expectations for student success, and feel that there is little they or the schools can do to help students (Payne, 2008). When students come from difficult family situations and poor communities, it is easy to blame their poor engagement and achievement on these outside factors and feel little control over the situation.

In this chapter we counter the myth that it is not possible to engage all students. First, we outline the individual factors associated with higher rates of disengagement among some groups of students. Next, we present some warning signs that teachers can use to identify disengagement in their classroom. Sections are presented on how to reengage groups that are particularly at risk for disengagement; these groups include boys, low-achieving youths, students with a history of behavioral problems, and African American, Hispanic, and low-income students. Finally, interventions that have been successful at increasing student engagement for at-risk groups of students are discussed.

WHY IS IT IMPORTANT TO RESIST DISENGAGEMENT?

Disengagement is key to understanding the gradual process by which students begin to withdraw from school. Dropping out of school is not an instantaneous event; it is a cumulative process that results from a series of negative school experiences (Finn, 1989). Research suggests that it is possible to predict who will drop out of school from their engagement behaviors in the elementary school years (Alexander, Entwisle, & Horsey, 1997). Therefore, all teachers can play a critical role in changing these educational trajectories so that students remain in school. It is important to resist disengagement in the classroom because of the severe negative individual and societal consequences of dropping out of school.

Dropout rates vary dramatically by racial/ethnic group, socioeconomic status, and school location. Hispanic and African American youths are significantly less likely to complete high school than are their white and Asian counterparts (Rumberger, 2011). In some urban centers, fewer than 30 percent of African American males graduate from high school (Smith, 2002). This is having devastating consequences on these individuals and their communities. Youths who do not complete high school are more likely to experience unemployment, underemployment, and incarceration. Failure to graduate from high school also results in lower earnings, poorer health, greater reliance on public assistance, and increases in crime (Rumberger, 2011). A sobering statistic is the finding that African American males have a higher likelihood of ending up in jail than in college (Smith, 2002).

RISK FACTORS FOR DISENGAGEMENT

Students enter every classroom with prior academic and social experiences that shape how they approach school. Teaching would be easy if all students were like Franco and Fiona, who have been discussed throughout this book as students with histories of positive experiences in school and high behavioral engagement and who like school and use cognitive strategies to make sure they understand the material. However, the reality is that most teachers also have students like Ryan and Rachel, who find school boring, have poor relations with their teacher and peers, and are already showing signs of disengagement as a result of their prior experiences in school.

Table 7.1 presents some demographic and individual factors associated with higher rates of disengagement. First, school can be a difficult place for many boys, who have been found to have higher incidence of behavioral problems, report more negative beliefs towards school, and have lower rates of school attachment than do girls (Martin, 2004; Voelkl, 1997). Furthermore, there is evidence that African American and Hispanic youths have higher rates of disengagement than white and Asian youths (Johnson, Crosnoe, & Elder, 2001, Ogbu, 2003). The level of school engagement has also been found to vary as a function of a family's economic resources. Students from poorer families experience lower rates of behavioral and emotional engagement and are at heightened risk of dropping out of school (Janosz, Archambault, Morizot, & Pagani, 2008; Li & Lerner, 2011). Finally, age matters. Students become more disengaged as they progress through school, with greater declines following the transition to middle school (Martin, 2007).

There are also a variety of individual factors that are associated with disengagement. Academic difficulties such as failing a class, having low grades, or having low achievement test scores are predictive of higher rates of disengagement (Balfanz, Herzog, & MacIver, 2007). Students who have a history of behavioral problems have a higher likelihood of disengaging from school

Table 7.1   Demographic and Individual Risk Factors for Disengagement

Demographic Factors
• Boys
• Hispanic, African American, or Native American
• Lower socioeconomic status
• English language learner
• Older grades
Individual Factors
• Learning disability
• Mental illness
• Low academic achievement
• History of behavioral problems
• Poor attendance
• Substance abuse
• Delinquency

(Finn & Rock, 1997). There is also a relation between disengagement and higher levels of problem behaviors, including substance abuse and delinquency (Wang & Fredricks, in press). Failure to engage in school may lead students to associate with delinquent friends and seek comfort in drugs, alcohol, and violence, which may in turn exacerbate their alienation from school.

Early Warning Signs of Disengagement

Teachers play a critical role in identifying students who are showing signs of disengagement and in intervening to prevent them from further disengaging and dropping out of school. Table 7.2 outlines signs of behavioral and emotional disengagement, which often precede cognitive disengagement. As outlined in Chapter 1, several scholars have developed early warning systems that identify youths who are showing initial signs of disengagement from school. Many of these early intervention

Table 7.2 Early Warning Signs of Disengagement

Behavioral
• Tardy
• Skipping classes
• Absenteeism
• Behavior referrals to the office
• Detention
• In-school suspension
• Out-of-school suspensions
• Not completing assignments
• Low expectation to graduate
Emotional
• Low perception of value of school
• No interest in school
• Boredom
• Anxiety
• Social isolation
• Poor peer relations
• Peer rejection

warning systems focus on behavioral indicators because these data are already being collected by schools. These warning systems collect information on attendance, achievement test scores, grades, and school behavioral problems. Students with a higher number of early warning signs have a higher likelihood of dropping out of school and higher rates of delinquency and substance abuse over time (Henry, Knight, & Thornberry, 2012; Neild, Balfanz, & Herzog, 2007). In addition to behavioral indicators, teachers should also monitor students' emotional reactions to school, to their teachers, and their peers. Students often disengage because they are bored, don't like school, feel alienated from adults, and have failed to develop positive relations with their peers.

WHY IS A STUDENT DISENGAGED?

Diagnosing the causes of disengagement is the first step in helping students to reengage. It is important to give students the opportunity to share their feelings about why they think they may be disengaged and work with them to develop experiences and strategies to change their beliefs and behaviors. Students need to view their teachers as supportive and not as part of the problem, but part of the solution. A list of questions to ask to determine the underlying reason(s) why a student may be disengaged is presented in Table 7.3.

Outside school factors. Students may be disengaged because of factors outside of classroom. Disengagement may be the result of a student not eating an adequate breakfast or lunch or not getting enough sleep. It is important to educate both students and their parents about the importance of nutrition and sleep for engagement and achievement. Family stresses such as a divorce, parental substance abuse, or the illness of a parent can also make it very difficult for a student to engage in school. In these situations, it is critical to enlist the support of social workers and psychologists in getting services to help the student cope with these stressors. It is also important to determine if disengagement is the result of a mental health or substance abuse issue. Linking students to

Table 7.3   Why Is a Student Disengaged?

• Is there any underlying family problem?
• Is the child sleep deprived or not getting proper nutrition?
• Is there any underlying mental health issue?
• Is the student using drugs or alcohol?
• Is the curriculum too hard?
• Is the student afraid to take chances?
• Is the curriculum too easy?
• Are the tasks boring?
• Does the student have the skills necessary to be successful at the task?

STOP AND REFLECT

1. What do you think are the biggest causes of disengagement? Do your responses emphasize characteristics of the individual child? Do you also consider contextual factors?

2. Use Table 7.2 to identify students who are beginning to show signs of disengagement in the classroom. How are they similar? How are they different?

3. Use questions in Table 7.3 to help diagnose why these students are disengaged. What other professionals need to be part of this diagnosis?

services to address their mental health and well-being can help to increase engagement.

Curricular factors. In other cases, disengagement is a result of the curriculum. Students like Rachel who have experienced limited academic success often feel like they do not have the skills to be successful. For these types of students, the threat of failure makes it unlikely they will take risks in the classroom, and not taking risks could have achievement consequences. It is important to reduce or even eliminate the risks of making a mistake by creating a safe, inviting, and respectful learning environment. It is also possible that students are disengaged because they perceive that the work is boring or too easy. For example, Ravet (2007) asked ten highly disengaged students why they had disengaged from school, and the most common reason given was that they were bored with the curriculum. In contrast, these students' teachers explained their disengagement in terms of a deficit perspective. They focused on individual factors, including students' attitudes, abilities, personalities, and family backgrounds, as the major causes of disengagement. Clearly, if these teachers had listened more closely to their students, they would have known the contextual reasons for the disengagement and would have been better able to intervene. For these students, adequate task challenge and a more engaging and meaningful curriculum may have helped to increase engagement (see Chapter 4 for information on tasks and engagement).

BOYS AND DISENGAGEMENT

We are currently facing a crisis in how we educate boys (Gurian & Stevens, 2005; Tyre, 2008). Rather than seeing the energy that many boys bring to school as an asset, some teachers view boys' behavior from a deficit lens (Sprung, Froschl, & Gropper, 2010). Many teachers expect their students to be able to sit still, pay attention, listen to directions, and make eye contact. However, the reality is that boys have more energy than girls and can have difficulty focusing and staying on task. They are more likely to fidget to work off steam and are less likely to make eye contact than are the girls in the classroom (Rao, 2009).

It is common for teachers to spend more time disciplining boys and ensuring they conform to school rules than they spend supporting boys' needs and evaluating how the structure of the classroom may be contributing to their engagement levels. Two common ways teachers have addressed concerns about boys' behavioral issues is to refer the boys to special education and/or to recommend medication. Although there are clearly cases where boys have an attention disorder and need treatment, many teachers are too quick in recommending a diagnosis and medication for problems that are primarily caused by environmental factors (Rao, 2009).

African American boys face additional challenges in school. To be both black and male puts these students at an even greater risk for placement in special education and results in higher rates of suspension and grade retention (Codrington & Fairchild, 2012; Smith, 2002). As outlined in Chapter 5 (see section on connecting to diverse students), white teachers often misunderstand the behavior of African American students, which can result in higher conflict in the classroom (Delpit, 1995). These teachers are more likely to view cultural differences in behaviors and interactions as indicative of deficiencies, which can result in unwarranted special education placements or disciplinary actions. Table 7.4 presents some statistics illustrating the challenges many boys are facing today in school.

How do the structure of the classroom and the nature of instruction contribute to the disengagement many boys are experiencing at school? High-stakes testing has changed the nature of instruction and has pushed the curricular expectations to earlier

Table 7.4   Challenges Facing Boys

• Boys are five times as likely to be expelled as girls. African American boys are three times more likely to be expelled than white children (Gilliam, 2005).
• Boys represent 70 percent of school suspensions, with higher rates for African American males in urban schools (Ferguson, 2000).
• 80 percent of children diagnosed with behavioral disorders are boys (U.S. Department of Education, 2003).
• 70 percent of children diagnosed with learning disabilities are boys (U.S. Department of Education, 2003).
• Boys are three times more likely to be diagnosed with attention deficit disorder and attention deficit disorder with hyperactivity than are girls (Froschl & Sprung, 2005).
• Boys score sixteen points lower in reading and twenty-four points lower in writing than girls (U.S. Department of Education, 2004).
• Boys get the majority of Ds and Fs in most schools (Guirian & Stevens, 2005).
• Boys make up less than 44 percent of the college population (Guirian & Stevens, 2005).
• Eighty percent of high school dropouts are boys (Guirian & Stevens, 2005).

and earlier grades. In many preschool and kindergarten classrooms, students spend much of their day doing seatwork, worksheets, and decontextualized literacy activities (Miller & Almon, 2009). This is very different than models of developmentally appropriate early childhood practice that include time for developing the socioemotional and self-regulatory skills for school. These environments can be stressful for boys, who often enter school at later stages of maturity than many girls.

To prepare for standardized tests, many schools have increased instructional time by reducing or eliminating recess, playtime, and physical education classes. The lack of physical activity can be particularly difficult for high-energy boys. These students are unable to release their pent-up energy during the day, which makes it more difficult for them to concentrate and increases the likelihood of behavioral problems. The American Academy of Pediatrics recently released a report titled *The Crucial Role of Recess in Schools* (2013) that highlights the social, cognitive, emotional, and physical benefits of recess. To compensate for limited recess and physical education, some schools have instituted **short exercise breaks** during lessons during which students get up and move (see www.instantrecess.com for one example of this approach). Research suggests that incorporating just fifteen minutes a day of exercise has benefits for on-task behavior and achievement (Barros, Silver, & Stein, 2009).

In the following *Engagement in Practice* section, Ellen describes one strategy she uses in her class with high-energy boys.

ENGAGEMENT IN PRACTICE: CREATING SKITS FOR HIGH-ENERGY BOYS

Ellen: When teaching *Romeo and Juliet,* I often have students act out skits to summarize important scenes. For instance, after we read Act I this year, I broke students up into five groups and assigned a scene to each group. I instructed students to abridge and modernize the text so that their performance would be accessible, entertaining, and informative. I distributed script organizers to each group member and gave them about ten minutes to draft their script. Upon completion, groups took the stage, introduced themselves as their characters, and acted out their scene using the scripts that they had prepared. The activity was successful because it allowed high-energy students to get out of their chairs and physically demonstrate their mastery of the plot of a very difficult text. It was also successful because I was able to use the activity as a formative assessment to detect areas of weakness.

Another challenge that many boys face in school is the need to conform to stereotypes of masculinity, which can limit their emotional and relational development (Froschel & Sprung, 2005). Some stereotypical qualities of boys include being independent, emotionally illiterate, aggressive, and not interested in developing intimate relationships. A recent book counters these stereotypes by illustrating the deep desire teenage boys have for intimacy in their relationships (Way, 2011). Teachers can help boys to counter stereotypes of masculinity and develop a broader notion of what it means to be a male in our society by teaching and showing them the value of expressivity, emotional literacy, and nurturing.

One of the challenges teachers face in countering these stereotypes, however, is the lack of male role models in many schools. Boys are significantly more likely to have white female teachers, especially during the elementary grades. This is problematic because research shows that male teachers are more able to create a boy-friendly learning environment (Rao, 2009). Unfortunately, for many young boys it is possible to go through the whole school day without interacting with an adult male. The lack of positive models to emulate is especially acute among African American boys living in urban areas. In the following *Engagement in Practice* section, Melissa describes how she exposes boys in her class to a range of role models from the community.

ENGAGEMENT IN PRACTICE: EXPOSING BOYS TO POSITIVE ROLE MODELS

Melissa: The majority of our staff is white and female. In order to expose a diverse group of boys to positive male role models, I ask community members to visit and work with them. Last year I invited a leader of a local human service agency to speak with us about homelessness. He brought two previously homeless clients with him who shared with the students their experiences and helped them shatter their preconceived notions about who is homeless. This year we had a visit from a young teacher and activist from Arizona. He shared how his students, mostly Hispanic, made changes in their community. At the end of this year, I invited a professor and slam poet from a local college to perform. He engaged the crowd, especially the boys, with his powerful words, his messages for black youth, and his connection to a local support group for families of incarcerated men. While I may be able to discuss these topics with my students, the stories are not mine. By accessing resources in our community, students can relate to broader range of adults, and the boys in my class are exposed to positive role models.

Finally, many boys face challenges related to literacy. Girls outpace boys in terms of language development and reading achievement, with this literacy gap increasing over time (U.S. Department of Education, 2004). Many children see reading books as a feminine activity (Porsche, Ross, & Snow, 2004). This gendered perception may be the result of boys having fewer opportunities at school and home to see men reading or being read to. Teachers play an important role in helping boys to both develop and retain a lifelong interest in reading. In the following *Engagement in Practice* section, Michele describes how she encourages the boys in her classroom to read.

ENGAGEMENT IN PRACTICE: ENCOURAGING BOYS TO READ

Michele: Every year when I add books to my classroom library, I try to include several choices that will appeal to the boys in my class. I also include books that tend to be popular among girls, but I have found a greater need to really look around and establish a vast collection for my boy readers. During conferences, parents often bring up concerns about their son's lack of interest in reading, and I try to share with them the various genres and titles that tend to be popular among boy readers. I do a beginning-of-the-year reading survey to assess student interest. Based on the results of this survey and what I have observed over the years, I make sure to include several action and adventure books, science fiction, fantasy, sports novels, biographies, mythology, science, and humorous books. One area that I've really expanded in my library is comics and graphic novels. These books are so popular with my fourth-grade boys each year that nearly every copy is constantly checked out. The students actually keep track of each book and who gets it next. I've learned to carry this interest over into writing, giving my students opportunities to write their own books during writing and choice times and then placing them in our classroom library. Many boys become prolific comic and graphic novel writers and illustrators. They often collaborate together to create series books.

I also make a conscious effort to include books that appeal to the boys in my class during my read alouds, both during lessons and when I do our daily chapter book read aloud. For the daily chapter book, I strategically include a few series books throughout the year, only reading the first book in the series and then telling the students they can read the rest on their own. This really piques their interest and gets them going in their independent reading. It also makes for some great informal discussions among the students who decide to finish the series.

In sum, these aspects of the school experience help to explain boys' higher rates of behavioral problems and lower levels of school attachment (Martin, 2004; Voelkl, 1997). As a result of the growing concern over the crisis in boys' education, there have been several books written about how to better support boys' learning (Gurian & Stevens, 2005; Rao, 2009; Sprung, Froschl, & Gropper, 2010; Tyre, 2008). Table 7.5 includes some practical strategies for increasing boys' engagement at all levels of schooling.

Table 7.5 Practical Strategies for Increasing Boys' Engagement

1. *Increasing opportunities for physical activity.* Over the last decade, cuts to recess and physical education have meant that students have less time for physical activity. Use of short (five-to-fifteen minute) in-class exercise breaks are one way to increase physical activity. Teachers can also give students the opportunity to move around the classroom during lessons and/or use a stand-up area to do seatwork. If possible, teachers in the younger grades can create an "exercise area" in the classroom where boys and girls can go if they need physical activity. Finally, taking children outside for some lessons provides another opportunity for physical activity. For example, a scavenger hunt can be effective way to both learn science concepts and get students moving.

2. *Countering stereotypes of masculinity.* One way to counter stereotypes is by connecting boys to a range of male role models who demonstrate both traditional masculine and feminine characteristics. It is important for both boys and girls to see the variability among individuals of the same gender and to realize that there are often more similarities than differences between the two genders. Teachers can also choose curriculum and books that help boys expand their idea of acceptable roles for males. Books where boys are the protagonists and that address a range of emotions are another way to foster discussions about masculinity. Exposing African American youth to

Table 7.5   (Continued)

positive role models is especially important as they have often fewer male role models to emulate outside of celebrities, rappers, and sports heroes.

3. *Connecting curriculum to boys' interests.* One reason boys may be disengaging is that the curriculum, especially in the earlier grades, is often not relevant to boys' lives. Teachers should build lessons around topics that are interesting to boys. For example, a teacher could use sports statistics to teach math concepts. Many boys also love to play video games. Several educational video games have been developed to teach math and literacy skills, science concepts, and history. These games can be a very effective way to engage boys.

4. *Supporting boys' literacy.* There are a variety of strategies that teachers can use to foster boys' interest in books and counter the stereotype that reading is a feminine activity. One is to choose books on topics that typically appeal to boys, such as fantasy, space, humor, mystery, sports, dinosaurs, mythology, superheroes. Another is to observe boys' literacy patterns to see the types of books and topics that are most interesting to them and use this information to make book selections for the classroom library. Boys should have time in their daily schedule to choose books or other literacy materials (e.g., magazines and graphic novels) to read on their own. Teachers can also use multisensory approaches to engage boys in literacy activities; these activities might include listening to a recorded story or writing or drawing on the computer. Finally, teachers can invite male readers into the classroom. Fathers, grandfathers, and males who work at the school can come into class to either share a favorite book or read a book that the teacher suggests.

STOP, REFLECT, AND TRY

1. What are your attitudes and expectations regarding boys' behavior? How does this differ from your expectations for girls?

2. Do you see boys' energy as an asset for learning? Why or why not? How can you increase their opportunities for active learning during the day?

3. Do you have boys in your class who are beginning to show signs of disengagement?

4. Using Table 7.5, evaluate the extent to which your instruction supports the needs of these boys.

5. What changes could you make to better meet the needs of the boys in your classroom?

6. Incorporate one of the recommendations in Table 7.5 for a boy who is showing signs of disengagement. How does he respond?

ACADEMIC PROBLEMS AND DISENGAGEMENT

One of the key predictors of disengagement is having academic difficulties. Students who struggle academically often lack the background knowledge and skills to be successful and, as a result, have had few opportunities to feel the sense of accomplishment that comes from achieving success in school. One common response for students who have experienced a history of failure is to believe that they lack the ability to succeed. These students often show a pattern of **learned helplessness**, where they have low expectations for success and give up quickly in the face of difficulty. Since they feel they cannot control the outcome and fear failure, they abandon any serious attempts to master tasks and instead concentrate on preserving their self-esteem and reputation (Brophy, 1996).

Low-achieving students frequently have difficulty following directions and completing their work (Brophy, 1996). As a consequence, these students often fall behind their classmates. This makes it more difficult to use instructional materials developed for their grade level and can result in students feeling frustrated because they do not know how to do the task and how to get the help they need. Rachel is a perfect example of this phenomenon because she feels like she lacks the skills she needs to be successful. Table 7.6 presents practical research-based strategies for helping students who are disengaged because of low achievement. These strategies are adapted from suggestions for working with low-achieving students (Brophy, 1996; McIntyre, 1989).

In the following *Engagement in Practice* sections, Michele and Ellen describe strategies they have used in their classrooms to support low-achieving students. First, Michele describes the use of guided math groups to provide differentiated instruction to

Table 7.6   Practical Strategies for Teaching Low Achievers

1. *Providing opportunities to achieve success.* It is important to set up tasks so that low-achieving students can experience success. Dividing assignments into smaller parts and making sure that the first part of the assignment is easy or familiar can help students to experience some initial success. This can also help students to feel less overwhelmed and see where they have done well and where they need to improve.

2. *Helping students to deal with frustration and failures.* Low-achieving students are more likely to become frustrated and give up easily. One way to minimize these frustrations and encourage students to persist is to make sure that students have the background knowledge and skills to be successful. It is also important to not single out students who are having difficulties or embarrass them in front of their classmates. Teachers should encourage effort and give students recognition for both their effort and individual progress. These students also may need individualized support so that they are willing to keep trying, especially when faced with difficulties.

3. *Adjusting task difficulty and reading levels.* It is important to give tasks that are within students' range of capabilities. In some cases, it may be necessary to reduce the difficulty of the task or adjust the reading level so that students can experience success.

4. *Providing clear directions.* Low-achieving students often have difficulty with instructions. It is important to provide students with clear and simple directions on what they need to do to complete a task and how they can achieve a desired outcome. Having the student repeat the directions is one way to make sure he or she understands the task. It is also important to provide clear time limits for completing the task, which may be longer than the time limits given to the rest of class.

5. *Offering tutoring and additional support.* Low-achieving students often have difficulty keeping up with their classmates. These students can benefit from tutoring or additional instruction from an aide, resource teacher, adult volunteer, or a high-achieving classmate.

6. *Setting realistic goals for task completion.* Low-achieving students often have difficulty completing assignments. Therefore, it is important to help students set realistic goals and evaluate their own accomplishments. The emphasis should be on effort and improvement, rather than how these students are doing relative to their classmates. Contracts can be an effective to way to help students chart and evaluate their progress. Students can receive "free time" or other rewards for completing an assignment or a predetermined goal outlined in the contract.

different ability levels. Next, Ellen describes how she makes task modifications to better support low-achieving students.

ENGAGEMENT IN PRACTICE: GUIDED MATH GROUPS

Michele: After a few years teaching, I realized that math was an area where my low-achieving students were really struggling and falling further behind. In reading, we were already using guided reading groups and literature circles to meet different learning needs and reading levels, but I was finding it difficult to take time out during math to help struggling students, especially those who were lacking in confidence and seemed unsure how to even approach the first problem. That's when I read about guided math groups and decided to try them out in class.

Guided math groups can be structured in various ways. In my class, I still included a short period of time for whole-group instruction when I introduced a new concept. Then I divided the class into three groups, with each rotating between three "stations." One group would meet with me to receive further small-group instruction and practice what we were learning, the second group would do a paired or group activity or game related to the concept, and the third group would do independent work related to the lesson. After the whole-group lesson, I would always meet with my struggling group first, in order to reinforce the lesson right away for them and make sure they understood the directions and what we were learning. The students who had a strong understanding of the concepts and moved quickly through the lesson were the last to meet with me. Our groups meetings usually involved problems and tasks to challenge them even further. Though it involves more work and preparation on my end, I like using math groups because I can actually check in with every student. When we come back together as a class, I can call on everyone, and students join in the discussion more readily because they have problems and tasks they know they have done successfully in their small groups. The best part is that the groups always change—there are a few students that may be in the struggling group most of the time, but I often find that students who really understand one area of math (e.g., geometry) may need more help in another (e.g., fractions). This constant change keeps students from being labeled in a "low" or "high" group, and they don't wonder why they are in a certain group.

ENGAGEMENT IN PRACTICE: MODIFYING TASKS FOR DIFFERENT ABILITY LEVELS

Ellen: For the past two years, I have taught five heterogeneously grouped classes. Students in my classes read and comprehend text at the third-grade level, the eleventh-grade level, and all levels in between. I have learned over time that it is imperative to try to teach to the middle and then differentiate content and activities to meet the needs of both the higher- and lower-achieving students. I often observe that students on both ends of the spectrum become disengaged because they feel that the content and skills are either too difficult or too easy. Rather than advocating for extra help or added challenge, some students succumb to their frustrations and give up altogether, alienating themselves from the rest of the class and the activity. Not only do the frustrated students disengage for the remainder of the lesson, but due to feelings of inadequacy, they often carry the frustration with them to the next class and the cycle continues to repeat.

In order to alleviate this problem, I carefully assess students to determine who will need modifications and what kinds of modifications they need. For instance, when teaching new vocabulary, I introduced students to a set of twenty words every other week. At the end of two weeks of practice, students were assessed on the set of twenty words. I quickly realized that assimilating twenty new vocabulary words in just two weeks was nearly impossible for some students, especially those whose primary language is not English. I remember passing out a vocabulary quiz to a student whose primary language is Haitian Creole. After glancing at the quiz, the student's energy changed instantly. His shoulders sank and he placed his head on the desk. When I asked him why he gave up, he told me that he was stupid and that he would have failed the quiz even if he had tried. Because the assessment was not tailored to help the student attain success, he became frustrated, disengaged, and ultimately failed. To prevent this from happening again and to boost the confidence of this student and students like him, I cut down the list to ten words with the intention of adding more words as students began to easily master the acquisition of ten. Modifying curriculum, assessments, and activities shows students that my goal is to help them succeed rather than fail, and rather than losing them completely, it allows me to reengage them.

STOP AND REFLECT

1. Do you have students who are disengaged because they are having academic difficulties? What are they like in terms of their behavior, emotions, and cognitive strategies? Which aspects of the curriculum do they struggle with?

2. Which aspects of Table 7.6 do you currently use with students who are having academic difficulties? Which aspects could you incorporate in your instruction to improve students' success?

3. Incorporate one of the strategies in Table 7.6 for a student having academic difficulties. How did he or she respond? Why did you choose this strategy for this particular student? What will you do next?

STUDENTS WITH A HISTORY OF BEHAVIORAL PROBLEMS

One of teachers' biggest concerns is how to manage the classroom to ensure that classes run smoothly and students' behavioral problems are minimized. This is important because the time spent addressing student misbehavior takes away from time that can be spent on learning. Prevention is the key to reducing behavioral problems. There will be fewer behavioral problems in a classroom with engaging tasks, a positive social climate, and clear expectations, rules, and routines. Students need to know what is expected of them and the consequences for failing to comply with these expectations. They also need to know that they can fail in a safe learning environment and that their success is expected and will be supported. Other keys to preventing student misbehavior include anticipating problems before they occur, intervening and redirecting off-task students before their behaviors become more severe, and dealing with a disruption with as little interruption as possible.

Even with these preventive measures, some teachers will still have students who are disruptive, distracting, or defiant. Many of these students have a history of behavioral problems and so they are acting or reacting as they have in the past. It is important to emphasize to these students that defiant, disruptive, and aggressive behavior is not acceptable and will not be tolerated. Equally important for these students is to identify the conditions that prompt and reinforce their negative behaviors. Teachers should determine when, where, and how often these misbehaviors occur. For example, teachers need to document whether these negative behaviors are more likely to occur at certain times of the day, during certain types of tasks, or during certain instructional arrangements (e.g., during small-group work, individual seatwork, or large-group discussions). In addition, teachers should track whether these misbehaviors occur in the presence of certain peers. This information can be used to determine the underlying cause(s) of student misbehavior and to develop a plan for either altering or removing the factors that trigger the misbehavior. This may mean changing the seating plan, using instructional small groups, offering a variety of instructional activities, or changing the pace of instruction.

When working with difficult students, it important to be calm and try to understand the situation to help to identify potential solutions. Not getting angry is not easy. These students often resist authority and know how to carry on a power struggle. However, getting upset has the potential to worsen the situation and takes away time from problem solving. Teachers should first reflect on their beliefs regarding student misbehavior to prevent negative cycles of teacher-student interactions from escalating (see Chapter 5 for more information on working with difficult students). It is important to remember that students' defiant behavior may stem from not having a supportive or caring adult role model or from a lack of consistency in their life. This misbehavior also may be the way students have learned how to get attention. In the end, disruptive and defiant students need compassion, understanding, and support from their teachers. Students like Ryan who have experienced failure and consistent confusion often have trouble believing that their teachers care about them, even when evidence suggests otherwise (Watson & Eken, 2003).

Critical to reengaging disengaged students is giving the students a voice. Students need opportunities to voice their feelings. Teachers need to respond that even though their behaviors are unacceptable, the students are cared for as individuals. A student like Ryan may benefit from the opportunity to explain his interpretation of an event and the triggers for his misbehavior. This may help the student to analyze his or her misbehavior and to begin to accept some responsibility. If the misbehavior persists, it may be necessary to organize a more formal conference to discuss the behavior, outline a specific plan to stop the behavior, and detail consequences that will result if behavioral changes are not made (Brophy, 1996). Finally, if a student's misbehavior is persistent, especially after intervention, it is important to enlist the support of administrators, psychologists, and social workers at the school. Many students could benefit from additional counseling or instruction on more effective ways to handle their frustrations, control their tempers, and resolve conflicts.

In the following *Engagement in Practice* section, Melissa describes how her school uses tribunals to deal with more severe student misbehavior.

ENGAGEMENT IN PRACTICE: USING TRIBUNALS TO DEAL WITH CHALLENGING STUDENT BEHAVIOR

Melissa: Sometimes the classroom teacher's intervention strategies do not result in any change in student behavior. In these cases, a tribunal is called. Parents, teachers, students, and an administrator gather to discuss the problem from all points of view. Goals are set for improvement, and each member of the group accepts some responsibility for the success of the plan. The plan is written up like a contract and signed by all parties. In this way, students feel supported by many different people. They know exactly what those supports are, and they understand their own responsibility to change behavior. Parents may learn about new resources to help their child (e.g., routines at home, counseling opportunities, and other supports) and come to realize their child's success is dependent upon them as well as the school. Tribunals reconvene every two weeks, and all members report on what they have done. Tribunals are reserved for more challenging students as a means of supportive intervention. Some issues addressed at tribunals include social skill development, aggression, and extreme withdrawal from school activities. This process is collaborative rather than punitive and has proved to be very effective.

STOP AND REFLECT

1. Identify students in your class (or in former classes) who have a history of behavioral problems. For each student address the following questions:

   a. What does this student get out of the behavioral problem?

   b. When, where, and how often do these behaviors occur?

   c. What could I do (have done) differently that would make this behavior less likely to occur?

2. If your class could be reduced by one student, who would you feel relieved to have removed? Why? What could you do to improve relationships with this student?

AFRICAN AMERICAN, HISPANIC, AND LOW-INCOME STUDENTS AND DISENGAGEMENT

African American and Hispanic youths have been found to have higher rates of behavioral problems and lower school attachment (Johnson et al., 2003). **Stereotype threat** is one theory that has been proposed to explain the higher rates of disengagement and underachievement by African American and Hispanic students (Steele, 1997). The basis of stereotype threat is that when a person's social identity, such as their race or ethnicity, is attached to a negative stereotype, the person will underperform in a manner consistent with this stereotype. Experimental research shows that under conditions when race is salient, African Americans and Hispanic students do worse than expected on standardized tests (Gonzalez, Blanton, & Williams, 2002; Steele & Aronson, 1995).

Another explanation given for African American and Hispanic students' lower engagement is experience with racial and ethnic discrimination. These students tend to experience two types of discrimination: 1) an awareness that they may encounter educational and job discrimination, which can undermine their beliefs in the long-term benefits of education (Fordham & Ogbu,

1986), and 2) daily experiences of discrimination by teachers and peers. Rosenbloom and Way (2004) interviewed African American, Asian, and Latino youths in an urban high school about their experiences with discrimination. The students talked about how no matter what their actual behavior was in the class-room, they felt they were stereotyped by teachers as "bad kids" or "kids who start trouble." Moreover, they felt that their teachers were uncaring, ineffective, and emotionally distant. Prior research has linked experiences of daily discrimination to declines in mental health and academic motivation (Wong, Eccles, & Sameroff, 2003).

One reason teachers may discriminate is they hold lower expectations for African American students, Hispanic students, and students from lower socioeconomic backgrounds. The reality is that most teachers are often unaware that they hold these differ-ential expectations and are treating groups differently. These pro-cesses are often unconscious and reflect stereotypes about different groups. In other cases, teachers do realize they have lower expectations but believe this differential treatment is appro-priate because of differences in students' ability level and home situations. Table 7.7 outlines both the overt and subtle ways that teachers communicate **differential expectations** to students (Good & Brophy, 1984; Cotton, 1989).

Low expectations are especially common for African American and Hispanic students in urban schools in high-poverty areas. Because these students often face such immense challenges in their family lives and communities, many teachers try to com-municate that they care about these students by demanding less and giving these students "one more chance" when they fail to comply with expectations. However, lower expectations are not going to help these students and may actually lead to them feeling more alienated from school. Instead, what is necessary for these students is a **warm demander**, a term that has been used to iden-tify teachers who are successful with poor students and students of color because they communicate warmth but also have a non-negotiable demand for student effort and respect (Kleinfeld, 1975; Ware, 2006). Irving and Fraser (1998) defined warm demanders as teachers "who provide a tough-minded, no-nonsense, struc-tured and disciplined environment for kids whom society has psy-chologically and physically abandoned" (p. 56).

Table 7.7   How Teachers Communicate Low Expectations

- Giving low-expectation students fewer opportunities to learn the material than high-expectation students
- Waiting less time for low-expectation students to answer a question than high-expectation students
- Calling on low-expectation students less frequently than high-expectation students
- Giving low-expectation students the answers or calling on someone else rather than helping them to figure out the answer
- Structuring low-expectation students' activities more closely
- Interacting with low-expectation students more privately than publicly
- Criticizing low-expectation students more often for failure and praising them less frequently for success
- Giving low-expectation students less positive interactions, including less eye contact, smiling, and head nodding
- Seating low-expectation students farther away than high-expectation students
- Asking high-expectation students more stimulating and cognitively complex questions
- Giving briefer and less informative feedback to low-expectation than high-expectation students

Scholars have concluded that a warm demanding style is a very effective teaching style, especially when applied to students of color, although to an uninformed observer it may appear harsh (Bondy & Ross, 2008; Ware, 2006; Irvine & Fraser, 1998). Table 7.8 lists characteristics of warm demanders. Although these teachers demonstrate compassion for students' situations, they demand that their students respect them and complete high-quality work. They do not accept excuses. Instead, they insist on students meeting high expectations. To make this possible, they provide support for the students to complete and improve their work. These teachers also approach students, especially those with behavioral problems, with unconditional positive regard and caring (Bondy & Ross, 2008). While warm demanders may become frustrated by students' behavior, they believe and communicate to their students that they can and will improve. These

Table 7.8   Characteristics of a Warm Demanding Teacher

- Establishes a caring relationship that convinces all students that he or she believes in them
- Insists that students treat the teacher and each another respectfully
- Demands for respect are non-negotiable
- Insists that all students complete tasks and perform at a high level
- Has a no-excuses policy for all students
- Demonstrates unconditional positive regard for all students, especially those who cause difficulty in the classroom
- Observes students to learn about their interests, experiences, and talents
- Recognizes how a student's cultural background guides values, beliefs, and behaviors
- Establishes supports to make sure all students will learn
- Collects data to understand a situation before acting
- Searches for solutions to problems rather than blaming students
- Is clear and consistent in expectations
- Reminds students of expectations. If students fail to comply, calmly deliver consequences
- Creates a climate where teachers are taken seriously

teachers reach out to students for help in understanding their behaviors and do not blame students or dismiss their concerns (Bondy & Ross, 2008).

There is evidence that urban students want to be in classrooms with warm demanders. Wilson and Corbett (2001) interviewed 200 students in high-poverty middle schools in Philadelphia about what they wanted in a teacher. They talked about wanting to be in classrooms in which:

- Teacher "stayed on students" to complete assignments.
- Teacher was able to control student behavior without ignoring the lesson.
- Teacher went out of his or her way to provide help.
- Teacher explained things until the "light bulb went on" for the whole class.

- Teacher provided students with a variety of activities through which to learn.
- Teacher understood students' situations and factored that into their lessons.

In the following *Engagement in Practice* section, Melissa describes a teacher at her school who personifies a warm demander.

ENGAGEMENT IN PRACTICE: MARY THE WARM DEMANDER

Melissa: Our middle school social studies teacher, Mary, is a warm demander. Each morning she greets children with a "hello" and then grills them about their homework. Before coming to middle school, younger students fear her. They have heard stories of how hard she is. But invariably students respond to her high expectations and consistently fair approach. They laugh in retrospect at their initial fears. The structure of Mary's class is predictable. She offers reading material across four grade levels to reach all learners. To give her students many opportunities to succeed, she prepares differentiated study guides for the learners in her room, from a scaffolded fill-in-the-blank to an outline form to free note-taking for advanced students. Mary has high expectations for all and they are non-negotiable. She understands that how she relates to the most troublesome students in her class will dictate a tone for how everyone else treats one another. She treats all of her students with respect. One student in particular struggled through both years of middle school. He underperformed and misbehaved. Refusing to give up on him, Mary offered after-school tutoring, visited prospective high school choices with him, and never lowered her expectations. She stayed on him and the rest of her class to meet these expectations. The student pushed back, declaring his dislike of her. By the year's end, he was not only improving performance, he declared his love for this teacher. She knew he needed her warm demanding before he did. When he graduated from the school, Mary promised to check with him periodically to monitor his progress. She truly went out of her way to provide to support to this and other students.

STOP AND REFLECT

1. In your teaching experience, have you had any obstacles developing relationships with particular groups of students?

2. How have your cultural values shaped your relationships with students of different groups?

3. How have you held or worked against holding differential expectations for students based on demographic characteristics (e.g., income level, gender, race, ethnicity) or ability?

4. Use Table 7.7 to evaluate how you communicate your expectations to students. Have a colleague observe your class to note whether you treat students differently based on factors such as race, gender, socioeconomic status, or ability.

5. Use Table 7.8 to evaluate your teaching style. Which qualities do you currently possess? Which of these are available for all students? Which are available for some students? Which qualities do you plan to incorporate more in your teaching?

INTERVENTIONS TO INCREASE ENGAGEMENT

There are several interventions that have been developed to increase engagement, especially at the middle and high school levels (see Chapter 1 for more information on interventions). These interventions are designed to either work with individuals who are showing signs of disengagement or work with schools to improve the overall level of student engagement. These reforms aim to increase student engagement by collecting data on early warning signs and engagement levels and by improving students' relationships with adults in the school. **Check and Connect**, developed by Sandra Christenson at the University of Minnesota, is an example of one such intervention program (www.checkand-connect.umn.edu). The program is designed to improve engagement and reduce dropout rates by maximizing personal contact and opportunities to build trusting relationships with a mentor or monitor. The Check component is designed to continually assess behavioral engagement (as reflected in attendance, grades, and suspensions). The Connect component involves program staff giving individualized attention to students and intervening when problems are identified. The monitor also advocates for students, coordinates services, provides ongoing feedback and encouragement, and emphasizes the importance of staying in school. Research has shown that students participating in the Check and Connect model showed increased attendance, persistence in school, accrual of credits, school completion, and decreased truancy, behavioral referrals, and dropout rates (www.ici.umn.edu/checkandconnect).

First Things First is another school reform model whose goal is to increase engagement and strengthen relationships between students and adults in secondary schools with a large number of disadvantaged students (www.irre.org). This reform was developed by James Connell and the Institute for Reform on Education and is now currently used in thirty-four high schools and eight middle schools. The program has three overarching goals: 1) students are cognitively, emotionally, and behaviorally involved in their academic work, 2) students are doing work that reflects the academic standards set by their district and state, and 3) teachers expect and support high levels of work from all students. They accomplish this goal through five different components: 1) strengthening instruction, 2) effective use of data, 3) personalized learning communities, 4) advocating for students and families, and 5) building capacity to strengthen and sustain reform. Evaluations of the First Things First model have shown improvements in student engagement, attendance, achievement, and graduation rates, as well as improvements in the quality of relationships between teachers and students (Gambone, Klem, Summers, Akey, & Sipe, 2004).

The **Talent Development** model is an early identification and intervention system whose goal is to reduce the likelihood that urban middle and high school students will disengage from school. Both the middle school and high school models were developed by colleagues at the Center for Research on the Education of Students Placed at Risk at Johns Hopkins University. These models combine research-based instructional programs and extensive teacher training and support to provide more active and engaging instruction with the goal of increasing the likelihood that urban students will stay in school. Another important emphasis is making structural changes to create learning environments in which teachers know and care about students (Balfanz et al., 2007). For example, the Talent Development high school encompasses five main features: 1) small learning communities, 2) curricula leading to advanced English and mathematics coursework, 3) academic extra-help sessions, 4) staff professional development strategies, and 5) parent and community involvement in activities that foster students' career and college development (Legters, Balfanz, Jordan, & McPartland, 2002). Researchers have shown that participation in Talent Development reforms is associated with higher levels of attendance, academic credits earned, promotion, and graduation rates (Legters et al., 2002; www .tdschools.org/research-results).

CHAPTER SUMMARY

The goal of Chapter 7 was to counter the myth that it is not possible to engage all students, especially the most difficult students who often have histories of disengagement. Although it is more challenging to engage certain students, teachers can and should make the efforts to increase all students' engagement levels. The consequences of disengagement for both the individual and society are too severe to not try. The chapter began with a discussion of the types of students who are most at risk for disengagement. Next, early warning signs teachers can use to identify students who are beginning to show signs of disengagement were outlined. Early identification is critical to reengaging students because of evidence linking school disengagement to dropping out of school. The chapter also provided the reasons why certain groups of students are at greater risk of disengagement and presented research-based strategies for reengaging these groups. These groups include male students, low-achieving students, and defiant, disruptive, and aggressive students. Finally, the chapter outlined strategies for working with low-income and African American and Hispanic students, who are at a higher risk of disengaging from school. Examples of intervention programs that have been designed to increase student engagement among at-risk students and schools concluded the chapter and provided evidence that there are ways to reengage struggling students. A central theme of this chapter is that with adequate support, all students can become engaged learners.

TEXT-TO-PRACTICE EXERCISES

TPE 7.1: **Case studies of disengagement.** Review the cases of Ryan and Rachel (outlined at the beginning of Chapter 1). Using the information in Chapter 7, outline their causes of disengagement and possible solutions.

TPE 7.2: **Identify and reengage disengaged students.** Use information from Chapter 7 to identify two of your students who are showing signs of disengagement and to diagnose the causes of this disengagement and identify possible strategies to reengage these students. Implement these strategies in the classroom. How do the students respond?

TPE 7.3: **Classroom observation.** Observe a classroom lesson (either in your classroom or in another teacher's). Can you identify students who are showing signs of disengagement? What are they doing? When and where is the disengagement most likely to occur? Use information in this chapter to identify possible causes of this disengagement and possible changes that could help to reengage these students.

TPE 7.4: **Supporting boys in the classroom.** Research lessons about masculine stereotypes. Adapt several to use in your classroom. Survey your students and their parents to find names of local community members, especially men, who might come to talk with your classes. Contact them and plan together an experience related to your curriculum.

TPE 7.5: **Encourage boys' literacy.** Take an inventory of the books in the classroom library. What books can you add to support boys' interests? Asking the school librarian and surveying students themselves can provide important information about the types of books to add to the classroom library.

KEY TERMS AND CONCEPTS

Check and Connect: An intervention program designed by Sandra Christenson at the University of Minnesota to increase engagement and reduce dropout rates by assessing attendance, grades, and suspensions (Check) and maximizing personal contact with a mentor or monitor (Connect).

Differential expectations: Either an unconscious or conscious process in which teachers hold lower expectations for some populations and treat students differently based on this grouping category (e.g., race, gender, socioeconomic status, ability).

First Things First: An intervention program developed by the Institute for Reform in Education to increase engagement in secondary schools. The program accomplishes this goal by 1) strengthening instruction, 2) effective use of data, 3) personalized learning communities, 4) advocating for students and families, and 5) building capacity to strengthen and sustain reform.

Learned helplessness: Students begin to doubt their abilities and, as a result, decrease their efforts, especially when faced with difficult material, which leads to a pattern of greater school failure. This motivational pattern is common among low-achieving students.

Short exercise breaks: Students take short breaks between lessons to do five to fifteen minutes of physical activity. These exercise breaks were developed to compensate for cuts to recess and gym classes and have been found to improve on-task behavior and learning.

Stereotype threat: Concern or anxiety that when a person's social identity, such as their race, is attached to a negative stereotype, the person will underperform in a manner consistent with this stereotype.

Talent Development Model: An early identification and intervention program developed by the Center for Research on the Education of Students Placed at Risk at Johns Hopkins University to reduce the likelihood that middle and high school students will disengage from school. Features of the program include 1) small learning communities, 2) curricula leading to advanced English and mathematics coursework, 3) academic extra-help sessions, 4) staff professional development strategies, and 5) parent and community involvement in activities that foster students' career and college development.

Warm demanders: A type of teacher who communicates warmth but also has a non-negotiable demand for student effort and respect. Warm demanders are especially effective for poor students and students of color.

RESEARCH-BASED RESOURCES

Books and Reports to Read

Beers, J. (2003). *When kids can't read: What teachers can do: A guide for teachers 6–12.* Portmouth, NH: Heinemann.

Brophy, J. (1996). *Teaching problem students.* New York, NY: Guilford Press.

Codrington, J., & Fairchild, H. (2012). *Special education and the mis-education of African American children: A call to action.* Position paper by the Association of the Black Psychologist. Retrieved on June 13, 2013, from www.abpsi.org/pdf/specialedpositionpaper021312.pdf.

Cotton, K. (1989). Education and student outcomes: School improvement Series. Northwest Regional Education Laboratory. Portland. Retrieved on June 13, 2013, from www.educationnorthwest.org/webfm_send/562.

Delpit, L. (1995). *Other people's children: Cultural conflict in the classroom.* New York, NY: New Press.

Ferguson, A. (2000). *Bad boys: Public schools in the making of black masculinity.* Ann Arbor, MI: University of Michigan Press.

Froschl, M., & Sprung, B. (2005). *Raising healthy boys: A report on the growing crisis in boys' education.* Academy for Educational Development.

Gambone, M. A., Klem, A. M., Summers, J. A., Akey, T. M., & Sipe, L. L. (2004). *Turning the tide: The achievements of the First Things First educational reform in the Kansas City, Kansas public school district.* Retrieved on July 15, 2013, from www.ydsi.org/ydsi/pdf/turningthetidefullreport.pdf.

Gilliam, W. S. (2005). *Prekindergarteners left behind: Expulsion rates in state prekindergarten programs.* Foundation for Child Development, Policy Brief, Series No. 3. Retrieved July 15, 2103, from www.challengingbehavior.org/explore/policy_docs/prek_expulsion.pdf.

Good, T. L., & Brophy, J. E. (1984). *Looking in classrooms.* New York, NY: Harper & Row.

Guirian, M., & Stevens, K. (2005). *The minds of boys: Saving our sons from falling behind in school and life.* San Francisco: Jossey Bass.

Legters, N. E., Balfanz, R., Jordan, W. J., & McPartland, J. M. (2002). *Comprehensive reforms for urban high schools: A talent development approach.* New York, NY: Teachers College Pres.

McIntyre, T. (1989). *A resource book for remediating common behavior and learning problems.* Boston, MA: Allyn & Bacon.

Miller, E., & Almon, J. (2009). *Crisis in the kindergarten: Why children need to play in school.* College Park, MD: Alliance for Childhood.

Ogbu, J. U. (2003). *Black American students in an affluent suburb: A study of academic disengagement.* Mahwah, NJ: Lawrence Erlbaum.

Payne, C. M. (2008). *So much reform, so little change: The persistence of failure in urban schools.* Cambridge, MA: Harvard Education Press.

Rao, A. (2009). *The way of boys: Promoting the social and emotional development of young boys.* New York, NY: HarperCollins.

Ravet, J. (2007). *Are we listening? Making sense of classroom behavior with pupils and parents.* London, UK: Trentham Books.

Rumberger, R. W. (2011). *Dropping out: Why students drop out of school and what can be done about it.* Cambridge, MA: Harvard University Press.

Sprung, B., Froschl, M., & Gropper, N. (2010). *Supporting boys' learning: Strategies for teacher practice, pre K–grade 3.* New York, NY: Teachers College Press.

Tyre, P. (2008). *The trouble with boys: A surprising report card on our sons, their problems at school, and what parents and educators must do.* New York, NY: Crown Publishers.

Watson, M., & Ecken, L. (2003). *Transforming difficult elementary classrooms through developmental discipline.* San Francisco, CA: Jossey Bass.

Way, N. (2011). *Deep secrets: Boys' friendships and the crisis of connections.* Cambridge, MA: Harvard Press.

Wilson, B. L., & Corbett, H. D. (2001). *Listening to urban kids: School reform and the teachers they want.* Albany, NY: State University of New York Press.

Web Sites to Visit

1. **Conscious Discipline** (www.consciousdiscipline.com). This site includes resources on programs that integrate classroom management with social/emotional learning, including information on workshops, books, and curriculums.

2. **Instant Recess** (www.instantrecess.com). This site includes information on an evidence-based model that incorporates ten-minute physical activity breaks into the daily routine.

3. **Check and Connect** (www.checkandconnect.umn.edu). This site includes information about Check and Connect, an intervention program designed to increase engagement and reduce dropout rates. The site includes research studies about the program and information on training and consultations.

4. **First Things First** (www.irre.org). The Institute for Research and Reform in Education site includes information on the First Things First intervention program.

5. **Talent Development Model** (www.talentdevelopmentsecondary.com). This site includes information on the Talent Development model at the secondary level, an early identification and intervention program designed to reduce the likelihood that urban students will disengage from school.

6. **Boys Read** (www.boysread.org). This is the site of an organization of parents, educators, librarians, mentors, authors, and booksellers whose goal is to increase literacy among boys.

7. **Getting Boys to Read** (www.gettingboystoread.com). This site provides resources for parents, teachers, and boys on how to increase boys' literacy.

8. **Guys Lit Wire** (www.guyslitwire.blogspot.com). This site provides book suggestions and other resources for encouraging adolescent boys' literacy.

CHAPTER EIGHT

MYTH 8: Student Engagement Is a Student Choice

Choosing to Make the Effort and
Not Waiting for Engagement to Happen

In this book, we asked teachers to reflect on how their beliefs about individual students, the types of tasks they choose for learning, and the social environments of their classrooms impact the level of their students' engagement. Our goal was never to blame teachers, but instead to empower them to see the variety of ways in which they can make a difference by creating engaging classrooms where deep learning can take place. The reality is that many teachers spend much of their time, effort, and emotional energy dealing with student disengagement in their classrooms. This reactive approach can be very frustrating and may help to explain the high levels of teacher burnout and attrition. However, rather than dealing with problems after they occur and waiting for engagement to magically happen, we wrote this book to encourage teachers to put their efforts into establishing more socially supportive and cognitively rich instructional contexts. Being proactive will result in fewer behavioral problems, students who are more interested and excited, and students who are more likely to use deep-learning strategies to try to understand the content.

We realize that student disengagement can seem overwhelming, but if teachers want to improve engagement, then the first step is to examine how teachers talk about students. In our experience, it is not uncommon to hear statements like these from teachers: "This student is disengaged because he doesn't care or is not trying hard enough!," "This student comes from a difficult family situation and there is only so much I can do!," or "It would be so much easier to create an engaging classroom if I just had more motivated kids!" Teachers often are quick to assume that the level of student engagement is a result of individual factors such as motivation or a student's family situation. Although individual factors do make it easier or harder to create an engaging classroom, the learning context matters. A central premise of this book has been that teachers have the power to increase engagement for all of their students by making changes to both their beliefs and practices based on proven research-based strategies.

In this book, we also have argued that engagement is a multidimensional construct that includes behavior, emotion, and cognition and that the most optimal achievement and learning outcomes occur when students are high on all three dimensions. Many educators emphasize the behavioral dimensions, such as whether students are on-task or compliant. However, just because students are participating and completing academic work does not mean they are emotionally and cognitively invested in deep learning. Unfortunately, many students just go through the motions. Although this may help them to achieve on low-level competency tasks and tests, it will not be sufficient to master the higher-level conceptual outcomes outlined in the Common Core and Next Generation Science Standards. In addition, low-level compliance will not ensure continued engagement in learning.

From our experiences, we have noted some challenges to creating engaging classrooms. First, the assessment culture has led many schools to focus efforts on standardized achievement test preparation at the expense of cognitively rich instruction. Unfortunately, this "culture of accountability" has resulted in many schools limiting the classroom practices that research has found to increase student engagement and result in deep learning. This emphasis on test performance is counterproductive and may backfire. By focusing so much on preparing students for testing, many schools may actually be contributing to lower achievement scores because many students find these environments so disengaging. Our hope is that as schools begin to adopt the Common Core Standards, which require deeper cognitive skills and more integrative understandings, they also will be placing more emphasis on teaching strategies that create behaviorally, emotionally, and cognitively engaging classroom environments.

In the following *Engagement in Practice* section, Michele describes the challenges she faces related to student engagement from the increased emphasis on standardized testing in the Chicago schools.

ENGAGEMENT IN PRACTICE: REFLECTIONS ON TESTING

Michele: As a fourth-grade teacher in Chicago, one of my biggest challenges with student engagement has been the increasing requirements and pressures from standardized testing. Since my first year of teaching, we have seen the number of tests that students are required to take each year increase. This is mainly due to the emphasis on data collection and measuring students' growth, as well as tying student performance to teaching evaluations. I think it is valuable to track students' growth, and I do just that in my own classroom when I observe and work with them during the year. The difficulty with all the testing lies in its lack of deeper meaning for students and the sheer amount of time spent on it—not only in terms of test preparation, but even simply the hours of test-taking.

Because of the overwhelming emphasis on testing in our district, as a teacher I have had to construct meaning for my students. For example, I have had to answer questions such as why is this test important, how will it help me, what does this have to do with what we learn in class, and why should I care? In the third, sixth, and eighth grades, many students are motivated by the prospect of summer school and failing their grade. I'm thankful

(Continued)

(Continued)

that my students do not have that fear, but the reality is that my students, my school, and I are being held accountable with real consequences if we don't do well. This, however, is not the message I want to give to my students. I want them to try their best in everything they do, and I've been trying to present testing as a challenge to them worth their efforts, but not one that determines their self-worth. When they panic or stress about it, I reassure them that everything we learn throughout the year will aid them in any endeavor, whether it's a test or their future career. There are some things that may show up on the test that we haven't learned yet, but I remind them that they have the tools that they can apply to any question in order to find the answer. We see these tests as puzzles or even games to solve, where we pay attention to how test makers might try to trip us up with wrong or misleading answers and where there are clues waiting to be found.

As a teacher facing testing pressure and the risks of student disengagement that accompanies it, I have found the best resources to be a supportive administration that trusts my judgment and allows me flexibility in the classroom, and colleagues both inside and outside of the school who are eager to share ideas, reflect, and learn alongside me as we seek out ways to enrich our instruction. These resources keep me from narrowing my teaching to simple test preparation and give me the same reminders I give my students—to look at the bigger picture and find deeper meaning in my teaching and our learning.

Another challenge is that implementing the types of instructional practices advocated in this book requires time, effort, and patience, even for the most experienced teachers. Student learning is complex; therefore, there are no quick fixes or simple solutions. Creating a culture of engagement requires time and an ongoing commitment to reflection and action. Examining one's practices can be especially challenging for inexperienced teachers. Successful implementation of research-based strategies will require support from administrators, adequate resources, and time for educators to discuss and reflect on these ideas. We encourage school personal (administrators, teachers, and staff) to read this book together and discuss what they can do collaboratively to create the most engaging environments for all of their students. Collecting data on the level of engagement (review Chapter 1 for specific suggestions) is the first step in this process.

Finally, although there is the rhetoric that all students can achieve, the reality is that many educators continue to believe it is not possible to engage all students (review Chapter 8 for examples of how the most difficult students have been reengaged). The working assumption appears to be that for some students, especially those who come to school facing individual and family difficulties, the problems of disengagement are too large and beyond the control of teachers to address. Unfortunately, many teachers continue to act on the belief that academic success is only possible for some students. However, engagement and achievement are correlated; you cannot achieve one without the other. Therefore, although it may seem difficult and even impossible at times to engage all students, teachers must continuously draw on both the examples from the intervention research literature and the practical examples of highly engaging classrooms and outside school activities (review Chapter 3 and 4). This growing research base shows that it is possible to increase engagement, even among the most disengaged youth.

In conclusion, students need to know how to think, reason, and solve problems in order to become engaged learners who are college and career ready. Unfortunately, many of our schools are not properly providing students with these higher-order thinking skills, and many students are not staying in school long enough to achieve this fundamental knowledge. We have a choice. We can continue to focus on ensuring compliance and providing superficial coverage of content, or we can invest our time, efforts, and talents into creating schools—classroom by classroom—where all students are deeply engaged. We know most teachers prefer the latter option, and the primary goal of this book has been to provide strategies to increase the level of student engagement. When students experience deep engagement, they will become lifelong learners and always seek out more engaging learning experiences.

References

Alexander, K. L., Entwisle, D. R., & Horsey, C. S. (1997). From first grade forward: Early foundations of high school dropout. *Sociology of Education, 70*(2), 87–107.

Altermatt, E. R. (2007). Coping with academic failure: Gender differences in students' self-reported interactions with family members and friends. *Journal of Early Adolescence, 27*(4), 479–508.

American Academy of Pediatrics. (2013). Crucial role of recess. *Pediatrics, 131*(1), 183–188.

Ames, C. (1992). Classrooms: Goals, structures, and student motivation. *Journal of Educational Psychology, 84*(3), 261–271.

Anderson, L., & Krathwohl, D. A. (2001). *Taxonomy for learning, teaching, and assessing: A revision of Bloom's Taxonomy of Educational Objectives.* New York, NY: Longman.

Asher, S. R., Rose, A. J., & Gabriel, S. W. (2001). Peer rejection in everyday life. In M. Leary (Ed.), *Interpersonal rejection* (pp. 105–142). New York, NY: Oxford University Press.

Assor, A., Kaplan, H., & Roth, G. (2002). Choice is good, but relevance is excellent: Autonomy-enhancing and suppressing teacher behaviours in predicting student's engagement in school work. *British Journal of Educational Psychology, 72*(2), 261–278.

Bafanz, R., Herzog, L., & MacIver, P. J. (2007). Preventing student disengagement and keeping students on graduation path in urban middle grade schools: Early identification and effective interventions. *Educational Psychologist, 42*(4), 223–235.

Baker J. A. (2006). Contributions of teacher-child relationships to positive school adjustment during elementary school. *Journal of School Psychology, 44*(3), 211–229.

Baker, J. A., Grant, S., & Morlock, L. (2008). The teacher-student relationship as a development context for children with externalizing or internalizing behavioral problems. *School Psychology Quarterly, 23*(1), 3–15.

Balfanz, R., Herzog, L., & MacIver, D. J. (2007). Preventing student disengagement and keeping students on the graduation path in urban middle-grades schools: Early identification and effective interventions. *Educational Psychologist, 42*(4), 223–235.

Barros, R. M., Silver, E. J., & Stein, R. E. K. (2009). School recess and group classroom behavior. *Pediatrics, 123*(2), 431–436.

Battistich, V., Schaps, E., & Wilson, N. (2004). Effects of an elementary school intervention on students' "connectedness" to school and social adjustment during middle school. *Journal of Primary Prevention, 24*(3), 243–262.

Battistich, V., Solomon, D., Watson, M., & Schaps, E. (1997). Caring school communities. *Educational Psychologist, 32*(3), 137–151.

Bempechat, J., & Shernoff, D. J. (2012). Parental influences on achievement motivation and student engagement. In S. L. Christenson, A. L. Reschly, & C. Wylie (Eds.), *Handbook of research on student engagement* (pp. 315–342). New York, NY: Springer.

Berndt, T. J., & Keefe, K. (1995). Friends' influence on adolescents' adjustment to school. *Child Development, 66*(5), 1312–1329.

Blumenfeld, P. C. (1992). Classroom learning and motivation: Clarifying and expanding goal theory. *Journal of Educational Psychology, 84*(3), 272–281.

Blumenfeld, P. C., Kempler, T., & Krajcik, J. S. (2006). Motivation and cognitive engagement in learning environments. In R. K. Sawyer (Ed.), *Cambridge handbook of the learning sciences* (pp. 950–984). New York, NY: Cambridge University Press.

Blumenfeld, P. C., Puro, P., & Mergendoller, J. (1992). Translating motivation into thoughtfulness. In H. Marshall (Ed.), *Redefining student learning* (pp. 207–240). Norwood, NJ: Ablex.

Blumenfeld, P., Soloway, E., Marx, R., Krajcik, J., Guzdial, M., & Palincsar, A. (1991) Motivating project-based learning: Sustaining the doing, supporting the learning. *Educational Psychologist, 26*(3–4), 369–398.

Birch, S., & Ladd, G. (1997). The teacher-child relationship and children's early school adjustment. *Journal of School Psychology, 35*(1), 61–79.

Bondy, E., & Ross, D. D. (2008). The teacher as warm demander. *Educational Leadership, 66*(1), 54–58.

Broh, B. A. (2002). Linking extracurricular programming to academic achievement: Who benefits and why? *Sociology of Education, 75*(1), 69–91.

Brophy, J. (1981). Teacher praise: A functional analysis. *Review of Educational Research, 51*(1), 5–32.

Brown, D. F. (2004). Urban teachers' professed classroom management strategies: Reflections of culturally responsive teaching. *Urban Education, 39*(3), 266–289.

Brown, B. B., & Larson, J. (2009). Peer relationships in adolescence. In R. M. Lerner & L. Steinberg (Eds.), *The handbook of adolescent psychology, Vol. 2: Contextual influences on adolescent development* (3rd ed.) (pp. 74–103). Hoboken, NJ: John Wiley & Sons Inc.

Buhs, E. S., & Ladd, G. W. (2001). Peer rejection as an antecedent of young children's school adjustment: An examination of mediating process. *Developmental Psychology, 37*(4), 550–560.

Buhs, E. S., Ladd, G. W., & Herald, S. L. (2006). Peer exclusion and victimization: Processes that mediate the relation between peer group rejection and children's classroom engagement and achievement? *Journal of Educational Psychology, 98*(1), 1–13.

Cohen, E. G. (1994). Restructuring the classroom: Conditions for positive small groups. *Review of Educational Research, 64*(1), 1–35.

Connell, J. P., & Wellborn. J. G. (1991). Competence, autonomy, and relatedness: A motivational analysis of self-system processes. In M. Gunnar & L. A. Sroufe (Eds.), *Minnesota Symposium on Child Psychology, Vol. 23* (pp. 43–77). Chicago, IL: University of Chicago Press.

Cordova, D. I., & Lepper, M. R. (1996). Intrinsic motivation and the process of learning: Beneficial effects of contextualization, personalization, and choice. *Journal of Educational Psychology, 88*(4), 715–730.

Crick, N. R., & Dodge, K. A. (1996). Social information-processing mechanisms in reactive and proactive aggression. *Child Development, 67*(3), 993–1,002.

Croninger, R., & Lee, V. (2001). Social capital and dropping out of school: Benefits to at-risk students of teachers' support and guidance. *Teachers College Record, 103*(4), 548–581.

Davis, H. A. (2006). Exploring the context of relationship quality between middle school students and teachers. *Elementary Educational Journal, 106*(3), 193–223.

Donohue, K. M., Perry, K. E., & Weinstein, R. S. (2003). Teachers' classroom practices and children's rejection by their peers. *Journal of Applied Developmental Psychology, 24*(1), 91–118.

Doyle, W. (1983). Academic work. *Review of Educational Research, 53*(2), 159–199.

Doyle, W, (1988). Work in mathematics classes: The context of students' thinking during instruction. *Educational Psychologist, 23*(2), 167–180.

Dweck, C. (1999). Caution—praise can be dangerous. *American Educator.* Retrieved from https://www.aft.org/pdfs/americaneducator/spring 1999/PraiseSpring99.pdf

Duke, N. K., Purcell-Gates, V., Hall, L. A., & Tower, C. (2006). Authentic literacy activities for developing comprehension and writing. *The Reading Teacher, 60*(4), 344–355.

Eccles, J. S., & Harold, R. (1996). Family involvement in children's and adolescents' schooling. In J. D. A. Booth (Ed.), *Family-school links: How do they affect educational outcomes?* (pp. 3–35). Hillsdale, NJ: Lawrence Erlbaum.

Eccles, J. S., Midgley, C., Wigfield, A., Buchanan, C. M., Reuman, D., Flanagan, C., & MacIver, D. (1993). Development during adolescence: The impact of stage-environment fit on young adolescents' experiences in school and in families. *American Psychologist, 48*(2), 90–101.

Eccles, J. S., Wong, C. A., & Peck, S. C. (2006). Ethnicity as a social context for the development of African American adolescents. *Journal of School Psychology, 44*(5), 407–426.

Eisenberg, N., & Fabes, R. A. (1998). Prosocial development. In W. Damon (Ed.), *Handbook of child psychology: Social, emotional, and personality development, Vol. 3* (pp. 701–778). New York, NY: Wiley.

Ennis, C. D. (1996). When avoiding confrontation leads to avoiding conflict: Disruptive students' impact on curriculum. *Journal of Curriculum and Supervision, 11*(2), 145–162.

Epstein, J. L., Coates, L., Salinas, K. C., Sanders, M. G., & Simon, B. S. (1997). *School, family, and community partnerships: Your handbook for action.* Thousand Oaks, CA: Corwin.

Feldman, A. F., & Matjasko, J. L. (2005). The role of school-based extracurricular activities in adolescent development: A comprehensive review and future directions. *Review of Educational Research, 75*(2), 159–210.

Finn, J. D. (1989). Withdrawing from school. *Review of Educational Research, 59*(2), 117–142.

Finn, J. D., & Rock, D. A. (1997). Academic success among students at risk for school failure. *Journal of Applied Psychology, 82*(2), 221–234.

Fordham, S., & Obgu, J. U. (1986). Black students' school success: Coping with the "burden of 'acting white.'" *The Urban Review, 18*(3), 176–206.

Fredricks, J. A. (2011). Extracurricular activities: An essential aspect of education. *Teachers College Record.* Retrieved August 8, 2011, from https://tcrecord.org/AuthorDisplay.asp?aid=21707

Fredricks, J. A., Blumenfeld, P. C., & Paris, A. (2004). School engagement: Potential of the concept, state of the evidence. *Review of Educational Research, 74*(1), 59–119.

Fredricks, J. A., & Eccles, J. S. (2005). Developmental benefits of extracurricular involvement: Do peer characteristics mediate the link between activities and youth outcomes? *Journal of Youth and Adolescence, 34*(6), 507–520.

Fredricks, J. A., Hackett, K., & Bregman, A. (2010). Participation in Boys and Girls Clubs: Motivation and stage environment fit. *Journal of Community Psychology, 38*(3), 369–385.

Gauvain, M., & Perez, S. M. (2007). The socialization of cognition. In J. Grusec & P. Hastings (Eds.), *Handbook of socialization: Theory and research* (pp. 588–613). New York, NY: Guilford.

Gay, G. (2002). Preparing for culturally responsive teaching. *Journal of Teacher Education, 53*(2), 106–116.

Garcia-Reid, P., Reid, R. J., & Peterson, N. A. (2005). School engagement among Latino youth in an urban middle school context valuing the role of social support. *Education and Urban Society, 37*(3), 257–275.

Gonzalez-DeHass, A. R., Willems, P., & Doan Holbein, M. (2005). Examining the relationship between parental involvement and student motivation. *Educational Psychology Review, 17*(2), 99–123.

Gonzales, P. M., Blanton, H., & Williams, K. J. (2002). The effects of stereotype threat and double-minority status on the test performance of Latino women. *Personality and Social Psychology Bulletin, 28*(5), 659–670.

Greene, B. A., Miller, R. B., Crowson, H. M., Duke, B. L., & Akey, K. L. (2004). Predicting high school students' cognitive engagement and achievement: Contributions of classroom perceptions and motivation. *Contemporary Educational Psychology, 29*(4), 462–482.

Greene, B. A., & Miller, R. B. (1996). Influences on achievement: Goals, perceived ability, and cognitive engagement. *Contemporary Educational Psychology, 21*(2), 181–192.

Greenwood, C. R., Horton, B. T., & Utley, C. A. (2002). Academic engagement: Current perspectives on research and practice. *School Psychology Review, 31*(3), 328–349.

Gregory, A., & Weinstein, R. S. (2004). Connection and regulation at home and in school: Predicting growth in achievement for adolescents. *Journal of Adolescent Research, 19*(4), 405–427.

Halpern, R. (1999). After-school programs for low-income children: Promise and challenge. *Future of Children, 9*(2), 81–95.

Hamre, B. K., & Pianta, R. C. (2001). Early teacher-child relationships and the trajectory of children's school outcomes through eighth grade. *Child Development, 72*(2), 625–638.

Hamre, B. K., & Pianta, R. C. (2006). Student-teacher relationships. In G. G. Bear & K. M. Minke (Eds.), *Children's needs III: Development, prevention, and intervention* (pp. 59–72). Washington, DC: National Association of School Psychologists.

Henderson, A., & Mapp, K. (2002). *A new wave of evidence: The impact of school, family, and community connections on student achievement.* Austin, TX: Southwest Educational Development Laboratory.

Henningsen, M., & Stein, M.K. (1997). Mathematical tasks and student cognition: Classroom-based factors that support and inhibit high-level mathematical thinking and reasoning. *Journal for Research in Mathematics Education, 28*(5), 524–549.

Henry, K. L., Knight, K. E., & Thornberry, T. P. (2012). School engagement as a predictor of dropout, delinquency, and problem substance use during adolescence and early adulthood. *Journal of Youth and Adolescence, 41*(2), 156–166.

Hill, N. E., Castellino, D., Lansford, J., Nowlin, P., Dodge, K., Bates, J., & Pettit, G. S. (2004). Parent academic involvement as related to school behavior, achievement, and aspirations: Demographic variations across adolescence. *Child Development, 75*(5), 1,491–1,509.

Hill, N. E., & Tyson, D. F. (2009). Parental involvement in middle school: A meta-analytic assessment of the strategies that promote achievement. *Developmental Psychology, 45*(3), 740–763.

Hughes, J. N., & Kwok, O. (2006). Classroom engagement mediates the effect of teacher-student support on elementary school students' peer acceptance: A prospective analysis. *Journal of School Psychology, 43(6)*, 465–480.

Irvine, J. J., & Fraser, J. W. (1998). Warm demanders. *Education Week, 17*(35), 56.

Jang, H., Reeve, J., Ryan, R. M., & Kim, A. (2009). Can self-determination theory explain what underlies the productive, satisfying learning experiences of collectivistically oriented Korean students? *Journal of Educational Psychology, 101*(3), 644–661.

Janosz, M., Archambault, I., Morizot, J., & Pagani, L. S. (2008). School engagement trajectories and their differential predictive relations to dropout. *Journal of Social Issues, 64*(1), 21–40.

Johnson, M. K., Crosnoe, R., & Elder, G. (2001). Students' attachment and academic engagement: The role of race and ethnicity. *Sociology of Education, 74*(4), 318–340.

Juvonen, J., & Murdock, T. B. (1995). Grade-level differences in the social value of effort: Implications for the self-presentation tactics of early adolescents. *Child Development, 66*(6), 1,694–1,705.

Kindermann, T. A. (2007). Effects of naturally existing peer groups on changes in academic engagement in a cohort of sixth graders. *Child Development, 78*(4), 1,186–1,203.

Kleinfeld, J. (1975). Effective teachers of Eskimo and Indian students. *School Review, 83*(2), 301–344.

Klem, A. M., & Connell, J. P. (2004). Relationships matter: Linking teacher support to student engagement and achievement. *Journal of School Health, 74*(7), 262–273.

Kohn, A. (1991). Group grade grubbing versus cooperative learning. *Educational Leadership, 48*, 83–87.

Krajcik, J., Blumenfeld, P., Marx, R., Bass, K., Fredricks, J., & Soloway, E. (1998). Inquiry in project-based science classrooms: Initial attempts by middle school students. *The Journal of the Learning Sciences, 7*(3–4), 313–350.

Krajcik, J., Blumenfeld, P., Marx, R. W., & Soloway, E. (1994). A collaborative model for helping science teachers learn project-based instruction. *Elementary School Journal, 94*(5), 483–498.

Ladd, G. W. (1990). Having friends, keeping friends, making friends, and being liked by peers in the classroom: Predictors of children's early school adjustment. *Child Development, 61*(4), 1,081–1,100.

Ladd, G. W., Birch, S. H., & Buhs, E. S. (1999). Children's social and scholastic lives in kindergarten: Related spheres of influence? *Child Development, 70*(6), 1,373–1,400.

Ladd, G. W., & Burgess, K. B. (2001). Do relational risks and protective factors moderate the linkages between childhood aggression and early psychological and school adjustment? *Child Development, 72*(5), 1,579–1,601.

Ladd, G. W., Herald-Brown, S. L., & Kochel, K. P. (2009). Peers and motivation. In K. Wenztel & A. Wigfield (Eds.), *Handbook of motivation at school* (pp. 323–348). New York, NY: Routledge.

Ladd, G. W., Herald-Brown, S. L., & Reiser, M. (2008). Does chronic classroom peer rejection predict the development of children's classroom participation during the grade school years? *Child Development, 79*(4), 1,001–1,015.

Langdon, C. A., & Vesper, N. (2000). The sixth Phi Delta Kappa poll of teachers' attitudes toward the public schools. *Phi Delta Kappan, 81*(8), 607–611.

Larson, R. W. (2000). Toward a psychology of positive youth development. *American Psychologist, 55*(1), 170–183.

Larson, R. W., Hansen, D., & Moneta, G. (2006). Differing profiles of developmental experiences across types of organized youth activities. *Developmental Psychology, 42*(5), 849–863.

Laureau, A. (2000). Home advantage: Social class differences in family-school relationships: The importance of cultural capital. *Sociology of Education, 60*(2), 73–85.

Li, Y., & Lerner, R. M. (2011). Trajectories of school engagement during adolescence: Implications for grades, depression, delinquency, and substance use. *Developmental Psychology, 47*(1), 233–247.

Linnebrink, L. A., & Fredricks, J. A. (2008). Developmental perspectives on achievement motivation: Personal and contextual influences. In J. Y. Shah & W. L. Gardner (Eds.), *Handbook of motivation science: The social psychological perspective* (pp. 448–464). New York, NY: Guilford Press.

Lynch, M., & Cicchetti, D. (1997). Children's relationships with adults and peers: An examination of elementary and junior high school students. *Journal of School Psychology, 35*(1), 81–99.

Mahoney, J. L., & Cairns, R. B. (1997). Do extracurricular activities protect against early school dropout? *Developmental Psychology, 33*(2), 241–253.

Mahoney, J. L., & Eccles, J. S. (2007). Organized activity participation for children from low- and middle-income families. In A. Booth & A. C. Crouter (Eds.), *Disparities in school readiness* (pp. 207–222). New York, NY: Lawrence Erlbaum.

Mahoney, J. L., Harris, A. L., & Eccles, J. S. (2006). Organized activity participation, positive youth development, and the over-scheduling hypothesis. *Society for Research in Child Development: Social Policy Report, 20*(4), 1–30.

Mahoney, J. L., & Stattin, H. (2000). Leisure activities and adolescent antisocial behavior: The role of structure and social context. *Journal of Adolescence, 23*(2), 113–127.

Malone, T. W., & Lepper, M. R. (1987). Making learning fun: A taxonomy of intrinsic motivations for learning. In R. E. Snow and M. J. Farr (Eds.), *Aptitude, learning and instruction III: Conative and affective process analyses*. Hillsdale, NJ: Lawrence Erlbaum.

Marsh, H. W., & Kleitman, S. (2002). Extracurricular school activities: The good, the bad, and the nonlinear. *Harvard Educational Review, 72*(4), 464–514.

Martin, A. J. (2004). School motivation of boys and girls: Differences of degree, differences of kind, or both? *Australian Journal of Psychology, 56*(4), 133–146.

Martin, A. J. (2007). Examining a multidimensional model of student motivation and engagement using a construct validation approach. *British Journal of Educational Psychology, 77*(2), 413–440.

Marx, R. W., & Walsh, J. (1988). Learning from academic tasks. *Elementary School Journal, 88*(3), 207–219.

Meehan, B. T., Hughes, J. N., & Cavell, T. A. (2003). Teacher–student relationships as compensatory resources for aggressive children. *Child Development, 74*(4), 1,145–1,157.

Midgley, C., Feldlaufer, H., & Eccles, J. S. (1989). Student/teacher relations and attitudes toward mathematics before and after the transition to junior high school. *Child Development, 60*(4), 981–992.

Middleton, M., & Midgley, M. (2002). Beyond motivation: Middle school students' perceptions of press for understanding in math. *Contemporary Educational Psychology, 27*(3), 373–391.

Mitchell, M. (1993). Situational interest: Its multifaceted structure in the mathematics classroom. *Journal of Educational Psychology, 85*(3), 424–436.

Monroe, C. R., & Obidah, J. E. (2004). The influence of cultural synchronization in a teacher's perception of disruption: A case study of an African American middle-school classroom. *Journal of Teacher Education, 55*(3), 256–268.

Murray, C., & Murray, K. M. (2004). Child level correlates of teacher-student relationships: An examination of demographic characteristics, academic orientations, and behavioral orientations. *Psychology in the Schools, 41*(7), 751–762.

National Research Council & Institute of Medicine. (2004). *Engaging schools: Fostering high school students' motivation to learn.* Washington, DC: National Academy Press.

Neild, R. L., Balfanz, R., & Herzog, L. (2007). An early warning system. *Educational Leadership, 65*(2), 28–33.

Newmann, F. M., & Wehlage, G. G. (1993). Five standards of authentic instruction. *Educational Leadership, 50*(7), 8–12.

Ng, F. F., Kenney-Benson, G. A., & Pomerantz, E. M. (2004). Children's achievement moderates the effects of mothers' use of control and autonomy support. *Child Development, 75*(3), 764–780.

Noddings, N. (1988). An ethic of caring and its implications for instructional arrangements. *American Journal of Education, 96*(2), 215–230.

Osterman, K. F. (2000). Students' need for belonging in the school community. *Review of Educational Research, 70*(3), 323–367.

Palinscar, A., & Brown, A. (1984). Reciprocal teaching of comprehension fostering and comprehension monitoring activities. *Cognition and Instruction, 1*(2), 117–175.

Paris, S. G., & Paris, A. H. (2001). Classroom applications of research on self-regulated learning. *Educational Psychologist, 36*(2), 89–101.

Peterson, P., Swing, S., Stark, K., & Wass, G. (1984). Students' cognitions and time on task during mathematics instruction. *American Educational Research Journal, 21*(3), 487–515.

Pianta, R. C. (2006). Classroom management and relationships between children and teachers: Implications for research and practice. In *Handbook of classroom management: Research, practice, and contemporary issues.* (pp. 685–709). Mahwah, NJ: Lawrence Erlbaum.

Pianta, R. C., Belsky, J., Houts, R., & Morrison, F. (2007). Teaching opportunities to learn in America's elementary classrooms. *Science, 315*(5820), 1,795–1,796.

Pianta, R. C., Steinberg, M. S., & Rollins, K. B. (1995). The first two years of school: Teacher–child relationships and deflections in children's classroom adjustment. *Development and Psychopathology, 7*(2), 295–312.

Pomerantz, E. M., Grolnick, W. S., & Price, C. E. (2005). The role of parents in how children approach achievement: A dynamic process perspective. In A. J. Elliot & C. S. Dweck (Eds.), *Handbook of competence and motivation* (pp. 259–278). New York, NY: Guilford Press.

Pomerantz, E. M., Moorman, E. A., & Litwak, S. D. (2007). The how, whom, and why of parents' involvement in children's academic lives: More is not always better. *Review of Educational Research, 77*(3), 373–410.

Porsche, M. V., Ross, S. J., & Snow, C. E. (2004). From preschool to middle school: The role of masculinity in low-income urban adolescent boys' literacy skills and academic achievement. In N. Way & J. Y. Chu (Eds.), *Adolescent boys: Exploring diverse cultures of boyhood* (pp. 338–360). New York, NY: New York University Press.

Raftery, J. N., Grolnick, W. S., & Flamm, E. S. (2012). Families as facilitators of student engagement: Towards a home-school partnership. In S. L. Christenson, A. L. Reschly, & C. Wylie (Eds.), *Handbook of research on student engagement* (pp. 343–364). New York, NY: Springer.

Reeve, J., & Halusic, M. (2009). How K–12 teachers can put self-determination theory into practice. *Theory and Research in Education, 7*(2), 145–154.

Reeve, J., & Jang, H. (2006). What teachers say and do to support students' autonomy during a learning activity. *Journal of Educational Psychology, 98*(1), 209–221.

Reeve, J., Jang, H., Carrell, D., Jeon, S., & Barch, J. (2004). Enhancing high school students' engagement by increasing their teachers' autonomy support. *Motivation and Emotion, 28*(2), 147–169.

Resnick, L. B. (1987). The 1987 presidential address: Learning in school and out. *Educational Researcher, 16*(9), 13–20, 54.

Resnick, M. D., Bearman, P. S., Blum, R.W., Bauman, K., Harris, K. M., Jones, J., Tabor, J., . . . Udry, J. R. (1997). Protecting adolescents from harm. Findings from the national longitudinal study on adolescent health. *Journal of the American Medical Association, 278*(10), 823–832.

Rogoff, B. (1994). Developing understanding of the idea of communities of learners. *Mind, Culture, and Activity, 1*(4), 209–229.

Rogoff, B. (1998). Cognition as a collaborative process. In D. Kuhn & R. S. Siegler (Eds.), *Cognition, perception and language: Vol. 2, handbook of child psychology* (5th ed.) (pp. 679–744). New York, NY: Wiley.

Rosenbloom, S. R., & Way, N. (2004). Experiences of discrimination among African American, Asian American, and Latino adolescents in an urban high school. *Youth and Society, 35*(4), 420–451.

Rubin, K. H., Bukowski, W. M., & Laursen, B. (2009). *Handbook of peer interactions, relationships, and groups.* New York, NY: Guilford Press.

Rubin, K. H., Bukowski, W. M., & Parker, J. (2006). Peer interactions, relationships, and groups. In N. Eisenberg (Ed.), *Handbook of Child*

Psychology: Vol. 3, Social, emotional, and personality development (6th ed.) (pp. 571–645) New York, NY: Wiley.

Ryan, A. M., (2000). Peer groups as a context for the socialization of adolescents' motivation, engagement, and achievement in school. *Educational Psychologist, 35*(2), 101–111.

Ryan, A. M., & Patrick, H. (2001). The classroom social environment and changes in adolescents' motivation and engagement during middle school. *American Educational Research Journal, 38*(2), 437–460.

Ryan, A. M., & Shim, S. S. (2008). An exploration of young adolescents' social achievement goals and social adjustment in middle school. *Journal of Educational Psychology, 100*(3), 672–687.

Ryan, R. M., & Deci, E. L. (2000). Intrinsic and extrinsic motivations: Classic definitions and new directions. *Contemporary Education Psychology, 25*(1), 54–67.

Shernoff, D. J., & Csikszentmihalyi, M. (2009). Flow in schools: Cultivating engaged learners and optimal learning environments. In R. Gilman, E. S. Huebner, & M. Furlong (Eds.), *Handbook of positive psychology in schools* (pp. 131–145). New York, NY: Routledge.

Skinner, E. A., & Belmont, M. J. (1993). Motivation in the classroom: Reciprocal effect of teacher behavior and student engagement across the school year. *Journal of Educational Psychology, 85*(4), 571–581.

Skinner, E. A., Kindermann, T. A., & Furrer, C. J. (2009). A motivational perspective on engagement and disaffection: Conceptualization and assessment of children's behavioral and emotional participation in academic activities in the classroom. *Educational and Psychological Measurement, 69*(3), 493–525.

Skinner, E. A., & Pitzer, J. R. (2012). Developmental dynamics of student engagement, coping, and everyday resilience. In. S. L. Christenson, A. L. Reschly, & C. Wylie (Eds.), *Handbook of research on student engagement* (pp. 21–45). New York, NY: Springer.

Slavin, R. E. (1991a). Group rewards make groupwork work: Response to Kohn. *Educational Leadership, 48*(5), 89–91.

Slavin, R. E. (1991b). Synthesis on research on cooperative learning. *Educational Leadership, 48*(5), 71–82.

Slavin, R. E. (1996). Research on cooperative learning and achievement: What we know, what we need to know. *Contemporary Educational Psychology, 21*(1), 43–69.

Smith, R. A., (2002). Black boys: The litmus test for "No Child Left Behind." *Education Week, 22*(9), 43.

Steele, C. M. (1997). A threat in the air: How stereotypes shape intellectual identity and performance. *American Psychologist, 52*(6), 613–629.

Steele, C. M., & Aronson, J. (1995). Stereotype threat and the intellectual test performance of African Americans. *Journal of Personality and Social Psychology, 69*(5), 797–811.

Stein, M. K., Grover, B. W., & Henningsen, M. (1996). Building student capacity for mathematical thinking and reasoning: An analysis of mathematical tasks used in reform. *American Educational Research Journal, 33*(2), 455–488.

Steinberg, L. D., Brown, B. B., & Dornbush, S. M. (1996). *Beyond the classroom: Why school reform has failed and what parents need to do.* New York, NY: Simon & Schuster.

Stuhlman, M. W., & Pianta, R. C. (2002). Teachers' narratives about their relationships with children: Associations with behavior in classrooms. *School Psychology Review, 31*(2), 148–163.

Turner, J. C. (1995). The influence of classroom context on young children's motivation for literacy. *Reading Research Quarterly, 30*(3), 410–441.

Turner, J. C., Meyer, D. K., Cox, K. C., Logan, C., DiCintio, M., & Thomas, C. T. (1998). Creating contexts for involvement in mathematics. *Journal of Educational Psychology, 90*(4), 730–745.

Turner, J. C., Midgley, C., Meyer, D. K., Gheen, M., Anderman, E., Kang, Y., & Patrick, H. (2002). The classroom environment and students' reports of avoidance strategies in mathematics: A multi-method study. *Journal of Educational Psychology, 94*(1), 88–106.

U.S. Department of Education (2003). Office of Special Education Programs. *25th Annual Report to Congress.* Washington, DC: Author.

U.S. Department of Education (2004). *Trends in educational equity of girls and women.* Washington, DC: Author. Retrieved on June 13, 2013, from http://nces.ed.gov/pubs2005/2005016.pdf

Valdés, G. (1998). The world outside and inside schools: Language and immigrant children. *Educational Researcher, 27*(6), 4–18.

Voelkl, K. E. (1997). Identification with school. *American Journal of Education, 105*(3), 204–319.

Vygotsky, L. S. (1978). Mind in society: The development of higher psychological processes. (M. Cole, V. John-Steiner, S. Scribner, & E. Souberman, Eds.). Cambridge, MA: Harvard University Press.

Wang, M. T., & Eccles, J. E. (2012). Social support matters: Longitudinal effects of social support on three dimensions of school engagement from middle to high school. *Child Development, 83*(3), 877–895.

Wang, M. T., & Fredricks, J. A. (in press). The reciprocal links between school engagement and youth problem behavior during adolescence. *Child Development.*

Ware, F. (2006). Warm demander pedagogy: Culturally responsive teaching that supports a culture of achievement for African American students. *Urban Education, 41*(4), 427–456.

Watson, M., & Battistich, V. (2006). Building and sustaining caring communities. In C. M. Evertson & C. S. Weinstein (Eds.), *Handbook of classroom management: Research, practice, and contemporary issues* (pp. 253–279). Mahwah, NJ: Lawrence Erlbaum.

Webb, N. M., Nemer, K. M., & Ing, M. (2006). Small-group reflections: Parallels between teacher discourse and student behavior in peer-directed groups. *Journal of the Learning Sciences, 15*(1), 63–119.

Wentzel, K. R. (1997). Student motivation in middle school: The role of perceived pedagogical caring. *Journal of Educational Psychology, 89*(3), 411–419.

Wentzel, K. R. (1998). Social relationships and motivation in middle school: The role of parents, teachers, and peers. *Journal of Educational Psychology, 90*(2), 202–209.

Wentzel, K. R. (2005). Peer relationships, motivation, and academic performance at school. In A. Elliot & C. Dweck (Eds.), *Handbook of competence and motivation* (pp. 279–296). New York, NY: Guilford.

Wentzel, K. R. (2009). Peer relationships and motivation at school. In K. Rubin, W. Bukowski, & B. Laursen (Eds.), *Handbook on peer relationships* (pp. 531–547). New York, NY: Guilford.

Wentzel, K. R., Baker, S. A., & Russell, S. (2009). Peer relationships and positive adjustment at school. In R. Gillman, S. Huebner, & M. Furlong (Eds.), *Promoting wellness in children and youth: A handbook of positive psychology in the schools* (pp. 229–244). New York, NY: Routledge.

Wentzel, K. R., Barry, C., & Caldwell, K. (2004). Friendships in middle school: Influences on motivation and school adjustment. *Journal of Educational Psychology, 96*(2), 195–203.

Wentzel, K. R., & Caldwell, K. (1997). Friendships, peer acceptance, and group membership: Relations to academic achievement in middle school. *Child Development, 68*(6), 1,198–1,209.

Wentzel, K. R., Filisetti, L., & Looney, L. (2007). Adolescent prosocial behavior: The role of self-processes and contextual cues. *Child Development, 78*(3), 895–910.

Wigfield, A., Byrnes, J. P., & Eccles, J. S. (2006). Development during early and middle adolescence. In P. A. Alexander & P. H. Winne (Eds.), *The handbook of educational psychology* (pp. 87–113). Mahwah, NJ: Lawrence Erlbaum.

Wigfield, A., Guthrie, J. T., Perencevich, K. C., Taboada, A., Klauda, S. L., McRae, A., & Barbosa, P. (2008). Role of reading engagement in mediating the effects of reading comprehension instruction on reading outcomes. *Psychology in the Schools, 45*(5), 432–445.

Wong, C. A., Eccles, J. S., & Sameroff, A. (2003). The influence of ethnic discrimination and ethnic identification on African American adolescents' school and socioemotional adjustment. *Journal of Personality, 71*(6), 1,197–1,232.

Wubbels, T., den Brok, P., Veldman, I., & Van Tartwijk, J. (2006). Teachers' interpersonal competence for Dutch secondary multicultural classrooms. *Teachers and Teaching: Theory and Practice, 12*(4), 407–433.

Yazzie-Mintz, E. (2007). *Voices of students on engagement: A report on the 2006 High School Survey of Student Engagement.* Bloomington, IN: Center for Evaluation & Educational Policy, Indiana University. Retrieved on February 1, 2010, from http://ceep.indiana.edu/pdf/HSSSE_2006_Report.pdf

Zimmerman, B. J. (2002). Becoming a self-regulated learner: An overview. *Theory Into Practice, 41*(2), 65–70.

Index

CORWIN
A SAGE Company

The Corwin logo—a raven striding across an open book—represents the union of courage and learning. Corwin is committed to improving education for all learners by publishing books and other professional development resources for those serving the field of PreK–12 education. By providing practical, hands-on materials, Corwin continues to carry out the promise of its motto: **"Helping Educators Do Their Work Better."**